Images of the Hunter
in American Life
and Literature

Studies on Themes and Motifs in Literature

Horst S. Daemmrich
General Editor

Vol. 54

PETER LANG
New York • Washington, D.C./Baltimore • Boston • Bern
Frankfurt am Main • Berlin • Brussels • Vienna • Oxford

Lynda Wolfe Coupe

Images of the Hunter in American Life and Literature

PETER LANG
New York • Washington, D.C./Baltimore • Boston • Bern
Frankfurt am Main • Berlin • Brussels • Vienna • Oxford

Library of Congress Cataloging-in-Publication Data

Coupe, Lynda Wolfe.
Images of the hunter in American life and literature / Lynda Wolfe Coupe.
p. cm. — (Studies on themes and motifs in literature; vol. 54)
Includes bibliographical references and index.
1. American literature—History and criticism. 2. Hunters in literature.
3. Hunting in literature. 4. Hunters—United States.
5. Hunting—United States. I. Title. II. Series.
PS173.H85C68   810.9'3526391—dc21   99-32032
ISBN 0-8204-4555-X
ISSN 1056-3970

Die Deutsche Bibliothek-CIP-Einheitsaufnahme

Coupe, Lynda Wolfe:
Images of the hunter in American life and literature / Lynda Wolfe Coupe.
–New York; Washington, D.C./Baltimore; Boston; Bern;
Frankfurt am Main; Berlin; Brussels; Vienna; Oxford: Lang.
(Studies on themes and motifs in literature; Vol. 54)
ISBN 0-8204-4555-X

Author photo by Michael Gillen

The paper in this book meets the guidelines for permanence and durability
of the Committee on Production Guidelines for Book Longevity
of the Council of Library Resources.

© 2000 Peter Lang Publishing, Inc., New York

Printed in the United States of America

Dedication

This book is dedicated to
my husband, John Coupe, who is my own Daniel Boone;
to my mother, Evelyn Wolfe;
and to the memory of my father, Donald Adams

Acknowledgments

I owe a great debt to so many people for supporting me through the process that ultimately resulted in this book. The topic of my dissertation upon which the book is based was inspired by my husband, John Coupe. Hunting and fishing with him has immersed me in the life of the woods where I have experienced the moments of clarity and self-knowledge that I describe in my discussion of hunter figures.

William Kelly, my adviser at CUNY, was indefatigable in editing my dissertation and urged me on with his kind but rigorous comments. I also wish to thank my dissertation committee, Joan Richardson and David Reynolds.

My editor, Debora Lyne, has been tireless in her meticulous work on the many drafts and endless revisions of the book manuscript. Her efficiency and good nature have rallied me through many setbacks.

My friends and colleagues at Pace University also contributed much appreciated moral and practical support over many years. Becky Martin, Ruth Anne Thompson, and Joe Franco assured me that completing the dissertation and the degree was indeed possible. Mike Gillen has been a wonderful colleague and mentor from whom I have learned valuable administrative skills. Bob Klaeger has kept me working in the Department of Literature and Communications so that I may pursue my love of teaching as well as writing.

My siblings, Sue, Gail, and Walt, have believed in me more than I could ever believe in myself. Of course, my mother, Evelyn Wolfe, is my hero. She has persevered through personal and health crises and continues to do so with rare strength and grace. I am just sorry my father, Donald Adams, did not live to see the publication of this book. I also wish to thank my many friends for their support, especially Donna D'Angelo, who was so happy for me when I told her the book had been accepted for publication.

There were also a score of people who suggested books, articles, and ideas to pursue that added so much to the depth and scope of this study. To all these and more I want to say thank you.

The following publishers have generously given permission to use extended quotations from copyrighted works.

Auel, Jean M. *The Clan of the Cave Bear*. New York: Bantam Books, 1980. Reprinted by permission of Jean M. Auel and the publisher.

Faragher, John Mack. *Daniel Boone: The Life and Legend of an American Pioneer*. New York: Henry Holt & Co., 1992. Reprinted by permission of the publisher. All rights reserved.

Tilton, Robert Steven. "American Lavinia: The Pocahontas Narrative in Ante-Bellum America." Ph.D. diss., Stanford, 1992. Reprinted by permission of the author. All rights reserved.

The mythology of a nation is the intelligible mask of that enigma called the "national character." Through myths the psychology and world view of our cultural ancestors are transmitted to modern descendants, in such a way and with such power that our perception of contemporary reality and our ability to function in the world are directly . . . affected.

Richard Slotkin in *Regeneration Through Violence: The Mythology of the American Frontier, 1600–1860*

Table of Contents

Introduction

The hunter is a liminal figure, traversing opposing worlds of wilderness and civilization, able to participate in both and yet not fully belonging to either. He is at once privileged and marginal. The hunter's practical skills, as well as his mythic connotations and the language used to describe him, all reflect a changing concept of American power.

Evolving across the span of American time, the hunter serves as a barometer of the social concerns of the nation. Initially, the hunter reflects American rebellion against the power of European aristocracy. Gradually, the hunter redefines the term *aristocracy* to accommodate American concerns with landscape, identity, and race and gender. But by the end of the nineteenth century, *individualism,* in the form of personal independence and initiative, replaces aristocracy—the hereditary claim to authority—as the basis of power in America. The hunter derives his power from his special place in the American culture.

Several studies have tried to capture the nature of the American experience with a single metaphor or system of symbols.[1] Many notable efforts have centered around the use of myth to explain conceptions of the American character.[2] This book does not try to define the American experience in terms of a single, unifying myth. Rather, it examines a cluster of images of the hunter. The hunter hero provides a focus for reading important cultural issues across the span of American time.

This study is organized chronologically, using pairs of representative figures from American literature, history, and popular culture. The pairs include Pocahontas and John Smith; Daniel Boone and Nathaniel Bumppo from James Fenimore Cooper's *Leatherstocking Tales;* Theodore Roosevelt and William "Buffalo Bill" Cody; William Faulkner's Ike McCaslin from "The Bear" and Ernest Hemingway; and author and screenwriter Thomas McGuane and Ayla from Jean Auel's *Clan of the Cave Bear.*

All are hunters, except Pocahontas and John Smith, who are "mythic compatriots" (Fisher vii) and "parents" of the American hunter. The pairs reflect oppositions of high and low, fictive and real, writer and figure, myth and history within the culture. They are actors in the unfolding events of their historical periods or representations of American power in art and culture. Many figures are simultaneously actor and artistic or cultural representation.

Chapter 1 looks at John Smith and Pocahontas as metaphorical progenitors of the American hunter figure; this hunter figure later emerges in the new Republic as Daniel Boone. The rescue of Smith by Pocahontas is a creation myth and an important founding moment. The rescue unites them in the popular imagination. Smith and Pocahontas represent the power to create a new, distinctly American identity that subverts European notions of aristocracy. *Myth* and *aristocracy,* as they apply to the role of the hunter, are discussed, as well as how they provide insight into the relationship between Pocahontas and Smith.

Pocahontas is a dual mother figure, at once symbolic mother to the hunter and literal mother, whose "descendants . . . became the 'nobility' of the Old Dominion," according to Robert Tilton ("American Lavinia" 4). Her dual role reflects the tension between an ideal of racial amalgamation and a fear of miscegenation. The idea of the melting pot, where a single national identity is forged from the combination of various ethnic backgrounds has served as a cultural ideal in the American psyche; however, the reality is a history of race prejudice and the practice of separation of the races. Pocahontas was unique in that she successfully crossed between the worlds of the Indian and the white settler. Although she finally married an English planter and not Smith, the story of her rescue of Smith has remained a legacy to the American imagination.

This resulting racial tension, in turn, establishes a borderline that the hunter crosses, one of many borderlines he crosses between different worlds. Thus, the hunter's primary characteristic is liminality. Pocahontas and Smith bestow traits on the hunter figure derived from their divergent cultures, as well as from their own experiences. That they crossed the barriers between their cultures and lived in each other's worlds is their primary legacy.

Chapter 2 looks at Daniel Boone as the first American hunter hero and Natty Bumppo as his literary reflection. Together they embody the power to develop the new nation. Their roles as hunter/scouts and settlers of the frontier became a model for American independence. Simultaneously, they rejected the European conception of aristocracy as inherited power.

As hunters, their power derived from individual prowess. Their ability to survive and, more importantly, to flourish in the wilderness inspired the settlers' confidence in them and in what they represented. During their "lifetimes," the United States became a nation. Just as separate colonies united into one country, the American hunter figure amalgamated Indian and European traits into one figure: Boone, followed by Bumppo, his image in literature.

We must understand the contemporary connotations of *wilderness* to appreciate the hunter's complex relationship with nature and the landscape. The Puritans believed that an *inner wilderness* accompanied the physical wilderness in America. The land held both promise and peril: On one hand, the land was rich and abundant; on the other, it was vast and savage. To the Puritans, the Indians were not simply unpredictable or dangerous neighbors; they were devils incarnate. The Puritans viewed the Indians' nature-based lifestyle as an invitation to damnation. Hunters who could go into the forest and successfully procure game were admirable, but they were also spiritually suspect because they were able to enter an alien world. Boone and Bumppo founded their identities upon their role as hunter. Both negotiated literal and figurative borderlines that were impenetrable barriers for those less able to adapt. But they frequently crossed between conflicting worlds as a result.

Chapter 3 discusses Theodore Roosevelt and William "Buffalo Bill" Cody as figures of physical and political expansion and control. Both men were hunters and cowboys. The hunter/cowboy figure became a metaphor for domestic and foreign power during their lifetimes. Cody and Roosevelt exemplify the hunter/cowboy's independence and self-reliance. Individuality as a source of power replaced the last vestiges of European aristocracy. Race and gender became important issues in the discussion of Roosevelt's view of the hunter/warrior ideal and, to a lesser degree, in the discussion of Cody's Wild West show. Roosevelt's hunter/warrior ideal is founded in Teutonic mythology, not the amalgamation of Euro-American and Native American cultures. The Teutonic or Germanic hero/warrior was the superman of his race, the leader who protected the people militarily as well as intellectually, charismatically subverting the lesser classes. The hunter/warrior of the New World combined the traits of Native American harmony with the wilderness environment and the European spirit of exploration and superiority of weapons. His views on race and gender are intricately tied to this hunter/warrior myth. Cody's views on race and gender become especially important when we look at how he organized his Wild West show. He constantly revised portions of the "exhibit," as he called it. His views and how they influenced his hiring practices and his treatment of the performers is examined.

With the growth of the nation as a world power came the closing of the frontier and the exploitation of its natural resources. Roosevelt's conservation efforts and Cody's Wild West show can be interpreted as ways of mitigating the ravaging effects of American expansion and excess. Representing American expansion and control in light of Manifest Destiny, Roosevelt and Cody are hunter figures; yet they also embody the contradictory images of conservationist and preservationist of a way of life that had all but disappeared—or some might say had never existed.

Chapter 4 examines William Faulkner's Isaac McCaslin and Ernest Hemingway, who represent the power to transcend degenerate forces in the culture through immersion in nature. Faulkner and Hemingway were part of the lost generation that had seen "the war to end all wars." Part of the legacy of war for Hemingway was dealing with his physical and spiritual wounds. The solace of hunting and fishing as a healing force is evident in his life and his art. Hemingway and his fictional characters leave the civilized world behind and escape into the natural world to convalesce. The Nick Adams stories, especially "Big Two-Hearted River," are the most familiar examples of this trope, but the pattern is repeated in several Hemingway works, including the autobiographical *Green Hills of Africa*. For Hemingway, hunting and fishing tested the sportsman's skill and provided opportunities to gain self-knowledge. Hemingway as hunter is more than a metaphor; his identity is inextricably linked with hunting.

Faulkner's voice chronicles the decay of the aristocratic Old South. The corrupt world of his fiction inscribes the culture in which he lived. His character, Ike McCaslin, is able to establish his identity as a hunter; his legacy is not the estate of his father but his education from the racially mixed Sam Fathers and "Old Ben," the bear he hunts. He also immerses himself in the natural world and, at least temporarily, is freed from those who would impose their standards on him. The deeper he journeys into the woods, and the farther behind he leaves the civilized world, the more self-knowledge he gains.

Both Faulkner and Hemingway depicted corrupt worlds that threaten and often overcome the individual. Yet, accompanying this cynical view is a nostalgia for a simpler life and time. Through hunting, their characters return to the uncorrupted values of the natural world. Crossing from the modern world into the world of nature provides an escape from degeneracy. But, even more importantly, it provides a way to find spiritual renewal and transcendence.

Chapter 5 examines Thomas McGuane and Jean Auel's protagonist, Ayla, from her Earth's Children series. These figures suggest the power to reinvent oneself in the face of postmodern concern with personal identity. Power in America is again revised in the latter part of the twentieth century to include not only those who have money and influence, but also those who succeed through individual initiative.

In his personal life and in his writing, McGuane uses hunting as a touchstone for developing a personal moral code. In *The Sporting Club,* he creates a picaresque world that illustrates the moral bankruptcy of the rich and privileged. His protagonist, Quinn, is torn between following the traditional, but corrupt, old guard of the club, or following Stanton, the spoiled, incredibly rich bad boy, who seeks to destroy it. Olson, an ideal sportsman, is the only positive model Quinn has. Olson is the club's caretaker, but he is fired early in the story. Quinn's predicament between equally unacceptable options reflects McGuane's own situation. McGuane is a scholar who wrote screenplays to support his art, and he was all but destroyed by Hollywood as a result. The glamorous life in the fast lane included not only money and recognition but alcohol, drugs, and a decadent lifestyle. His health, marriage, and mental stability were threatened to such a degree that he eventually reached a point where he could no longer function. McGuane finally found balance in Montana, where he now writes, ranches, rides cutting horses, fishes, and hunts.

Ayla embodies the increasingly powerful women's movement of the 1970s and 1980s. Ayla is a Cro-Magnon child adopted by a Neanderthal tribe, the Clan of the Cave Bear. Physically and mentally different from those in her society, she suffers ostracism of the cruelest kind. She is beaten, raped, and separated from her young son when she is cast out of the clan to wander alone. She teaches herself to hunt, an activity strictly forbidden for women of the Clan. Hunting gives Ayla power over her environment and a sense of self-worth. By the end of the novel, she knows she will be able to survive on her own.

The social and literary rebel and the "new" woman are recent examples of American individuality. Hunting gives McGuane and Ayla the insight and confidence to redirect their lives. Like other American hunters before them, they cross many borders, both literal and figurative.

In the course of this book, rhetorical as well as mythic approaches to the significance of the hunter are examined. As Philip Fisher has pointed out, "[r]hetoric is the place where language is engaged in cultural work, and such work can be done on, with, or in spite of one or another social group." Fisher has traced a shift in emphasis among Americanists from myth to rhetoric. He points out that myth is "fixed, satisfying, and stable," and normalizes our social life, while "rhetorics are . . . part of what is uncertain or potential in culture" (vii).

Images that recur in the hunting motif are especially important. For the American hunter, his solitary nature is reinforced by his isolation. He is immersed in nature, and happy to be there; nonetheless, he is alone. Isolation is a proving ground for testing the hunter's merit. Isolation is also an important pattern in mythical portrayals of hunters, reinforced by the language of the hunt, which is usually singular. The hunter looks for "sign" of one or more animals. Rhetorically, a *sign* is a unit of meaning. It may be an utterance or some other single entity that communicates. The hunter speaks of the hunting "trail," although that trail may actually be several trails. The hunter conventionally hunts and kills one animal at a time. The seriousness and specialness of the occasion is underscored by the use of the singular. Even group hunting among primitive peoples concentrated on cooperatively harvesting one large animal. Hunting recognizes the individual: the hunter and the hunted.

This recognition of the individual is the underlying principle of the American experience. The hunter figure is an amalgamation of Indian and European cultures, and this makes him an American original. But, above all, he is a liminal character. He crosses borders of landscape and race and, consequently, establishes a unique national and personal identity. Most recently, the hunter in America is a symbol and a sign of crossing gender boundaries. The hunter demonstrates that the power to subvert social authority, to develop, to expand and control, to transcend degenerate forces, and to reinvent oneself resides in the individual. Self-knowledge, finally, is power.

Notes

1   Among the major studies are Richard Slotkin's trilogy: *Regeneration Through Violence: The Mythology of the American Frontier, 1600–1860; The Fatal Environment: The Myth of the Frontier in the Age of Industrialization;* and *Gunfighter Nation: The Myth of the Frontier in Twentieth Century America.* Also of interest are *Virgin Land: The American West as Symbol and Myth* by Henry Nash Smith; *The American Adam: Innocence, Tragedy, and Tradition in the Nineteenth Century* by R. W. B. Lewis; *The Frontier Mind* by Arthur K. Moore; and *Wilderness and the American Mind* by Roderick Nash.

2   Especially Slotkin and Smith.

Chapter 1

Pocahontas and John Smith: Metaphorical Parents of the American Hunter Figure

. . . and with cudgels raised they were about to aim their blows, when Pocahontas, the daughter of Powhatan, when she could not prevail upon her father with ardent entreaties, rushed at Smith like a mad woman and, embracing his head with her arms, asked to receive in his stead the blows aimed at his head. (Wharton 72)

. . .

After some six weeks fatting amongst those Savage Courtiers, at the minute of my execution she hazarded the beating out of her brains to save mine; and not only that, but so prevailed with her father, that I was safely conducted to Jamestown; where I found about eight and thirty miserable, poor and sick creatures, to keep possession of all those large territories of Virginia. Such was the weakness of this poor Commonwealth, as had the Savages not fed us, we directly had starved. And this relief, most gracious Queen, was commonly brought us by this Lady Pocahontas. (John Smith, qtd. in Barbour, *Three Worlds* 330)

. . .

It is as a rescuer that Pocahontas is best known, and much of the mythology that has been built up around her continues to be associated with this crucial founding moment in American history. (Tilton, "American Lavinia" iv)

John Smith and Pocahontas represent an ideal amalgamation of European and Native American. Even though this ideal was never realized, the connection between Smith and Pocahontas has remained fixed in the American imagination over the centuries. Robert Tilton argues convincingly that the rescue story is the basis for the appeal of these figures, that it acts as a creation myth for America. The pair incorporates traits from European and Indian cultures essential to the hunter hero who comes to symbolize American independence.

The Rescue

The rescue of Smith by Pocahontas is part of the larger history of the initial settlement at Jamestown, Virginia, 1606–1607. Henry Wharton describes Smith's involvement in the Virginia colony in his laudatory *Life of John Smith* (1685).[1] He describes how Smith found the colony in shambles "because of factionalism, carelessness, and over confidence among the settlers." Between the attacks of the Indians and the ineptitude and lethargy of the colonists, expectations of prosperity soon disappeared. The social make-up of the colonists consisted of "a few leaders" who were willing to help in the work of settling Jamestown, which included fighting the "barbarians" and doing hard, physical labor to scratch out an existence. Many of the new citizens of Virginia were these "who had escaped the gallows or had completely squandered their inheritance in brothels and inns." And although Smith was sent with the responsibility to "remedy the situation," he wasn't given the authority of complete control. He was to serve as a council member with the governor (64).

Many of those whom Smith found in the struggling colony would not work even to save their own lives; they seemed incapable or unwilling to do what was necessary to survive. Wharton describes the problems Smith encountered and the treachery that jealousy of Smith inspired.

> The Governor and the greater part of the leaders . . . spread slander about Smith here and there among the sailors and the soldiers, cast suspicions upon him, accused him of having ambitions to become king, and, as their boldness increased, deprived him even of the membership in the Council with which he had been entrusted. (64–65)

Smith, however, decided to act with bravado. He laughed at the insults and insinuations and did not try to pursue any legal claim against them. Finally, the fear of the Indians was so great that no one would venture outside the fort, with the result that food and provisions were exhausted and the colony faced starvation. Whether they liked it or not, the governor and council members had to trust Smith's administration or perish (Wharton 64–65).

Although Wharton's style is dramatic in relating this series of events, the basic facts of the situation have been substantiated by others.[2] Smith's reputation as a hero prior to the Pocahontas incident sets the stage for the events that unfolded. Smith is portrayed as a practical and courageous leader who took on the task of saving the floundering colony in a methodical way.

First, Smith worked on the barracks and fortifications and, although the governor still retained ultimate authority, Smith was responsible for all military affairs. Leaving the colonists with forty-four of the fifty armed men in the fort, he took six soldiers to foray through the forest to find Indians who would trade for grain. According to Wharton, along the way Smith and his men encountered "savages [who] laughed at this insane boldness and, sure that the English would anyhow soon perish, gently proffered Smith a handful of grain." Smith and his men answered by dispatching a hail from their guns. A skirmish ensued in which the Indians had superiority of numbers, but the colonists "repaid the arrows with bullets, and their superior effects were matched by their higher morale." The standard bearer for the Indians fell to the ground and with him an idol that had been carried into battle. The Indians then desisted. The English snatched the idol and exchanged it "for a very great amount of grain" (65–66).

These preliminary adventures are important for several reasons. Despite conflicting views of Smith, no one has denied that he acted bravely in the New World. He was fighting the jealousy, laziness, and incompetence of those who, although more highly born, were less able to cope with the problems they encountered. Wharton strongly suggests the aspersions cast on Smith's reputation by the "gentlemen" in his party were not based so much on his failings but on his status as a commoner (64–66).

Smith had to function in a situation where traditional European values, which emphasized the privileges of aristocracy, were unworkable. First, the settlers were physically removed from English political and social influences. Second, the talents needed to survive in the New World were in opposition to the complacent aristocratic assumptions about labor. What the colonial setting required was self-reliance and common sense, qualities Smith possessed. These traits were foregrounded by the necessities of wilderness living and would eventually make the hunter figure the ideal representation of that experience. In the wilderness, physical self-reliance and independence also fostered mental self-reliance and independence. Smith developed confidence as a result of his abilities, which in turn endowed him with a form of power unknown to commoners under the European power structure. He was especially critical of the cowardly acts by those who considered themselves his betters.

When Smith returned to the fort, he found the governor and others planning to desert Virginia and sail for England. Writing in the third person,

since he included materials he acquired from others along with his own
adventures and observations, Smith described this incident in the third
book of his *Historie of Virginia:*

> Wingfield and Kendall . . . in the absence of Smith, . . . strengthened themselves
> with the sailers, and other confederates . . . abord the Pinnance, (being fitted to
> saile as Smith had appointed for trade) to alter her course and goe to England.
> Smith unexpectedly returning had the plot discovered to him, much trouble he
> had to prevent it, till with store of sakre and musket shot he forced them stay or
> sinke in the river, which action cost the life of captaine Kendall. (94–95)

Smith prevailed, and in the spring of 1607 he went in quest of the
sources of the Chickahominy River. When he was prevented from sailing
farther upstream by overhanging foliage, he led a small party to explore
the interior of the province. He and his men, who included two Christian
Indians, encountered and battled a large group of three hundred Indians,
led by Opechancanough, brother of Powhatan and King of the Pamunkey.
Smith conducted himself with audacity. At one point, he tied one of his
Indian allies to him as a shield. His other Indian ally had fled, and the two
other Englishmen were killed. He was finally wounded, captured, and
transported to Powhatan, the Emperor. Along the way, he impressed the
Indians by presenting his watch to Opechancanough and lecturing on
"the movement of the heavens, the measurement of time, and the alterna-
tion of days and nights" (Wharton 70).

Eventually, Smith was brought to Powhatan, and it was then that his
famous rescue occurred. According to Smith's account, Powhatan's favorite daughter, the princess Pocahontas (whose name means "playful"
or "lively"), saved him from death by physically placing herself between
him and the poised clubs of her tribe members.

In 1624, Smith recounted how tribe members brought him to
Meronocomo, where he met the Emperor Powhatan. While more than
two hundred "Courtiers" gawked at Smith, the emperor and his entourage made their entrance. Powhatan was dressed in a robe of raccoon
skins with the tails "hanging by." On each side of him sat a young girl of
about sixteen to eighteen years old, along with rows of men and, behind
them, women along the sides of the "house." The heads and shoulders of
the attendants were painted red, and many were adorned with the white
feathers of birds on their heads and necklaces of beads around their necks.
As the emperor entered, his subjects shouted and the "Queene of
Appamatuck was appointed to bring him water to wash his hands, and
another brought him a bunch of feathers, in stead of a Towell to dry

them." Next was a great feast and, afterward, a long consultation. "But the conclusion was, two great stones were brought before Powhatan: then as many as could layd hands on [Smith], dragged him to them, and thereon laid his head, and being ready with their clubs, to beate out his braines, Pocahontas the Kings dearest daughter, when no intraty could prevaile, got his head in her armes, and laid her owne upon his to save him from death" (J. Smith, *Generall Historie of Virginia* 101).

What has been remembered from Smith's account of this incident is the rescue scene. Other significant information is not as well known.[3] For example, Pocahontas was a young girl of perhaps twelve years old and Smith was twenty-seven. In 1612, she was held captive in Jamestown— the taking of captives by Indians and whites was a political tool used by both. While in captivity, she converted to Christianity and was christened "Rebecca." She subsequently married and had a son by John Rolfe, an English planter. After her marriage to Rolfe, she traveled to England, where she was presented at court to King James I and Queen Anne as a princess in her own right.

The rescue itself presents a problem of interpretation. Barbour, Tilton, Frances Mossiker, and others offer a possible explanation for Smith's rescue by Pocahontas, which might not have been obvious to Smith. There is also the possibility that Smith may have been aware of such explanation, but did not articulate it in his writing. In fact, he did not even mention the rescue in the initial account of his adventures.

The alternative explanation to Smith's belief that his imminent execution was halted by Pocahontas is that the actions of the Powhatans and Pocahontas may have been rites in an elaborate adoption ceremony, which Smith did not understand was taking place. The "death" of Smith (as a white man) and his "rebirth" (as an Indian) by virtue of Pocahontas's "sacrifice" may have been staged to initiate him into the tribe. But, whatever the circumstances of the rescue may have been, it acquired an enduring fame. The figures of Smith and Pocahontas became inextricably linked in the popular imagination.

Tilton and several other critics hold the view that portrayals of this incident during the colonial period may have been attempts to rally antimonarchial sentiment.[4] If indeed Pocahontas did defy her King/father with impunity, her example teaches a dangerous lesson: If the monarch/father is unjust, he can and should be challenged. Viewed retrospectively from the time of the American Revolution, the story becomes even more powerful.

Tilton sees a correspondence between the "myths" of George Washington and the cherry tree and the rescue of Smith by Pocahontas in that both narratives involve "an incident from the youth of the protagonist that in some way explains or predicts the adult actions of Washington and Pocahontas." He explains that in each story the young person shows bravery when facing a powerful adversary, with the most important ingredient being a challenge to "patriarchal power" no matter what the result of such a challenge. Finally, there is "an appeal to honesty as the key to unlock an expression of paternal love." Pocahontas is willing to sacrifice herself to save Smith and exhibits overt defiance of her father's wishes. The result is that her father shows his love for his daughter by sparing Smith. In such a context Pocahontas becomes an example of rebellion against father and King, which turns out to be justified and has positive results (101–102).

This view has two interesting implications. First, the figure of Pocahontas as a rebellious woman inspires admiration rather than resentment. Second, the connection is made between Washington and Pocahontas as icons and appropriate role models who were nevertheless rebellious characters. Additionally, the liminal position of youth caught between childhood and adulthood figures significantly here. As a metaphor of transition, it has obvious resonances for the new nation itself. That the appeal of Smith's rescue by Pocahontas has endured hundreds of years suggests that the story speaks in a lasting fashion to the American psyche.

In his *True Relation of such occurrences and accidents of noate as hath hapned in Virginia since the first planting of that Collony* (1608), John Smith casts himself as the father not only of Jamestown but also of his own image. Smith's self-portrait is unabashedly heroic. He was not unduly burdened by modesty, of course, but the fulsome descriptions of his exploits in America may have been a form of self-defense because his leadership was often questioned and challenged. The need to justify what he did would have been very much on his mind. His enemies were everywhere, constantly seeking to discredit him. Smith may have been suspect because he spent a great deal of time with the Indians, unlike most of the other early settlers. Like the Indians, he developed a respect for the natural way of life that ensured survival in the wilderness.

Seeing Smith as the "other" in his society is especially interesting when considering the nature of the American hunter figure. The hunter is relied upon by, but not fully accepted as a member of, the "civilized" society. When Smith went into the wilderness to find food for the colony, only to be captured and eventually accepted by the Powhatans, he became even more alien to those he left behind in "civilization."

Smith, the Indians, and Hunting

Smith described the hunting habits of the Indians in detail and with obvious admiration. He explained how hunting skills were necessary for the "industry" of the tribe, the methods of hunting in a company, and the disposition of the various portions of harvested game. And he made reference to his own captivity by a large hunting party in a swamp along the Chickahominy River. "In one of these huntings they found me in the discovery of the head of the river of Chickahamania, where they slew my men, and tooke me prisoner in a Bogmire, where I saw those exercises, and gathered these Observations" (*Generall Historie of Virginia* 66–67).

The cooperation among tribe members to carry out the hunting activity—the distribution of work to process the various products of the hunt with the accompanying division of labor—highlights the status of the hunter/warrior. Smith emphasized the skill required by the various tribe members, particularly the details of stalking deer.

> One Salvage hunting alone, useth the skinne of a Deere slit on one side, and so put on his arme, through the neck, so that his hand comes to the head which is stuffed, and the hornes, head, eyes, eares, and every part as artificially counterfeited as they can devise. Thus shrowding his body in the skinne by stalking, he approacheth the Deere. . . . If the Deere chance to find fault, or stand at gaze, he turneth the head with his hand to his best advantage to seeme like a Deere. (*Generall Historie of Virginia* 67–68)

Here the Indian hunter immerses himself in the animal world and even dresses as the animal, identifying with his prey. The Indian perception of the animal and human worlds has been described as joined (Kerasote 52–60). Man is not seen as superior to his fellow creatures; they are all inhabitants of the same family. Animals and men are brothers necessary for the other's survival. Men need to understand the habits of their brother creatures and appreciate their "sacrifice" in the hunt. The practice of preserving the head and horns of deer originally was a salute to the animal, not the hunter. The hunter took only what he needed and thus a balance was maintained. The pride of a hunter was not based on individual prowess or competition, but rather on being able to participate in the process. To be a hunter was a grave responsibility and an honor. Man was part of the cycle of nature, not in charge of it. Dangerous animals could hunt the human hunter—man was part of the food chain. Techniques for pursuing game, killing it, and processing it represented important aspects of the Indian culture and way of life. They were at once practical and symbolic. Smith understood this.

Smith observed both group and single hunting techniques, noting the contributions by different members of the tribe. He carefully noted the uses to which the animals were put, and how bows and arrows and knives were made. He described how they used bows and arrows to hunt and fish, detailing their construction. "They bring their bowes to the forme of ours by the scraping of a shell. Their arrowes are made some of straight young sprigs, which they head with bone, some 2 or 3 ynches long." Smith explained that crystal splinters, sharp stones, turkey spurs, and the bills of birds were also employed for cutting implements. Cutting up deer and making shoes and other clothing required sharp knives, which the Indians crafted out of reeds. The nochs on the arrows were cut out using a beaver's tooth, which had been set in a stick. Glue was made from the sinews of deer and a jelly obtained by boiling antlers (*Generall Historie of Virginia* 65).

There is no indication that Smith adopted the methods of the Indians, but he certainly admired the useful aspects of much of their craft.

Pocahontas and Smith After the Rescue

Frances Mossiker thoroughly reviews the research on the figure of Pocahontas in history and fiction. She sees Pocahontas as a catalyst in establishing the first settlement in America because, after the rescue, Pocahontas was instrumental in saving the struggling colony. She visited Jamestown herself, bringing supplies. When her father objected to these visits, she helped Smith arrange trade with other branches of her tribe. Such trade was crucial for survival because the colonists had not adapted to the demands of the New World. Smith realized the value of the princess's practical and political significance for the future of the colony.

Aside from Smith and a few others, the English settlers refused to see the necessity of adopting Indian methods for hunting and farming. Their stubborn attachment to European notions almost destroyed the colony. Adopting aspects of the Indian lifestyle and husbandry was as crucial to survival as negotiating peace with the Indians.

The Virginia colony's harsh first years illustrate these two important lessons. First, the colonists had to learn the practical skills necessary for thriving in their new environment—skills they could learn from the Indians. Second, they had to understand, if not accept, aspects of Indian culture that could make cohabitation possible. Pocahontas and Smith were the first to cross the cultural barriers separating Indian from European. The American hunter figure is heir to this legacy of crossing cultures.

Smith's captivity exemplifies the European immersed in Indian culture. Although this immersion was not voluntary, it provided him with insight that served him well in later dealings with the Indians. Pocahontas crossed cultures several times in her short life and provides an even more dramatic example of liminality.

Pocahontas represents the ideal of the hunter/warrior in her role as princess of a hunting people. She also reflects the Indian's connection to the world of nature because the hunter/warrior is mythically joined to the earth and its life forms. The Indian hunter considers himself part of nature, and his hunting represents his participation in the cycle of life and death. Unlike the European view of man as apart from the animals and having dominion over them, Indian cosmology locates man as interdependent with—not superior to—other creatures.

A number of components came together to form the traits of the American hunter figure. He emerged from a combination of the Indian hunter/warrior embodied in Pocahontas and her people and the European adventurer/settler embodied in Smith. But the key to seeing Smith and Pocahontas as parent figures for the hunter lies in their crossing into each other's world. Smith and Pocahontas survived and flourished as a result of crossing barriers, while others struggled or perished by remaining static and separate. Smith and Pocahontas were the first to make the transition and adapt in both Anglo and Indian worlds. This mobility surely undergirds their enduring place in the American imagination.

Once Smith was "rescued," he still had to negotiate the treacherous politics of the colony. Jamestown was in a precarious position. Smith was careful not to let the Indians know that permanent settlement, let alone expansion, was the purpose of the crown. After the rescue and Pocahontas's help to the settlers, relations between the Indians and the English took several turns for the worse. Smith was also still contending with malcontents who sought to undermine him. Although Powhatan suspected the true intent of Smith and the English was to settle in America and displace his people, Pocahontas remained loyal to Smith. When Powhatan planned an attack on Smith's life, Pocahontas warned him at considerable risk to her own. If her father had found her out, she would have been killed. She delivered the message, refused any reward, and slipped away into the forest. This visit under cover of night was the last between Pocahontas and Smith in the New World; he did not see her again until they met during her trip to London several years later.

Smith had ambitions beyond Jamestown. He wanted an appointment to some important post in New England, and his connection to Pocahontas could prove inconvenient. He wrote that his feelings for her were "brotherly" or "fatherly," but indicated that she might characterize hers for him quite differently. After their last meeting, when she warned him of treachery, he allowed her to think him dead. Her subsequent marriage to Rolfe may have been possible only because she held this belief.

Pocahontas and Smith met in England years after the rescue. According to Smith, he wrote to Queen Anne upon the visit of Pocahontas to London and praised her. His addressed a "little book" (i.e., a formal epistle or memorial) to Queen Anne praising the qualities of Pocahontas. The importance of this surviving abstract is not whether it is verbatim, but that it shows Smith's attitude toward Pocahontas. He wanted to make clear the extent to which Pocahontas had gone to save Jamestown, and his tone was affectionate in a brotherly, if not fatherly, way (Barbour, *Three Worlds* 329).

Smith offered some useful insight to the monarch in suggesting the vital role Pocahontas might yet play in Great Britain's success in the New World. After detailing the numerous services Pocahontas rendered to the struggling colony of Virginia, he suggested the role she might yet play in solidifying Great Britain's interests in the New World. The kingdom might be extended through Pocahontas, who was royalty in her own right. But, should she be alienated, she might forget her love for England and Christianity. Smith added that the Queen's aid could bring about what she and the King's subjects most earnestly desired (Barbour, *Three Worlds* 330).

If, through marriage to an Englishman, Pocahontas could bring about peaceful relations between the settlers and the Indians, Great Britain could then profit from the alliance. Smith was only too aware of the delicate hold the settlers had in the colony of Virginia. But he may not have been aware of the effect of his supposed death on Pocahontas. When Pocahontas saw Smith again in England, she

> was visibly disturbed when [he] . . . arrived, turned aside from her guests, and remained silent for so long that Smith, as he puts it, repented "to himself to have writ she . . . could speak English." Rolfe and Smith and the others then left her for awhile, "as not seeming well contented," but an hour or two or three later returned, to find her in a more talkative mood. (Barbour, *Three Worlds* 331)

A rendition of the conversation between Smith and Pocahontas at this meeting appeared in Smith's *Generall Historie of Virginia*. He recounted that she spoke to him about his relationship with her father and their agreement that "what was yours should bee his, and he the like to you; you called him father being in his land a stranger, and by the same reason so must I doe you." Smith explained he would not allow her to call him "father" since she was a king's daughter. She replied that he had come to her father's country and caused fear in him and all his people with the exception of herself, adding that he should not fear her calling him "father." She said she would continue to do so and insisted that he call her "childe," thus signifying their being countrymen. Smith also told us that Pocahontas had reports of his death and believed them; her father had tried to find out the veracity of these reports "because your Countriemen lie much" (*Generall Historie of Virginia* 238–239).

This account reveals Pocahontas as an articulate and intelligent young woman. Her comment on the veracity of Englishmen is particularly pointed, considering Smith's deception about his death. Even though this dialogue was reconstructed by Smith, he seemed unaware of the barbs she was flinging him. The verbal sparring in this scene clearly shows Pocahontas to advantage.

Shortly after this encounter, when she was about to sail back to America, Pocahontas took ill and died at Gravesend, where she was buried. Twenty-one or twenty-two years old, she was survived by her husband, John Rolfe, and their son, Thomas.

Pocahontas negotiated vastly different cultures at a time when her gender and youth usually posed insurmountable barriers. That she was able to cross between these worlds and flourish is testament to her legend.

Pocahontas as Mother

Although no one before has paired Pocahontas and Smith as metaphorical progenitors of the American hero, Pocahontas has been read as the mother figure by several critics. Philip Young, Vachel Lindsay, Mary Dearborn, and Frances Mossiker are only a few of those who have discussed "our mother, Pocahontas." And there are numerous references to Smith as the "American Aeneas." These important allusions underline the mythic aspect of the Pocahontas-Smith relationship as parents and founders. Further, Pocahontas as mother figure comes from the wilderness. She crosses over into the world of civilized Christianity but still retains her tie to the natural world.

Tilton addresses the issue of amalgamation in the colonial period in his book, *Pocahontas, The Evolution of an American Narrative.* This work originally appeared as his dissertation, entitled "American Lavinia: The Pocahontas Narrative in Ante-Bellum America." (The title of the dissertation is more relevant to Smith's and Pocahontas's roles as parent

figures than the title of his book.) Tilton sees a connection between the
Roman and American founding "myths," which explains the title of his
dissertation.

Princess Lavinia of Latium married the hero Aeneas, who had invaded
her country. Their descendants inhabited the glory that became Rome a
thousand years later. "Her race survived the war between two nations,
and was merged with the Trojans to form the Roman people." Aeneas
and Lavinia were considered the parents of the Roman nobility. The parallel between Lavinia and Pocahontas stems from the same pattern. Princess Pocahontas eventually married one of the "invaders," John Rolfe
(not Smith), and their union begat the "nobility" of the "Old Dominion."
In both cases, marriage of a princess brought a period of peace between
warring factions (Tilton, "American Lavinia" 4).

The parallel is helpful in providing a context for the Pocahontas narrative. Although it would be ideal to see Smith and Pocahontas as marriage
partners after the rescue, the story of the American Lavinia works out
differently from that of the Roman Lavinia, and the reasons for this difference are quite important. Tilton continues:

> However, while Anglo-Americans often hypothesized about a peaceful merging
> with the Indians and the creation of one people, Pocahontas's race was not given
> the opportunity granted to the Latins to join with their conquerors, and their
> survival to this day owes little to the efforts of the European invaders. On a
> figurative level, however, as one can argue that as Lavinia was the "mother" of
> the Roman Empire, so the princess of Virginia is for all Americans, as Vachel
> Lindsay put it, "Our mother, Pocahontas." ("American Lavinia" 4)

Amalgamation presented the possibility of resolving a number of problems. The access to land could most easily be accomplished by marriage
between European settlers and Indian inhabitants, although attitudes toward ownership and land usage were quite different for Indians and whites.
While the Indians used the land for hunting, cultivating, and inhabiting,
they did not think of specific parcels as belonging to them, let alone
inheriting land from their ancestors or willing land to their heirs. The
emphasis was on the land's use, and freedom to range over it for whatever purpose was pressing at the time. Ownership of land would seem as
ridiculous as ownership of the sunrise or the sunset, the ocean or the
seasons. Once the initial connection could be made through marriage,
however, the chances of land inheritance over a period of time would
make redistribution and further settlement more palatable for everyone.
Once a people composed of both Indian and European bloodlines evolved

into a blended whole, the spectre of warring over land rights could be exorcized.

In reality, however, the possibility of amalgamation remained an elusive ideal, circumscribed by issues of both race and gender. The union of a European man and an Indian woman, for example, was far more acceptable than the union of an Indian man and a European woman. Others have discussed this bias, and Tilton skillfully summarizes these views. He tells us that the significance of Pocahontas is mythic. The story of her rescue of Smith was accompanied by a realization that she was "an actual, flesh-and-blood woman" who had left her position and her people, married an Englishman, born a son, and "whose descendants were highly visible members of the colonial Southern aristocracy." Although the pattern of Red and White marriage was not followed by others, it did prove that such amalgamation was possible ("American Lavinia" 19–20).

Despite the attraction of interracial marriage and its promise of amalgamation, the fear of miscegenation predominated. Indeed, the racial anxieties of the colonists were firmly in place before they left England. Of course, there are notable exceptions to this rule. The Southern aristocracy's claims to descendence from the Pocahontas-Rolfe marriage are the most striking example, all the more so for its uniqueness in a country that has traditionally embraced the "melting pot" as a central metaphor. Tilton argues that one reason why the story of the rescue of John Smith has survived and predominated over the story of the courtship and marriage of Pocahontas and John Rolfe is that the rescue is a much less threatening narrative for those who fear miscegenation.

Another explanation for the rescue story's appeal is that it seemed to resolve miscegenation: It satisfied the appeal of amalgamation but avoided the threatening reality of consummation. It satisfied the American conflict between rebelling against authority and the need for tradition.

Pocahontas as metaphorical mother of the American hunter operates in two ways. First, many hunters who subsequently inhabited the frontier were racially mixed progeny of European men and Indian women. (The reverse combination also occurred, but not as often.) Second, even if not racially mixed, hunters were culturally amalgamated. This amalgamation was reflected in their commerce with the Indians, their lifestyle, and their mode of dress. Hunters incorporated the traits needed to survive and flourish from the colonial period and into the new Republic.

The American hunter shares a common heritage with other mythic hunters and several similarities with his European counterparts. But the

American hunter is unique to the American landscape, both literal and mental. His ability to negotiate cultural chasms was the defining trait that distinguished this American hunter figure.

In effect, the hunter in America redefined the nature of aristocracy. In Smith's case, his association with Pocahontas, who is princess of the "savage" world, a world of hunters and warriors, placed him in a position between European nobility and "savage" nobility. He functioned in both worlds, but he was fully embraced by neither. Smith hunted, but he is not known as a hunter; Pocahontas was the princess of a hunting people, but she is not known as a hunter either. Rather, these figures are combined in the popular imagination and can be viewed as progenitors of the figure who later emerged as the American hunter figure.

Daniel Boone was the first hunter to embody this figure. Richard Slotkin argues that the image of Daniel Boone lies in his ease in adjusting to meet certain basic needs of the people of frontier America. The flexibility of this image is the key to its strength and endurance. Tilton links Boone's flexible image to the figure of Pocahontas. He argues that both figures possess the ability to "express multiple, and at times contradictory agendas" ("American Lavinia" 1–2).

The Pocahontas narrative that "address[ed] a number of racial, cultural, and gender-related issues" is as relevant today as it was during the colonial and ante-bellum eras. Its "cultural usefulness" is indeed the key to its pervasiveness. Pocahontas is not only a mother figure but, additionally, a model of female power and self-determination. This power is usually found only in goddess figures, and Pocahontas is such a goddess figure.

Frances Mossiker addresses the role of Pocahontas in relieving racial anxiety. Mossiker implies that Pocahontas is a mythic figure largely because she embodies the ideal of amalgamation of the races through marriage, which the Europeans saw as the only possibility for redeeming the fearful "savage." Pocahontas is the prime example of the romantic "noble savage": royal, dignified, athletic, one with nature. At the same time, she is the Christian convert: intelligent, able to speak English and adopt European manners, a paragon accepted by King James I and Queen Anne at court.

Although the England Pocahontas visited was closer to the Renaissance than the Enlightenment, she prefigured the noble savage. Apparently her royalty as a princess was so thoroughly accepted by the court of King James I—and the King himself—that she was admitted to an audience with the King and Queen Anne. Her husband, a mere middle-class farmer, was excluded. Mossiker also indicates that King James was highly displeased with Rolfe for having married so far above him.

Apparently King James was furious that a mere commoner like Rolfe would marry a royal princess. Tilton points out that the King was "offended that this was a corruption of the royal blood of America," but the deeper reason for his anger could have been a fear that Rolfe might claim his own kingship through his marriage to Pocahontas, or if he did not, his son might, thus thwarting England's claim to the colony ("American Lavinia" 29–30).

Tilton's comments about Rolfe have several implications. Class distinctions were much more than social snobbery. Nobility and the lines of inheritance determined land ownership and entitlements. Claims to royalty carried political power. Therefore, the threat of a prior claim, such as one by Rolfe based on his "royal" marriage to Pocahontas, conceivably was a threat to the English monarchy's claim to Virginia.

Rolfe's situation also had implications for Smith. A commoner, no matter how talented, could not ascend to noble status except through marriage—and then the elevation in rank would usually pertain only to offspring. The aristocracy was a closed and self-protective group, with long tradition dictating their rights and privileges. Wharton stresses that notions about aristocracy shaped the contemporary view of Smith. Wharton's translator, Laura Polanyi Striker, comments that Wharton believed Smith's commoner status was the main reason for derision by the gentry. The nobility was unable to appreciate the merits of one not of their class. Further, they were threatened by the very idea that a commoner could outstrip them (3–31).

In Virginia, Rolfe was considered something of a martyr for having taken the responsibility of amalgamating with the Indian to ensure peace. Rolfe himself wrote a lengthy letter to Governor Thomas Dale in the form of an apology, explaining his motives for wanting to marry Pocahontas, and history has taken a dim view of his sanctimonious attitude toward his bride. He apologized for loving her and wrote that he suffered and prayed over the matter to determine whether or not he had experienced lust or true love, and only after great moral self-examination in the Puritan tradition did he decide that it was indeed God's will driving him to such action.

Lett therefore this my well advised ptestacon, wch here I make betweene God and my owne Conscience be suffifient wyttnes . . . (noe waye leade soe farr foorth as mans weaknes may pmytt, wth the vnbridled desire for Carnall affection) for the good of the Plantacon, the honor of or Countrye, for the glorye of God, for myne owne salvacon, and for the Cnvertinge to the true knowledge of God and Iesus Christ and vnbeleivinge Creature, namely Pocahuntas To Whome my hart and best thoughts are and have byn a longe tyme soe intangled & in thralled in soe intricate a Laborinth that I was even awearied to vnwnde my selfe thereout. (Mossiker 345)

That Pocahontas was viewed so differently in America and England illustrates opposing connotations of the Indian princess. As American royalty and a possible vehicle for British claim to American land, she was aligned with European aristocracy. In this persona, too, she was mythic mother figure to the hunter. As an Indian girl who married a Euro-American farmer, she was a racial and religious threat to the settlers. A century would pass before Southern "aristocrats" happily traced their lineage to Princess Pocahontas.

Pocahontas did not leave any written record of her experience. She has been written about, however, and portrayed by many in ways that reflect their own agendas. Of course, Smith is the most notable. He recounted what she said, but there is no word directly from the princess herself. Pocahontas spoke in other ways. Her actions provide a text that has several interpretations, but stands as her direct utterance. She inspired the love of her father, rescued Smith, helped the colonists, converted to Christianity, married Rolfe and bore a son, traveled to England, and impressed the court. Yet her position in the worlds she traveled between was precarious: She left her own people to become the "other" in Anglo-European Virginia, the first female ethnic figure.

"Otherness" was another condition linking Pocahontas and Smith. Smith was the "other" in his culture because of his status as commoner and his commerce with the Indians and Pocahontas.

Myth, Aristocracy, and the Hunter

The narrative of Pocahontas, especially the rescue of Smith, is in essence our first national myth. And since a main function of myth is to supply an emotionally satisfying story whose psychic underpinning reinforces the culture, the Pocahontas–John Smith narrative is the ideal American creation myth for several reasons. Main concerns in American culture over the span of time have been and continue to be landscape, identity, and race and gender. Permutations of the hunter figure unite these concerns and provide models that serve as focal points. The forms the hunter figure takes during different stages of the country's development are expressions of those cultural concerns.

In terms of the mythic aspects of the hunter figure, the most useful work is Richard Slotkin's critical trilogy, *Regeneration Through Violence: The Mythology of the American Frontier, 1660–1860* (1973); *The Fatal Environment: The Myth of the Frontier in the Age of Industrializa-*

tion, 1800–1890 (1985); and *Gunfighter Nation: The Myth of the Frontier in Twentieth Century America* (1992). In these seminal studies, Slotkin argues that "the reigning American frontier myth is the tale of a superior . . . man . . . securing his own regeneration, and often that of the nation, through violent conflict. In these books, the frontier myth . . . serves as a sort of American creation story, played out in endless variations" (Pascoe 20).

Landscape is an essential element in the American experience, especially the concept of wilderness. Wilderness represents both the literal and figurative stages for the drama of American exploration and development. The hunter's identity grows out of his relationship to the land he traverses. Like an epic hero, the hunter journeys through the physical landscape and gains knowledge and skill. He is tested and proves himself worthy, a process that establishes his identity.

The hunter figure emerges in American history and literature precisely when Americans are most preoccupied with their own landscape. Unlike the Spanish who came to the Americas for conquest and trade with little intention of permanent settlement, the English sought to establish colonies. The settlers who hunted had to adopt many of the skills of the Native Americans. The figure who emerges after combining the traits of the European adventurer-settler and the Native American becomes the "American hunter."

The hunter figure becomes virtually the only "comfortable" amalgamation of the two peoples. The settlers had conflicting loyalties between England and America. They were not ready for the demands that the physical landscape presented: the severe weather; the intimidating topography of forests and mountains; the uncooperative inhabitants who were surprisingly reluctant to have their land wrested from them. Only through adaptation did the settlers progress from mere survival to gaining a foothold in the New World and, ultimately, to thriving in it. The hunter was the first to make this transition.

Spanish philosopher Jose Ortega y Gasset, in *Meditations on Hunting* (1942), offers insights on the relationship of the hunter to the land, drawing some interesting conclusions about the nature of aristocracy and the central role of land ownership. Hunting is emblematic of aristocracy. In European society, Ortega argues, it is the nobility and landed gentry who determine hunting rights, with the emphasis on sport rather than subsistence. He points out "the almost universally privileged nature of the sport of hunting" and believes it is part of the human condition to yearn to hunt. Further, class hatred evidenced in periods of revolution grows out of the limitations placed on hunting by the upper class to prevent the lower class from pursuing the activity: "The first thing that the 'people' have done was to jump over the fences of the preserves or tear them down, and in the name of social justice pursue the hare and the partridge" (30).

In addition to providing a physical setting for the hunter, the landscape is a symbol of power. Those who impose limitations on the landscape wield social power. As America grew, land rights were defined to fit circumstances in the New World. Three factors came into play: the granting of land by monarchs who were far removed in physical distance and direct experience, the presence of native inhabitants whose conception of land rights was quite different from European notions of ownership, and the vastness and variety of the terrain. Although not unscathed, the hunter negotiated the land itself and its accompanying ownership issues. He succeeded in the New World and emerged as a new type, developing skills and attitudes needed to meet the special demands of the American wilderness.[5] The basis for his ability to cross these literal and political borders was his intimate tie to the natural environment. Hunting allowed him to move through the landscape, feeding himself and sometimes making a profit.

The key role of landscape in the American experience is treated in Jane Tompkins' *West of Everything: The Inner Life of Westerns*. She sees the rekindling of interest in the western as significantly tied to physical landscape. Tompkins argues that the landscape is the genesis of almost any western and, particularly when well illustrated by desert locations in film, "we have the sense of being present at a moment before time began" (70). In her view, emptiness represents another repeating American motif. Attention to landscape emphasizes the creation, or more exactly, the conscious re-creation of a world in order to begin again, to find a fresh setting for action. Physical movement through the landscape from Europe to America, from the East to the West, from stasis to mobility, is a pattern in American culture. Tompkins' point about the western landscape can be readily expanded to embrace the entire process of settling the frontier.

The relative ease of mobility is again an American distinction. Pocahontas and Smith established a precedent for movement between landscapes, both literal and figurative. Philip Fisher comments that a "unifying force [within American society is] mobility itself," since moving from place to place interrupts the notion of tradition within any ethnic ghetto (xiii). Specific identification with any group depends upon that group remaining intact, passing on the culture from generation to generation. Even one move geographically tends toward the "melting pot" (xiii).

A basis of American national identity is that other identities are left behind when the individual moves. What is striking when examining the hunter figure is that he defines who he is largely through his ability to move through the landscape, interacting with it and with those who inhabit it. He does not leave part of his identity behind, however, but enhances and reinforces it. The hunter redefines the European notion of aristocracy from Ortega's inheritor of land with the "privilege" of hunting to one who "inherits" the land through his prowess in negotiating it, harvesting its animals, and forming a relationship with the land that transcends the proprietary. The hunter and the land are linked; the hunter is part of the land and the land is a part of the hunter.

Parallels to mythic hunters, especially those who are in transition or are transformed or come to grief as a result of transgressing taboos are applicable in a discussion of liminality. In his essay, "The Black Hunter and the Origin of the Athenian Ephebia," Pierre Vidal-Naquet discusses the liminal quality of young men in the Athenian Ephebia—a two-year period of military service described by Aristotle (106). The Ephebia served on the "frontier" before taking up the responsibilities of marriage and full citizenship. Vidal-Naquet sees the position of these young men as marginal, poised between opposing forces in society. He bases his premise on the myth of the Black Hunter.

Several versions and interpretations of this myth exist but, in general, it has to do with a contest between Melanthos (the black one) and Xanthos (the fair one) to settle a dispute arising during a festival, the Apaturia. Melanthos wins by means of a trick and eventually becomes King of Athens.

The myth has been found in texts as far back as the fifth century B.C. The setting is the frontier, called an *eschatia,* which is at the end of a city's boundary. It is a mountainous region between Athens and Boeotia. Such a frontier area was the haunt of shepherds and hunters, and the boundaries tended to be in constant dispute. During this period, the Athenians and Boeotians were fighting and the Boeotian King Xanthos, "the fair one," was to settle the matter in a duel with Thymoites, King of Athens and last descendant of Theseus. But Thymoites was old, and in his place the warrior Melanthos, "the black one," was to fight "the fair one" (Vidal-Naquet 109–110).

The key to the incident as Vidal-Naquet sees it is the deception or trick Melanthos used to defeat Xanthos. During the fight, Melanthos cried out to Xanthos that someone was beside him. Xanthos turned to look and was killed by Melanthos as a result of the distraction. Melanthos then became King of Athens (110).

Vidal-Naquet explores the significance of the trick. Connotations of hunting permeated Greek society, and hunting was crucially connected to the Ephebia. He looks particularly at three aspects of the myth: the idea of the frontier, the trick itself, and the stress on blackness.

> [H]unting is linked fundamentally with the *argos* in Greece, the land that lies beyond the cultivated area, that is, with the *eschatiai*, the borderlands of Greek cities. Plato calls his ephebe, the person who defends the frontier area, an *agronomos* (*Laws* 6.760e–61a). More generally, hunting was so normal for heroes, whom the ephebes emulated, that F. Orth remarked that "heroes are hunters and hunters heroes." In a sense, hunting is on the side of the wild, the "raw," of night, and the skills employed in the Spartan *krypteia* [which is like the Ephebia] were those of hunting. (117)

In several ways the motif surrounding the Black Hunter in the classical world can be likened to the figure of the American hunter, essentially in the liminal quality that defines him. Both are part of the world of the frontier; both are associated with certain dualities, on the one hand admirable (cleverness), on the other questionable (wiliness); both are discussed in ambiguous language in which references to "darkness" or "blackness" abound. Finally, both are associated with transitional conditions, the Athenian Ephebia and colonial America.

However, the distinguishing factor for the American hunter is his flexible nature, which ensures his survival and defines his persona. Hunters who do not follow the strictures of the established order in the classical world most often meet with disaster. Also, unlike the classic hero or European hunter, the American hunter is rarely a member of the aristocracy or landed gentry. His power comes from his personal skill rather than from the will of the gods or the accident of heredity.

Vidal-Naquet describes various types of hunting and ascribes positive characteristics to mature, socialized hunters who use "manly" weapons, like spears. These individuals hunt in groups by the light of day. He ascribes negative characteristics to solitary, adolescent hunters who pursue game at night, using nets and snares. It is as if youth connotes not only the transitional phase of the hunter, but the negative pole of oppositions between dark and light, youth and age, solitary and social, cowardly and brave.

To take Vidal-Naquet's observations a step further, we can link the hunter figure and his country. European hunting was an aristocratic and highly organized activity, while American hunting was an independent, individualistic one. The hunter figure who emerges from the colonial period reflects the transition of America from British colony to new Republic. Daniel Boone and his fictional counterpart, Natty Bumppo, embodied the power to throw off aristocratic authority and develop this new nation.

Notes

1   Laura Polanyi Striker has translated the original Latin manuscript, "Vita Johannis Fabricii Militis Angli," *The Life of John Smith, English Soldier,* handwritten by Henry Wharton in 1685. Ms. Striker obtained permission from the Archbishop of Canterbury to microfilm the manuscript, which resides in Lambeth Library in London. She brought a microfilm copy to the United States in the 1950s, and it is available today at the Forty-second Street branch of the New York Public Library. Copies made from the microfilm are not good quality, but the film can be studied effectively on a viewer in the library. No printed copy of the Latin manuscript is known to exist.

2   Wharton emphasizes the negative influence of Smith's status as a commoner on public opinion. According to Striker, Wharton's defense of Smith is based on Wharton's religious conviction that humble origins are reflective of the examples set by Jesus and the apostles. The corrupt gentry was largely responsible for the defamation of Smith. Wharton likens the passions that motivated attacks on Smith—by those referring to themselves as "gentlemen" in Smith's company—to the jealousy and fear that spurred the betrayal and denial of Jesus.

3   Tilton cites a number of portrayals of the rescue in drama, pictorial representations, and the other arts in Ante-Bellum America.

4   See Tilton's chapter, "The Pocahontas Narrative in Post-Revolution America," pages 71–114, for the full discussion.

5   See Richard Slotkin, "A Gallery of Types," ch. 8 in *Regeneration Through Violence: The Mythology of the American Frontier, 1600–1860* (Middletown, CT: Wesleyan University Press, 1975), 223–367.

Chapter 2

Boone and Bumppo:
The Emerging Hunter Figure

This account of my adventures will inform the reader of the most remarkable events of this country.—I now live in peace and safety, enjoying the sweets of liberty, and the bounties of Providence, with my fellow-sufferers, in this delightful country, which I have seen purchased with a vast expense of blood and treasure, delighting in the prospect of its being, in a short time, one of the most opulent and powerful states on the continent of North-America; which, with the love and gratitude of my countrymen, I esteem a sufficient reward for my toil and dangers. (Daniel Boone qtd. in Filson 81–82)

. . .

The general Boon, back-woodsman of Kentucky,
Was happiest amongst mortals anywhere;
    For killing nothing but a bear or buck, he
Enjoy'd the lonely, vigorous, harmless days
Of his old age in wilds of deepest maze.
(Byron, *Don Juan*, Canto 8, LXI–LXII)

. . .

On the human imagination events produce the effects of time. Thus, he who has traveled far and seen much is apt to fancy that he has lived long, and the history that most abounds in important incidents soonest assumes the aspect of antiquity. In no other way can we account for the venerable air that is already gathering around American annals.
(Cooper, *The Deerslayer* 9)

Daniel Boone and James Fenimore Cooper's Natty Bumppo, embody the rugged individualism so central to American self-fashioning. Boone and Bumppo's lifetimes cover the period from colony to nation. They reflect a movement in American culture away from inherited power and toward individual prowess. The basis for Boone's and Bumppo's power lies in the hunter's ability to negotiate the landscape and to lead others across the continent.

Daniel Boone and the National Destiny

Boone: The Myth and the Man

John Mack Faragher's biography of Daniel Boone addresses the problems of sorting fact from folklore in Boone's life. Faragher concludes that fact and legend are entwined and, furthermore, the folklore evidence is not simply a way to reconstruct the facts of Boone's life (xvi). The first composite American hunter and hero is a model of possibility.[1] He provides a series of bridges between opposing forces in the culture during the colonial period and the new republic.

Boone as hunter provides a bridge first between the old world and the new. From adolescence, Boone inhabited a world that consisted of a mix of cultures. Hunters from varied backgrounds crossed paths in the woodlands, and smoked and talked together, exchanging trade, news, and information. Boone met many of these hunters and they became his "forest teachers." Some of these hunters were descended from European settlers "whom the Delawares called nittappi, or friends." Also among the hunters were several Indians of different "ethnic varieties"; these were the men, both red and white, who taught young Boone "a way of life that combined elements of both cultures and bridge[d] many of the differences between Indian and European. . . . This way of life . . . centered on hunting" (Faragher 19–20).

The original interaction between Indian and European seen in the model of Pocahontas and John Smith entered a new phase with Boone. He combined the Indian's ability to survive in the wilderness with the white man's desire for settlement and ownership. The hunter in America was quite different from the hunter in Europe, primarily because the American landscape seemed limitless.

The term *wilderness* connotes a number of images. The physical wilderness and its accompanying motif of an "inner wilderness" has been discussed elsewhere, especially in regard to the Puritan experience in the New World.[2] The New World was seen by the Puritans as a "New Eden" that held the opportunity for a "New Adam"[3] to perfect himself spiritually and prosper in the "Virgin Land."[4] The Puritans are most closely associated with the concept of the outer physical landscape reflecting an inner emotional or spiritual landscape. However, this relationship between the individual and his environment is repeated throughout the American experience and is exemplified in the figure of the hunter.

Perhaps the very traits enabling the hunter to set a foot in each of these two worlds deny him a full life in either. There may be an ease in traversing these worlds, but the liminal figure must be dynamic and cannot remain fixed for a long period of time. The hunter is the agent of change, the tool of transition, and, therefore, incapable of stasis. The worlds he traverses are in opposition, and he who negotiates them is constantly placed in the line of fire. He may pause, but he does not take up permanent residence. This restiveness is reflected outwardly by physical movement and inwardly by contemplation.

Numerous studies have addressed the subject of wilderness, including Henry Nash Smith's *Virgin Land: The American West as Symbol and Myth;* R. W. B. Lewis's *American Adam: Innocence, Tragedy, and Tradition in the Nineteenth Century;* Arthur K. Moore's *Frontier Mind;* Roderick Nash's *Wilderness and the American Mind;* David E. Shi's *Simple Life: Plain Living and High Thinking;* and Max Oelschlaeger's *Idea of Wilderness: From Prehistory to the Age of Ecology.* These works treat the importance of the concept of wilderness, and consider its initial and continuing effects upon American life and literature.

In his preface to the third edition of his book, Nash discusses how wilderness served as the "basic ingredient of American civilization." The physical wilderness provided the building materials for construction and simultaneously provided a symbolic identity and meaning. Appreciation of the wilderness is crucial to our intellectual history and its expression in America is unique in the experience of the world. He further points out that the psychological aspect of human beings urges them to try to "understand, order, and transform the environment." Wilderness stands for the unknown and uncontrollable in nature and in the human mind, with the prime directive being to tame what is "wilderness." He suggests that European colonists (as opposed to the hunters) "reexperienced" the ancient bias toward wilderness in America, which made them feel fearful and insecure (xi–xii).

Nash argues that American national identity is inextricably tied to wilderness. Because the hunter is linked to the environment, he is an appropriate lens through which to examine national identity. The hunter's identity resides in his relationship with the landscape. He is part of nature and he hunts to survive. But his skill does more than allow him to eat. Hunting is a way of life integrating survival with spiritual development. The hunter's lifestyle in the wilderness challenges him to explore his inner world as well. Indeed, the connection to an "inner wilderness" is reinforced by his physical experience. Especially for those who are unable to cope with the harshness of the topography and weather, the experience raises questions of purpose and often self-doubt. For those who are able to cope and, further, to meet the challenge of the new land and excel, there is a coinciding self-confidence.

The first figure to represent the American hunter hero, one who embodies both the physical and spiritual aspects of wilderness life, was Daniel Boone. The historical Boone and his legendary recreations provide an important model of the hunter. Stories ranging from truth, half-truth, and surmise to outright tall tale are interwoven with the facts. But there is something more significant than extricating fact from fiction in the accounts of Boone. Faragher comments:

> The record of Daniel Boone largely consists of the stories of humble American men and women, written out laboriously with blunt pencils on scraps of paper, or told aloud in backwoods cabins or around campfires and taken down verbatim by antiquarian collectors. The materials for Boone's biography not only document the life of an American frontier hero but reveal the thoughts and feelings of the diverse peoples of the frontier. (xvi)

According to Simon Kenton, the reason "they say the things they do" comes from a need to define themselves and their world in terms that are reaffirming and reassuring (Faragher xvi). Daniel Boone was at once larger than life and approachable. He was a hero, but he was also a neighbor. Faragher captures this quality in his biography and resolves the confusion in Boone lore by presenting various accounts of Boone with commentary, indicating sources and degrees of reliability. His treatment has the advantage of inclusion; when he says, "The things people choose to say about Boone provide clues to their own concerns," he captures Boone's elusive essence. Boone is a reflection of the diverse people of the frontier and their equally diverse concerns. His liminality as hunter hero invites this flexibility.

In his review of Faragher's work, David Herbert Donald, "whose ancestors immigrated to Kentucky with Daniel Boone," summarizes the problem with Boone's images (11). He concludes there were really two Boones. One image depicts the illiterate man in his famous coonskin cap (which in reality he never wore). This was the pioneer who crossed the Appalachian Mountains into Kentucky, leading the settlers who dared to inhabit a land that in 1775 was peopled with Indians who savagely defended their hunting grounds against the white men. This Boone made a name as a fierce Indian fighter and as a man who found neighbors within 70 miles to be too close. This Boone ended his days in Missouri lonely and unhappy (11).

The other popular portrait of Boone was as an agent who helped the successful land speculator Richard Henderson sell vast tracts of land and who betrayed white settlers to the Shawnees. Captured by Chief Black-fish, this Boone became his adopted son and was renamed *Sheltowee,* which means "Big Turtle." This Boone was brought up on charges of treason for helping the British during the Revolutionary War. After being tried, he escaped to the frontier of Missouri, where he spent the rest of his life as a bitter old man (Donald 11).

"Both [of these portraits] are wrong in general, and they are wrong in detail." Boone's character was much more complex than the opposing stereotypes would indicate. Boone loved to read, and his favorite book was *Gulliver's Travels* by Jonathan Swift; he hated fur hats; and he did not work for Henderson when he conducted his initial journeys into Kentucky (Donald 11).

Boone is a pervasive presence in American lore precisely because his image is so capacious. He is a composite of the often disparate elements of frontier life in America and, as such, is quite literally the quintessential "American."

The label "American" was and remains problematic. Americans questioned their national identity before there was a nation. J. Hector St. John Crevecoeur, an American author and agriculturist born in France, asks, "What is an American?" Americans (and non-Americans, for that matter) have been trying to answer this question ever since. Ludwig Lewisohn addresses the problem of the questioner first. He emphasizes that Crevecoeur was French and, as such, possessed "the strong social instinct of his race." Lewisohn sees Crevecoeur's answer to the question of what defines an American as "delightful literature, but fanciful sociology." Lewisohn clearly states that "the hardworking colonial farmer" who did not have any refined civilizing influences of the Old World was isolated and probably "no very delectable type." And he agrees with Professor Wedell's view that the Ideal American farmer is as unreal as Voltaire's "ideal savage" (Faragher xix–xx).

Crevecoeur's question and Lewisohn's reaction are instructive for examining the hunter's image. The question and reaction center around two things: the farmer as exemplary American and how the reality of the farmer's life compares with the ideal. Not only is there disparity between the ideal farmer and his real-life counterpart, but the farmer and the hunter are often juxtaposed in American history. The relationship between the two is most often one of opposition. The farmer, no matter how "rough," becomes domesticated as the hunter never can. Even in later refinements of the hunter figure seen in William "Buffalo Bill" Cody, Theodore Roosevelt, Ernest Hemingway, and William Faulkner, an element of wildness remains. The hunter paves the way for the farmer, yet the hunter who tries to be a farmer is an anomaly.

Boone is an example of this dynamic. He establishes homestead after homestead, only to leave it to the care of his family for long periods of time, even years, while he hunts and scouts new territory. He and other early hunters make settlement possible but are personally unable to enjoy the life they secure for others. Yet the merit of the settled life is never in question as an ideal—hunters just do not seem capable of partaking in it. We see this also in Cooper's character, Natty Bumppo, who embodies the American movement west. He helps create a world he cannot inhabit because it rejects him. But Boone is perceived as both farmer and hunter, while Bumppo is not. Boone's image is more flexible than Bumppo's because Boone's has been created by many forces. Bumppo is the fictional creation of only one author.

Richard Slotkin points out that John Filson's version of the Boone myth was infinitely adaptable. Boone's fame is directly attributable to John Filson, a thirty-year-old schoolmaster who, according to Faragher, was very much an Icabod Crane figure. Filson taught school during the Revolutionary War and afterward began speculating in land. The original source from which the Boone legend grew is Filson's *The Discovery, Settlement, And present State of Kentucke: And An Essay towards the Topography, and Natural History of that important Country: To which is added, An Appendix, Containing, I. The Adventures of Col. Daniel Boon, one of the first Settlers, comprehending every important Occurrence in the political History of that Province*. There are three other appendices, but the Boone material is the most famous.

Looking at what historians call "Filson's Boone," the section of the account in which Boone supposedly tells his own story, reveals how this narrative forms the basis for the Boone legend.[5] Filson's treatment, which proved mythic in proportion, was powerful because it adjusted to and reflected "local values or cultural assumptions," with the result that the Boone narrative became a cultural barometer. The different images of Boone traced "the emergence of American national consciousness, the process of cultural differentiation that finally divided the Euro-Americans from the Europeans" (Slotkin, *Regeneration Through Violence* 313).

Robert Tilton expands this point and applies it to Pocahontas. Perhaps we can conclude that "a body of texts" will be pervasive if they have the "ability to express multiple, and at times contradictory agendas" ("American Lavinia" 1). This is another basis for viewing Pocahontas as the metaphorical matriarch of Boone. Many of the same forces making Pocahontas so intriguing are also active in the creation of Boone's figure. "Contradictory agendas" pervade issues of land ownership, national identity, and race and gender throughout the colonial and early republic periods.

Pocahontas is a multi-valient figure. In one sense, she was the mythic mother figure from the pagan world of the wilderness. Fear of racial amalgamation with the savage was mixed with admiration for the beautiful Indian princess rescuer. She crossed the cultural barriers between Indian and European, pagan and Christian, loyalty to her father and loyalty to her husband. She was superior because she was royal, but she was inferior because she was non-white and female. Boone was white and male, but he was the son of English tradespeople. He spent extensive time in the wilderness, lived with the Indians, and was adopted by them. That alliance, however, did not prevent him from becoming a military leader and an advocate of American expansion.

Annette Kolodny makes the point that when we view the past we cannot divorce ourselves from the present; in effect, we re-create the past to explain and fit the context of the present. She argues that "the choices we make in the present inevitably alter our sense of the past that led to them. . . . [T]he further removed the author is from us, so too must be her or his systems of knowledge and belief, points of view, and structures of vision" ("Dancing Through the Minefield" 280). This observation is even more apt when applied to figures in the past. When we read historical texts, we overlay them with the issues of the present.

If we expand the concepts of "reading" and "text" to mean deciphering and interpreting information or signs, Kolodny's observations become even more pertinent. In the case of Boone, where the greatest number of texts are written about him rather than by him, he is re-created endlessly to fit the needs of the present reader—whenever that "present" happens to be.

In his own time, Boone's family and religious experience fostered attitudes that enabled him to communicate with the Indians. His family's religious background was Quaker. The Quakers were the one religious sect that had good relations with the Indians. He naturally took to life in the woods and easily formed relationships with Indian and backwoods hunters. But he was associated with farming as well as hunting. As a member of a large immediate and extended family, he embodied domesticity as well as adventure. He was one of eleven children, and he and his wife had seven of their own. His dual identities linked him to both Indian and Euro-American cultures, raising questions of his loyalty to each. He was at once a self-sufficient loner and a valued member of the community.

By his fiftieth birthday, Boone had acquired an international reputation. He had been a leader in the struggle against the Indians as they tried to defend their hunting grounds, and he was appointed Lieutenant Colonial of Militia by Virginia and elected to the state assembly. He became what might be termed an *American aristocrat*. He was a formal part of government and, therefore, part of the power structure. His hunting skill made him a key figure in land acquisition, especially in Kentucky.

In the first section of Filson's work, Boone introduces himself and Kentucky:

> The settling of this region deserves a place in history. Most of the memorable events I have myself been exercised in; and, for the satisfaction of the adventures, and scenes of life from my first movement to this country until this day. (50)

He goes on to describe the scene, referring to the landscape and the activity, number, and variety of wildlife.

> We found everywhere abundance of wild beasts of all sorts, through this vast forest. The buffaloes were more frequent than I have seen cattle in the settlements, browsing on the leaves of the cane, or cropping the herbage on those extensive plains, fearless, because ignorant, of the violence of man. Sometimes we saw hundreds in a drive, and the numbers about the salt springs were amazing. In this forest, the habitation of the beasts of every kind natural to America, we practiced hunting with great success until the twenty-second day of December following. (51)

Richard Slotkin sees *Kentucke* as Filson's attempt to create a viable market for land sale and development. Filson employed Boone's adventures as a vehicle for speaking to prospective settlers. He carefully organized and orchestrated a powerful document of propaganda designed to influence people to settle in Kentucky. However, there were problems with writing an inspirational tract that would not mislead the public about the hardships involved in settlement.

Filson began to tour the country, looking for men of prominence to interview for his book to inspire emigrants to face the hardship of life on the frontier. Filson was extremely persistent in his quest. Those reluctant to be interviewed claimed that the only way to get rid of him was to give in and talk to him. Filson interviewed several Kentuckians, including Boone. Faragher tells us that this was a pivotal time for Filson to meet Boone since Boone was living in crowded quarters with his own family and other relatives. The time Boone spent away from the small log cabin in the relatively spacious and quiet rooms where Filson was staying provided him with time to reflect on his adventures as Filson listened to him with rapt attention (Faragher 3).

As Boone told his stories, Filson saw the potential for more than the "compleat guide" he had originally planned. "Filson structured Boone's narrative to read like an epic" (Faragher 3–4). Each episode of Boone's journey into Kentucky contains danger and time for reflection. He crosses mountains, has numerous adventures, faces death. He returns home determined to lead his family and a party into the wilderness to found a new settlement. There are further adventures and setbacks. One of his sons is killed and his daughters are kidnaped by Indians. He himself is captured by Indians and escapes. After Indian attacks, including a massacre, and "after General Clark rages across the Ohio with his army, destroying the native towns, are the Indians finally 'made sensible of our superiority'" (5). After the Revolution, Boone reflects on his endeavor and the narrative ends.

As Faragher writes, "Filson also told Boone's story as romantic myth. In so doing he demonstrated his thorough familiarity with the perennials of colonial American literature—narratives of Indian warfare and captivity and journals of spiritual revelation and growth" (5). *Kentucke* is structured much like a Puritan sermon and this structure is itself an underpinning for reading the narrative as myth. What is significant as well is that Boone's character is the central ingredient in this myth-making process (Slotkin, *Regeneration Through Violence* 272).

Slotkin also comments that while the Puritan sermon begins with a biblical text, Filson "takes the map of Kentucky for his text." The Puritan sermon "exfoliates" the meaning of the biblical text, and Filson plans to develop the meaning inherent in the land. "The map itself is watermarked with a plowshare and the words 'Work & be Rich'" (*Regeneration Through Violence* 272). The necessity of settling Kentucky was almost a moral duty that would benefit both the landscape and the settler alike. "One of the major themes of Filson's Boone narrative is, in fact, the ability of the wilderness to redeem man" (270).

In Filson's *Kentucke,* Boone is portrayed as a contemplative man, a natural philosopher who reflects upon his experiences. One effect of these contemplative sections is to provide an intellectual and philosophical link between Boone's development and that of the nation. Through Filson's careful treatment, Boone's journey into the wilds of Kentucky became a rationale for Manifest Destiny. Physical action was followed by mental reflection, which was followed by more physical action and reflection. With each cycle of physical and mental action, Boone learned more about himself and reaffirmed his and, by implication, the nation's goals. Boone's movement through Kentucky became a blueprint of westward expansion.

Probably the most famous passage of *Kentucke* involves Boone viewing the territory from a ridge. His brother had returned to the settlement for much-needed supplies, and Boone was alone, lacking even the company of a horse or a dog. He spent the time brooding on the absence of his wife and family. It is a moment of revelation for himself and for the future of America.

> One day I undertook a tour through the country, and the diversity and beauties of nature I met with in this charming season, expelled every gloomy and vexacious thought. Just at the close of day the gentle gales retired and left the place to the disposal of a profound calm. Not a breeze shook the most tremulous leaf. I had gained the summit of a commanding ridge, and, looking round with astonishing delight, beheld the ample plains, the beauteous tracts below. On the other hand, I surveyed the famous river Ohio that rolled in silent dignity, making the western boundary of Kentucke with inconceivable grandeur. At a vast distance I beheld the mountains lift their venerable brows, and penetrate the clouds. All things were still. (qtd. in Filson 54–55)

Boone goes on to describe roasting the loin of a buck he killed and how he was able to lie down and sleep peacefully until the next morning. His skill as hunter allowed him the freedom to roam at will because he could provide for himself. His philosophical nature could be exercised because his basic wants were met.

He continued his tour for several days, finally returning to his camp to find that Indians had visited but not disturbed it. He further reflected that he had been in constant danger and, were he a man who was "tormented with fear," he would have suffered terribly. However, he was able to deal with the threat of howling wolves and countless other dangers and yet remain quite content. Boone further reflected:

> Thus I was surrounded with plenty in the midst of want. I was happy in the midst of dangers and inconveniences. In such a diversity it was impossible I should be disposed to melancholy. No populous city, with all the varieties of commerce and stately structures, could afford so much pleasure to my mind, as the beauties of nature I found here. (qtd. in Filson 56)

After this contemplative section, the narrative moves rapidly forward. His brother returned in July, and they proceeded to the Cumberland River, naming the "different waters" along the way. He finally returned to his home and family and prepared to lead them west. Eventually Boone's family and other families came to Kentucky, establishing a pattern of westward expansion. Boone's experience is a template; he serves as a focus, forthright and accessible.

For Slotkin, "Filson's tale . . . dramatize[s] convincingly the interdependence of Boone's destiny, the historical mission of the American people, and the destiny appointed for the wilderness by natural law and divine Providence" (*Regeneration Through Violence* 269). Slotkin points to Boone as "the archetypal hero of the American frontier, [and] the Boone narrative, in fact, constituted the first nationally viable statement of a myth of the frontier" (268–269). Davy Crockett, whose name is often linked with Boone's, may be "King of the Wild Frontier," according to the popular song, but Boone came first.[6]

Mary Lawlor traces the history of Daniel Boone, which she asserts is the history of a cultural figure and a literary figure whose authenticity is a dominant feature. Examining several rhetorical aspects of representations of Boone found in the works of Filson, Hall, Flint, and Cooper, she argues that, upon close analysis, the ideal of Boone is ultimately a vehicle of rhetoric employed by different authors to promote their subjective agendas (29).

In Filson, Lawlor also sees the connection between the development of the country and Boone's own life. She writes that around 1782, Filson went to Kentucky, where he met Boone and heard his story, which was also the history of Kentucky. She points out that Filson called attention to the "rustic quality" of Boone's speech while "not exactly claim[ing] that Boone was himself illiterate." She sees in Filson a stress on the naturalness of Boone, a quality that could not be designed, much as the history he tells could not be designed. Rather, it emerges from and with him (31). She observes that

> [g]enerating the wilderness that generates him, Boone becomes the quintessential figure of the West, imaging the whole field of its possibilities in his presence or in the simple sound of his name. . . . Boone thus provides a representative image for the already-functioning modality of the hybrid American self: Land, money, and biography inextricably entwined in each other's meaning. (33)

So the landscape, Boone's rustic speech, and the figure of Boone as "seen" or "imaged" by Filson are all part of Kentucky, which is part of the nation and the "hybrid American self." Defining the *self* is part of the larger issue of identity and the American character. And conflict is often central in such discussions.

William Kelly has examined the Leatherstocking Tales as a series in which tension between American originality and a search for origins binding characters to the past are unresolved. Anxiety about being too late in a new country accompanies a preoccupation with re-creating the American self. As soon as one realizes the value of a particular event, it is over. By the time the frontier is opened, whichever frontier that happens to be, its unique potentiality is violated.

What is "real" or authentic does not necessarily have anything to do with verifiable facts. In fact, the truth becomes almost totally subjective when reading Boone narratives. Meaning is derived from the needs that the narratives fulfill rather than from any objective content. As with Pocahontas, the story or stories have been created and re-created by others, not by the historical figure. The extant Boone material, written in his own hand, is very small. A number of dictated "autobiographies" exist, along with testimony of witnesses to certain events and other second- and thirdhand accounts of episodes from Boone's life. The character of such material is valuable in its contribution to a legend that is as various as it is pervasive. Consistently apparent is the construction of meaning from these sources, according to the writer's desire and the need his narrative is created to meet. Boone's changing image is yet another example of Kolodny's point that we re-create historical and legendary materials to satisfy the needs of the present.

In James Hall's *Letters from the West* (1828), for example, Boone is portrayed "as a solitary individual, and exemplary instance of the 'backwoodsman'; and this type is itself understood to subsume and magnify several traits of what Hall attempts to articulate as the 'national character'" (Lawlor 33). Furthermore, the rhetorical aspects of Hall's work underline the mythic aspects connecting Boone's character with the country.

Lawlor points out that in letter 16 of Hall's work, Boone as backwoodsman is the solitary figure who "faces the dark interior of the continent." Hall emphasizes the deprivation Boone experienced and attributes his suffering to his purposely excluding himself from the commercial activities of the general public, thereby making his sacrifice literal. Boone suffered physical and mental torment in his efforts to explore Kentucky, which is poignant when one translates the word *Kentucky* from its Indian meaning, "Bloody Ground" (Lawlor 35–36).

Lawlor sees the wilderness as a sort of underworld akin to that of the Greek and Roman myths where the hero descends into the world of the dead (36). The idea of crossing borders from one world into another is thus reinforced. In Hall, Boone as the American hunter travels from civilization into the wilderness, assuming the rites of sacrifice and death. His journey is directed toward the good of the emerging American people. He is the ideal leader, the noble heart seeking to inspire those who will follow. He must cross the border of the unknown and face danger.

This notion is also reminiscent of the borderline between the frontier and civilization where the young Athenian Ephebe were posted. The myth of the Black Hunter carries connotations of doubt and duplicity. The oppositions of youth/age, frontier/civilization, West/East, black/white are present in the language. Boone is contrasted with the inhabitants of the civilized East. Lawlor argues that the metaphor system of interiority, darkness, danger, and death used to represent the landscape of the forest in Hall is related to the economic system of eastern trade that prosperous citizens enjoy and that Boone himself is denied (37).

In Timothy Flint's widely read *Biographical Memoire of Daniel Boone* (1833), the figure of Boone is very much the same character as Natty Bumppo of Cooper's Leatherstocking Tales, which Flint had read. He had also read Filson's Boone. In contrast to Hall's portrayal, which depicted Boone's service as painful and self-sacrificial, Flint places Boone in a "paradisiacal wilderness" that nurtures him and depicts him as a "naming Adam." He is like Cooper's Leatherstocking, who goes before the civilization that will force the unknown land to bow to its progress (Lawlor 37).

Justification for progress is found in nature itself. In Flint, one can read a pre-Darwinian version of "survival of the fittest," where the superior Boone overcomes adversity and ushers in progress in his very person. In this view, nature is a commissioner of Boone's actions, delegating him political authority. Lawlor points out that Flint's narration speaks as that of the culture and the law; it is symbolic order that finds nature in its own expression (38). Boone functions alone in the wilderness, a model of innocence, but linked to the national destiny. As a hunter, he not only moves through the forest successfully, he blazes trails for others.

Lawlor discusses the place of marking and erasing in "reading" the wilderness. Boone's ability to read signs in nature and especially the language of "Indian passages" is crucial to his success in the forest. Flint emphasizes "Boone's negotiation of woodland trails [which] involves as much if not more attention to erasing and placing his own marks as it does to deciphering those of others" (Lawlor 38).

What Lawlor doesn't say is reading signs in the forest initially and finally has to do with hunting. The reading of animal sign is essential to survival because a hunter needs such skill to locate game. Even the deadly game of Indian and white settler tracking one another is based on skills learned in the hunt. This tracking process becomes metaphoric on several levels. Discussions of Boone frequently employ the terminology of hunting. Moreover, a hunting motif is active in the Boone narratives and in the literature and writings that grow from it. Boone's source of power is hunting, and hunting becomes emblematic of life in the wilderness.

Oppositions found in the Boone material highlight extremes and borderlines between extremes. Lines of demarcation denote actual borders. Indeed, a study could be made of all the surveying accounts found in the Boone narratives. Borderlines impact Boone's life throughout his career as surveyor and scout, and indicate his liminality in other arenas. The ambivalence of literal and figurative borders and the crossing of borders are concerns of the hunter figure.

Boone as Hunter

From the time Boone was fifteen, he was known as one of the best hunters in his Pennsylvania countryside (Faragher 9). Boone's love for the woods and for hunting began even earlier. Faragher tells us that in his old age Boone often repeated stories of his childhood in Pennsylvania (11). These remembrances reveal a touching closeness to his mother. He was one of eleven children, and in the summers he would go with his mother to tend the cows in open pasture. Boone recounted how, when he was ten and eleven years old, he would help his mother with a herd of milk cows that they drove to summer pastures north of the family homestead. The summer quarters included pens for the cows and a small dairy house. Although in reality it is likely his mother would have included his younger siblings in such a journey, Boone recalls there being just the two of them. After the chores of the day, they would sit by the fire and she would sing Welsh songs to him. He would provide their supper by hunting with a club he had fashioned. Because factual details such as his mother still nursing his brother and another baby being on the scene within the year were not part of his memory, these episodes can be seen as an idyllic adolescent fantasy where he and his mother inhabited a special woodland world (Faragher 14–15).

Although his mother returned home to store her butter and cheese, Boone remained in the pasture, and there he developed a love of solitude. Having ten siblings at home might explain the deep family feeling balanced by a strong need for privacy. In his adult life, Boone repeated this pattern: His devotion to family was offset by frequent absences. For him, these departures took the form of questing in the wilderness. In a sense, Boone leaving his family in one place—he leaves his father and siblings at their farm—is a way of establishing a new level of family intimacy in an-other place. He grows closer to his mother in the woodland setting. The world of the woods is associated with fond memories, grounded in hunting.

> As he looked back from the vantage of old age, he recalled those summers as the point when his life's course had been determined. His "love for the wilderness and hunter's life," he reminisced, began with "being a herdsman and thus being so much in the woods." (Faragher 14–15)

When Boone reached the age of twelve, his father gave him his first gun, and he soon became an excellent marksman. His father was a weaver by trade, and his family had come from England and settled in Pennsylvania. The family was Quaker and, although they were at odds with their sect at times, the influence of the Society of Friends had a lasting influence on Boone, particularly in terms of his empathy for Native Americans. The Quakers historically had peaceful relations with their Indian neighbors, and Boone would have been comfortable with the notion of brotherhood with them. In fact, his grandfather opened his home to Indians caught in conflicts with settlers.

Later in his life, Boone was adopted by an Indian chief and his wife during one of his captivities. Although his son and brother were killed and his daughter kidnaped by Indians, Boone's fondness for this "family" was never compromised. Boone's predisposition toward the Indian way of life may have had its roots in his relationship with his mother. Indian mothers often instructed their very young sons with bow and arrows. Although Boone's mother is not described as a hunter, she was responsible for his link to nature and the life of the woods. Like Pocahontas, she was the source of both comfort and adventure.

The early description of his mother singing before the open fire paints an intriguing picture. In the cosmos of the Native Americans, songs and dances, which were expressions of their spiritual world, were performed in their forest home. Nature and the earth were associated with the nurturing mother principle, and all beings and objects were imbued with spirits. Boone's ease with the forest world throughout his lifetime reinforces his image as a "son" of the wilderness.

Once again, the basis for Boone's citizenship in the forest is hunting. That he is nurtured by the wilderness and associates it with both his birth and adoptive mothers is important, but his ability to hunt enables him to live in the wilderness. Boone developed his hunting skills without the instruction of his immigrant father. Most emigrants to America came without any hunting experience. In Europe, hunting was reserved for the nobility. In America, therefore, the hunting way of life that developed in the backwoods depended largely on Indian knowledge and skill (Faragher 20).

Boone's relationship with the land is again fraught with oppositions. The Indian view of the land was centered around use rather than ownership. Boone held conventional European attitudes toward ownership, but he also realized that in the American landscape other operative principles existed. His immersion in Indian culture gave him some understanding of the Native American view, and the landscape itself in America was quite different from the limited land available for hunting in Europe. Furthermore, the land itself, with its often fear-inspiring topography, presented a challenge for anyone to negotiate.

Boone's skill allowed him to explore the land. A recurrent theme in *Kentucke* is his joy in the landscape, where others feared and dreaded it. In *Kentucke,* the genesis of many of Boone's adventures is a hunting expedition. Hunting becomes the reason for crossing borders. It is Boone's passport. He regarded hunting as his occupation from the time he completed his first long hunt.

Boone's physical appearance has been variously portrayed. His "business of life" involved practicality above all else. Although Boone in buckskin with a coonskin cap on his head is a popular image, it is inaccurate.

Indian and white hunters tended to mingle their style of dress, especially when they had commerce together. Faragher describes the outfit of the hunter. The details and the associations which accompany the items of dress are enlightening. Although the Europeans adopted more of the Indian dress than vice versa, the Indians did come to use European tools like the awl for making and repairing moccasins. They also adopted some of the clothing of the backwoodsmen, such as the hunting shirt, which was loose fitting and could be knotted. Indian warriors shaved or plucked their heads, leaving a single strip of hair down the middle of the scalp that would be treated with bear grease and adorned with feathers and other things for ceremonies or warfare. European hunters might let their hair grow as did the Indian men and treat it with bear grease. Some frontiersmen adopted the breechclout and leggings in the Indian style, which left thighs and hips bare, and presented a rather shocking sight to the folk in town. "Boone adopted these styles as a youth in Pennsylvania, and they remained his through the whole of his long life" (Faragher 20–21).

Boone is described as powerfully built and about five feet eight inches tall, "with broad shoulders and chest, strong arms, and thick legs." He weighed about 175 pounds, had a "high forehead and heavy brow, prominent cheekbones, a tight mouth, [and] a long and slender nose." Faragher tells us Boone had his father's "penetrating blue eyes and fair, ruddy complexion but his mother's dark hair, which he always kept plaited and clubbed in Indian fashion" (30–31).

Many of these physical details are reproduced in Cooper's Leatherstocking Tales. Natty Bumppo's hunting shirt of buckskin and his moccasins are frequently described, as is Chingachgook's calico shirt. The hairstyles of the Indians, in connection with tribal or individual identity, are also repeatedly brought to the reader's attention.

Beneath the physical details of dress is the issue of identity. Faragher tells us that American frontiersmen were often characterized as hybrid Indians by their contemporaries, and that hybridization was an internal condition as well an external expression (22). He further comments that there were Americans like Boone who went far toward seeing the Indian point of view (23). This comment reflects the distinction between those who were connected to both Indian and white worlds and those who resided exclusively in one world or the other. In truth, it was probably not possible to be untouched in some way by the opposing world. However, the hybrid hunter, whether mostly Indian or mostly white, resided squarely on the borderline.

The type of hunting Boone pursued underscores his liminality. Who hunted, what one hunted, and how one hunted had significant implications: whether one hunted alone or with a group, for subsistence or sport or market. During the course of his lifetime, Daniel Boone hunted small game, deer, bear, and buffalo; and trapped beaver, otter, and muskrat. The stages of his life are reflected in his hunting and trapping habits. Small game hunting and trapping were activities usually associated with youth or old age, while big game was the pursuit in manhood.

Again the Black Hunter comes to mind with its mythic connections between youth and forms of hunting. Hunting at night as a youthful and covert activity is linked with duplicity and doubt. Hunting during the day is an overt activity signifying forthrightness and social adjustment. That youth hunts alone and in darkness is negative in the mythic world of the Black Hunter. But, in American culture, the lonely hunter, especially in the case of Boone, is a positive figure. Independence and self-sufficiency are desirable traits. One admires the strength of character allowing the exceptional loner to prevail. These distinctions between European and American aspects of hunting individuate the American hunter.

Distinctions between male and female hunters in America are important, too. Historically hunting has been a pre-eminently male activity, associated with masculinity, the role of provider, and a test of physical and intellectual skill. However, evidence is coming to light that hunting activity among women has always been part of the American experience.

Although not stressed in most sources, women did their fair share of subsistence hunting while their menfolk were off on more glamorous adventures, usually hunting and trapping for profit. Boone's wife, Rebecca Bryan Boone, often was left alone for long periods of time (once for two years), as were many women who were married to professional hunters.

> Needing fresh meat for the stew pot, many was the time that Rebecca herself hunted small game in the woods near the house. In the nineteenth century men along the Yadkin still told of the time she rode north to a salt lick on Deep Creek, her gun loaded with buckshot, and "fired a gun from nearly the top of a tree and killed 7 deer and her mare that she rode there." It was an improbable tale, and coupled with a male barb about the dead horse, yet the story testified to the strength and determination of an able and intelligent woman. (Faragher 50)

That women hunted, and have always hunted, but have not been recorded as doing so is broadly suggestive. Annette Kolodny addresses the subject of women in the wilderness and considers their absence from the literature and history of the American frontier. Her comments about Mary Jemison and Rebecca Bryan Boone are particularly germane. Mary Jemison dictated her life's story to James Everett Seaver. The resultant text, The Narrative of the Life of Mrs. Mary Jemison, became the bestseller of 1824 ("Dancing Through the Minefield" 81). Although Kolodny discusses the alterations Seaver no doubt made to the oral history of Jemison, what nonetheless comes through any censorious efforts is the woman's ability to live happily in the wilderness. She married twice, both times to Indians. Subsequently she was a single parent to seven children. She was able to successfully settle on the Gardau Flats of the Genesee River and build a house with only her children's help. Thereafter, she consistently brought in a corn crop and flourished in her chosen home. She lived to old age, with her children and grandchildren settling nearby. Furthermore, she had white families as tenant farmers to whom she rented land to till ("Dancing Through the Minefield" 76–79).

Kolodny wryly comments that when Richard Slotkin refers to Seaver's Life, he conveniently ignores Jemison's gender as significant to her accomplishment. That a woman would want to enter the world of the "male hunter-adventurers" and, perhaps more significantly, that a woman could do so involved the crossing of very significant borders indeed ("Dancing Through the Minefield" 80).

In general, the narratives about white male hunters take the form of a human lover engaging the landscape as the beloved entity. The language used to describe the hunter and his relationship with the land is erotic and uses metaphors and other specifically sexual imagery. The vocabulary includes references to the land as female and "virgin"; the hunter in the wilderness is said to be in "her embrace"; the condition of the land is "uncontaminated" with no hint of "violation" (Kolodny, *The Land Before Her* 3). Although some women in the frontier wilderness adapted to the landscape, the idea of women engaging the wilderness was regarded as inappropriate and/or unthinkable.

In accounts of Boone's life, Rebecca Bryan Boone appears as an appendage to her husband. It is obvious that she is an important presence, however, if only by implication. In *Kentucke,* Boone gives her credit for being able to move the family back to her father's house when Daniel is away from the family for two years and believed dead. Timothy Flint writes that Boone's young son was the leader of the party that removed the family. But Boone himself clearly stated that Rebecca led the family through its long and difficult journey. The simultaneous existence and absence of Rebecca Boone implies she accomplished many exceptional things, but has not been given credit for them. Many women must have hunted during the settling of the frontier, yet this fact is consistently omitted. Hunting connotes masculinity and power. Who hunts remains a culturally defining question.

Who hunted in America during the colonial and early republican periods is a key to understanding the dynamics of the time. The Indians hunted first, and controversy over use and ownership of Indian hunting grounds was a major factor in the evolution of relations between Indians and settlers. The arrangements made between the French and the Indians, the British and the Indians, and the Americans and the Indians were highly problematic. Boone's experience is emblematic of these major conflicts. In the French and Indian Wars, Boone sided with the British against the French. As the settlers became alienated from England, Boone tried to remain neutral in the escalating conflict. His wife's people, the Bryans, were loyalist in sympathy, and he was not anxious to be in the forefront of rebellion against the crown. However, by the time he had founded Boonesborough (1775), rescued his kidnaped daughter and her friends from the Shawnee (1776), and was wounded (1777), he became aware of the delicate balance of the new country.

A copy of the Declaration of Independence reached Boonesborough in August of 1776, but the struggle for America was far from over. Two years later, Boone was captured along with a number of other men as they were on a salt-making expedition. Boone negotiated with the Indians and the British in an attempt to save his settlement from destruction. Various accounts and interpretations of this incident exist. However, the result was that he was charged with treason. His acquittal followed, but the spectre of uncertainty regarding his character was never fully erased during his lifetime.

The subsequent struggles for control of the land repeated the pattern of whites encroaching on traditional Indian hunting grounds, fierce but ultimately futile resistance by the Indians, and their further removal to locations where the process began again. Boone understood the Indians' feeling for the land, but his notions of ownership were aligned with those of the white settlers. The excesses of market hunting, which would soon decimate the buffalo herds, were already marked in Kentucky, where plentiful game was an invitation to slaughter. Even before his Kentucky days, Boone was hunting on the Yadkin, where

> [t]he country of the Upper Yadkin teemed with game. Bears were so numerous, it was said, that a hunter could lay by two or three thousand pounds of bear bacon in a season. The tale was told in the Forks that nearby Bear Creek had taken its name from the season Boone killed ninety-nine bears along its waters. The deer were so plentiful that an ordinary hunter could kill four or five a day, and it was said that Boone and a companion once took thirty between sunup and sundown near the head of the Yadkin. Deer were best when they were "in the red," during summer or early fall, before they acquired their blue winter coats. The deerskin trade was an important part of the regional economy. In 1753 over thirty thousand skins were exported from North Carolina, and thousands more were used within the colony for the manufacture of leggings, breeches, and moccasins. A "buck" was the standard of the trade, and by 1750 the term had already become a synonym for its monetary equivalent, the widely circulating Spanish peso, known by its German name of "thaler," or dollar. (Faragher 31–32)

This passage points out that the plentiful game was viewed as inexhaustible and that the economy was linked to wildlife in the American landscape in actuality and in metaphor.

The close connections between the environment and the people who inhabit it are emphasized by the accompanying reflection in the language. The "buck" is simultaneously the animal, its own processed skin, and its monetary value. A "Boone" was another name for a good hunter during the nineteenth century in the mountains of Kentucky (Faragher 54). "Boone" is synonymous with a powerful cluster of images. His figure as hunter is at the heart of this power.

Natty Bumppo, Literary Reflection of Daniel Boone

The protagonist of Cooper's Leatherstocking Tales is a literary reflection of Daniel Boone. Since his first appearance in *The Pioneers* (1823), a number of studies of the Tales and their main character have centered on issues of American national identity and the iconic nature of Natty Bumppo. Although Bumppo's figure is not perfectly analogous with Boone's because Boone's is more complex and flexible, Bumppo's relationship with the changing landscape, his own identity and (by implication) the nation's, and his attitudes toward gender and race mirror Boone's in important ways. Furthermore, Cooper's manipulation of *time* and *language* underscored Bumppo's status as an American.

Time

In the first paragraph of *The Deerslayer,* Cooper pondered time's role in providing a framework for experience.

> On the human imagination events produce the effects of time. Thus, he who has traveled far and seen much is apt to fancy that he has lived long, and the history that most abounds in important incidents soonest assumes the aspect of antiquity. (9)

Here, Cooper manipulated time in several ways. He emphasized that time is skewed by individual human experience and the life of nations. It can seem longer or shorter than it really is. It is distorted by one's perception. When many events happen in a short space of time, they seem to occur over a longer period. But time also restores a sense of balance; Cooper further suggested that "what seems venerable by an accumulation of changes is reduced to familiarity when we come seriously to consider it solely in connection with time" (*The Deerslayer* 9). Cooper is telling us that experience can deceive. The "accumulation of changes" is not in itself trustworthy unless we know how to view it properly.

William Kelly argues that "Myth is history's antithesis" (159). Historic time and mythic conception are opposing forces in the Leatherstocking Tales. Kelly sees the Tales as "a point of cultural reference and a source of national identity" (vii). He points out that critics and cultural historians have converted the five Tales into a single myth, thereby reducing their complexity and "denaturing" them. "This reshaping of the series is particularly ironic," Kelly argues, "because the tales represent Cooper's ardent attempt to conceptualize rather than transcend America's history. Across the five volumes of the series, Cooper addresses his culture's relation to the past and struggles to achieve a coherent sense of historical form" (vii–viii). Time is a key ingredient because Cooper had to constantly reshape it to accommodate his needs over the course of the Tales, which cover a significant period of time. What is more, Cooper began near the end of his protagonist's life and re-created his character's past and future. Cooper's temporal manipulations suggest the hunter figure's ability to transcend limits.

Kelly shows Cooper was driven by opposite desires—simultaneously wanting autonomy and tradition. Cooper constructs and continually revises a pattern in the Tales that suggests his attraction to the idea of fleeing restrictions imposed by time (viii). Cooper was at once arguing for American originality and trying to establish some link with the past. The tension between these opposing desires is evident throughout the Tales. And this tension is once again the basis for seeing the hunter on the borderline. The nature of the borderlines the hunter crosses is contradictory. Kelly discusses numerous contradictions that reveal a failure to reconcile the "origin versus originality" issue. However, he argues that a progression of Cooper's vision takes place over the course of the Tales.

"Wary of both radical originality and subservient dependence, Cooper begins the Tales by depicting America as both free from and bound to the past. In *The Pioneers* and *The Last of the Mohicans*, he is able to sustain that contradictory perspective by offering an illusory synthesis that purports to reconcile freedom and restraint," according to Kelly (viii). In these first two novels, Cooper's double vision serves to heighten the reader's sense of how the culture responded to the burden of the past. As the series progresses, Cooper reformulates his patterns to reshape history through his narratives, thus dealing with any logical inconsistencies in his conception of American growth. He frees the Tales from mythic readings and restores their American historical dimension (viii–ix). Freeing the Tales from mythic readings is unnecessary. That they invite multiple interpretations is stimulating rather than limiting. Cooper's fascination with aspects of time and his rebellion against any limitations imposed by it are illustrated by his integration of events in Leatherstocking's life.

Restrictions of time abound in American literature. Establishing legitimacy through longevity pervades Cooper and many other writers from Washington Irving to the present. In a new country, establishing a sense of the ancient and, therefore, a claim to legitimacy is a difficult task. Equally difficult is capturing the elusive spirit of a particular time that has passed. However, both the ancient and the timely are a focus in the Tales.

Much of the problem with looking at Cooper's first two Leatherstocking novels is confronting a schizophrenic perspective, one desperate for historical context while simultaneously too late to experience the imagined pristine world of the past. The Tales are complicated chronologically. The order in which they were written and published—*The Pioneers* (1823), *The Last of the Mohicans* (1826), *The Prairie* (1827), *The Pathfinder* (1840), and *The Deerslayer* (1841)—differs significantly from the chronological lifetime of their hero, Natty Bumppo. Bumppo's lifetime is portrayed in *The Deerslayer* (1740), which covers his early twenties; *Mohicans* (1757), his mid-thirties; *Pathfinder* (1759), his late thirties; *Pioneers* (1793), his early seventies and *Prairie* (1805), his early eighties.

Looking at the Tales according to the chronological life of Natty Bumppo instead of the publication date offers two advantages. Cooper's vision of the series can be seen more fully because (1) *The Deerslayer* is the last book written and (2) it deals with the earliest stage of Bumppo's life. Cooper implied that a character's meaning can only be determined in retrospect after knowing his ultimate outcome. Bumppo's lifetime reinforces Annette Kolodny's point that "the choices we make in the present inevitably alter our sense of the past that led to them" (*The Land Before Her* 278).

Kolodny discusses *The Deerslayer* and its relation to the other Tales in the series. She looks at Natty Bumppo's development over the course of the five volumes. She comments that Cooper had been searching for the "substance and meaning" of Bumppo's character and, when he finished *The Deerslayer,* this search finally came to an end (*The Lay of the Land* 109).

Furthermore, Cooper's diction is important. In particular, Cooper "named" Bumppo at different stages in his development. These names are significant and describe Bumppo's role at specific times in his life. He is "Deerslayer" in the first stage of his life because he has only slain animals, never man. When he finally kills a man, he is dubbed "Hawk-eye" by the very man he kills in that man's dying breath. However, Cooper constructs this incident carefully to fully absolve Bumppo of any bloodthirstiness. By the time he is forced to dispatch his enemy, an Indian brave, Bumppo has already given the man numerous opportunities to withdraw. Bumppo only kills the Indian when convinced the man will not relent until one of them is dead.

Overall, Bumppo is "Leatherstocking." Cooper introduces him as such in *The Pioneers*, then re-creates him over the course of the series, supplying him with appropriate and transitional names. As with Boone, naming Natty Bumppo as a hunter provides the crucial definition of his character.

Language

Louise K. Barnett examines the work as a novel where speech itself raises many issues. She discusses the nature of speech in *The Deerslayer* and the relationship between speech and silence. Although she examines all of the main characters in the novel, she focuses on Natty Bumppo. In "*The Deerslayer,* language is envisioned as adequate to the needs of speakers. The ever-present dialectic between speech and silence is repre-sented only in terms of intentionality: that is, when characters speak they are able to express themselves eloquently, but they may choose silence as the preferable course" (19). Bumppo chooses silence at a critical point in the novel, but even before this critical point he establishes himself as a man whose words are to be marked and pondered.

When he does speak, Natty Bumppo defines himself as a hunter first and foremost. During the course of *The Deerslayer*, he becomes a warrior as well, but his initial and his enduring identity is that of hunter. Cooper's narration reinforces this definition, literally referring to Bumppo only as "Deerslayer" or "the hunter" throughout the novel. Bumppo soliloquizes using the metaphor of the hunt. For instance, he comments that there is "little manhood in killing a doe" (13). Hurry Harry's character is labeled "reckless" when he misses a buck at the beginning of the book, and Deerslayer upbraids him for his hasty shot. Several discussions take place where the habits of deer are used as examples of particular behavior, and frequent comparisons between hunting and warfare are drawn to emphasize the experience of Bumppo. After all, the subtitle of *The Deerslayer* is *The First Warpath.* That Bumppo proves to be a valiant warrior is not surprising, although he voices his own concern at his lack of experience in war.

Bumppo's private life is examined as well. Natty's celibacy is admirable since it indicates his restraint, but his refusal to mate is unnatural in the natural world he inhabits. He is a reflection of the untapped potential of the landscape. As with a virgin forest, the land is untouched, holding the allure of beauty and the promise of fertility, but its uncultivated aspect is in conflict with the national interest in development and "civilization." Bumppo is "pure," but this purity may not be virtue but, instead, sterility or a refusal to grow up. Virginity is desirable because it connotes purity, but it is useless if it remains too long intact.

Ironically, virginity is a state associated with the female rather than the male. The land is usually referred to in female terms. The role of hunter in America is usually thought of as male, and the hunter's relationship with the land is often portrayed in sexual terms.

The virgin hunter in the mythological world is most strikingly portrayed as female, exemplified by the huntress Artemis (Greek) or Diana (Roman). She is desirable because she is beautiful (and perhaps because she is dangerous to mortals); yet she is untouchable because she is immortal, and no mere human has any power over her. The consequence for any male who violates her chaste state, even by viewing her, is gruesome death. She is notorious for changing her would-be violators into deer, which are then torn apart by their own hunting dogs in the chase or shot with arrows by ignorant humans who are unaware of the true nature of their prey.

The story of Actaeon is a prime example. As a young hunter he spies on Artemis and sees her bathing. He cannot keep silent, snickering as he observes the goddess. Furious, Artemis transforms him into a stag, and he is destroyed by his dogs. Despite this pitiless aspect of Artemis, she is simultaneously the goddess of childbirth, baby animals, and the moon, and the twin sister of Apollo, the sun. Nicole Loreaux argues that Artemis "is the most eroticized of the three [virgin goddesses; the other two are Hestia and Athena] and perhaps also the most terrifying . . . hunters keen on living must forbear to gaze on the beautiful body of the naked goddess in her bath—as Actaeon learned to his peril" (24).

Natty Bumppo, by contrast, is all too human but he maintains his chaste state. He is an anomaly—at once a strong, talented young hunter with a certain primitive appeal yet innocent of the baser vices of humanity, although not ignorant of the forces in the world he has chosen to inhabit. In *The Deerslayer*, he rejects marriage through silence: Judith Hutter reveals her desire to marry him and any civil word of his would indicate compliance. Celibacy can be viewed as *not* acting, not marrying; in this sense, silence can be viewed as not acting. By not speaking, Bumppo maintains his celibate state. His is a rather passive celibacy in contrast to the fierce and overtly destructive chastity of Artemis.

The two figures have in common a proprietary relationship with the forest. They may not mate as do the humans and animals who inhabit this setting, but they protect those within their domain and participate in the other cyclical aspects of the woods. They hunt, they are skillful in their craft to the point where they seem almost magical, and they are in harmony with the environment. In a sense both Artemis and Natty Bumppo are virgin parents to those they protect in the forest. After all, Artemis is the goddess of childbirth and baby animals. Bumppo acts as instructor and father to younger men in his older years; in his younger years, he is the emblem of correct standards and behavior. The maternity and paternity of these two figures is reminiscent of the clerical appellations of "mother" and "father." In fact, as Barnett points out, Bumppo is called a "Moravian" by Hurry Harry for his "frequent citing of the Moravian missionaries and his adherence to their teachings" (20).

The forest of *The Deerslayer* is an untouched wilderness "not the howling desert of the Puritan imagination, . . . but a nurturing presence whose pristine existence is superior to any other environment" (Barnett 20). Bumppo has chosen to live in and identify with his woodland environment, yet he is the spokesman for conventional social hierarchy. Judith Hutter, whom Bumppo rejects as a suitable marriage partner, is doomed by her nature and family history. Her mother had children out of wedlock because she chose someone above her on the social scale. Her mother then married below her social level. The clear implication is that Judith will go astray because her mother did. Her mother's primary error was violating the boundaries of her social class. Barnett argues that "Deerslayer's commentary on such violations of hierarchy asserts the superiority of rigidly maintained class distinctions." She further comments that "nothing is suitable that is out of character . . . is simply . . . the principle that governs *The Deerslayer's* perfect economy" (20).

When adherence to class distinctions is expressed in speech in the novel, it reveals and reinforces an acceptance of society's standards. Strict observance of social order and class lines would seem more appropriate in a European setting than in the American wilderness. But Deerslayer is in an America still tied to Britain. The perspective is skewed, with the British portrayed as unattractively as the French. The point for Cooper is establishing the sterling character of Bumppo. Bumppo backs up his words with action and, although he has proven himself in prior Tales, he is largely untried in this book. Barnett sees in *The Deerslayer* a "commitment to speech, more than action" because it is "a public commitment to the values of the word and an ultimate test of character in which a man's word literally becomes his bond." Further, she says, it "invoke[s] a central conflict of the American experience—the tension between wilderness and individual freedom." What is more, she stresses "the pastoral is the ideal genre for Cooper's acute sense of these polarities." While the pastoral is the ideal type or genre for exploring the polarities between the wilderness and individual freedom, she argues that looking at the text as a romance is to read it as an exploration of the familiar issue of identity. Who the characters are predominates the novel, and this preoccupation is revealed first through their speech, and only later through other behavior (19–20). And although language is capable of corruption, Barnett sees Cooper as confident that language has the power to "achieve an ideal discourse" (20).

According to Barnett, the way ideal discourse is achieved is through categorizing and the authorial voice. Categorizing people, situations, and events defines them. Bumppo is at once categorizing and defining, and is himself categorized and defined through language. Barnett sees the keyword of the novel's discourse as "nature," and the keyword of its metadiscourse as "truth" (21). The primary consideration of Natty Bumppo as *hunter* underlies both.

Bumppo is the touchstone of what is right, although he is not perfect. Through his speech or silence he is able to order the world of *The Deerslayer*. This novel is the culmination of Cooper's vision; in it he has reconstructed Bumppo's youth. *The Deerslayer* is both the first and last of the Leatherstocking Tales. The appellation of "Deerslayer" refers to Bumppo's skill as a hunter, and to his not having killed a fellow human creature. This point is emphasized in the beginning of the novel as he talks with Hurry Harry.

> "'Tis true, the Delawares call me Deerslayer, but it's not so much because I'm pretty fatal with the venison as because that while I kill so many bucks and does, I've never yet taken the life of a fellow creatur'. They say their traditions do not tell of another who had shed so much blood of animals that had not shed the blood of man." (36)

Bumppo was also formerly known as "Straight-tongue." Bumppo says of himself early in the novel that "you will find me as plain-dealing in deeds as I am in words" (20–21). His rifle is called "Killdeer," indicating its primary function. The other titles or appellations for Bumppo are all associated with his skills as hunter and woodsman, with the exception of his family name, "Bumppo." Hetty Hutter asks him to recite all his names because, in her simplicity, she believes they will reveal what he is really like. The occasion also provides Cooper with an opportunity to have Bumppo list his pedigree.

> "Tell me *all* your names," repeated the girl earnestly, for her mind was too simple to separate things from professions, and she *did* attach importance to a name; "I want to know what to think of you."

"Well, sartain; I've no objection, and you shall hear them all. In the first place, then, I'm Christian, and white-born, like yourself, and my parents had a name that came down from father to son, as is a part of their gifts. My father was called Bumppo; I was named after him, of course, the given name being Nathaniel, or Natty, as most people saw fit to tarm it." (59)

Bumppo goes on to explain the provenance of his various names. He starts with his surname, Bumppo, and declares that although it is not a lofty sounding name, "men have bumped through the world with it." He further elaborates that "Straight-tongue" came from the Delawares when they found out Bumppo was not given to lying. "Pigeon" is the name given him when the Indians saw he was quick of foot, and he adds that the pigeon is known to have a swift wing and fly in a straight line.

Cooper's humor is evident when he has Bumppo explain his least appealing name. "'From carrying messages, and striking blind trails, I got, at last, to following the hunters, when it was thought I was quicker and surer at finding the game than most lads, and then they called me the *Lap-ear*, as, they said, I partook of the sagacity of a hound.'" To which Hetty responds, "'That's not so pretty . . . I hope you didn't keep *that* name long.'" He then goes on to explain the name that becomes the novel's title, *Deerslayer*: "'Not long after I was rich enough to buy a rifle,' returned the other, betraying a little pride through his usually quiet and subdued manner; 'then it was seen I could keep a wigwam in ven'son; in time, I got the name of Deerslayer, which is that I now bear; homely as some think it, who set more valie on the scalp of a fellow mortal than on the horns of a buck'" (59–60).

Bumppo's discussion with Hetty reveals a gently mocking attitude, while not diminishing the importance of naming and its influence in "reading" character. The emphasis is self-conscious and underscores again the role of language, specifically, categorizing and defining through naming.

The most important naming takes place when Bumppo is rebaptized "Hawk-eye" by the warrior he meets on shore. They have a lengthy discussion over ownership of a canoe, which ends in a life and death battle. The incident happens less than a quarter of the way through the novel. Cooper deemed it necessary to show the reader that Bumppo is already worthy of the title, even at this preliminary stage of his development. He kills his first fellow creature, but only after repeated attempts to forestall the inevitable. Ultimately, he must be true to his "gifts" and survive in his environment.[7]

Along with his inherent goodness, Cooper stresses Bumppo's sound judgment. Those around him are flawed but, despite his youth, he is serious, not reckless. Hurry Harry is reckless in his attitudes toward the law and the Indians, and he compounds his flaw through his rash behavior. Judith is reckless with her person; her reputation is sullied because she is unable to control her "gift" of beauty. Hetty is not reckless in the sense that she knowingly does wrong, but her mental weakness yields a flawed view of reality. She is pious, but she is dangerous because of her simplicity. Tom Hutter, very much like Harry, is lawless. He has decided to create his own world, a flawed god whose kingdom is doomed. Nature will recapture his castle and ark.

The reader is carried through Cooper's exploration of acceptable and unacceptable alternatives by Natty Bumppo, and Cooper's voice becomes Bumppo's voice. That Cooper is speaking through Bumppo explains why many of the passages involving dialogue take on the characteristics of narrative. Rather than an exchange between characters, the dialog is transformed into a philosophic discourse. Many critics, most notably Mark Twain, have mocked the long-winded, awkward speeches of Bumppo.[8]

In *Beneath the American Renaissance*, David Reynolds discusses subversive humor and language, specifically in regard to the Crockett almanacs. He argues that language illuminates a mind set.

> Reputable humor . . . was conservative and restrained, harking back to the smooth wit and polished periods of Goldsmith and Addison. It championed a moral and predictable universe and upheld decorum and a rigid social hierarchy. . . . Subversive humor . . . reveled in disorder, violence, amorality. (442)

Although Cooper aligned himself with the reputable and polished school of humor in his narrative, he drew Hurry Harry and Thomas Hutter as rascals who violate the decorum of society and the law. Natty Bumppo is no drawing-room dandy, but his moral fiber is never in question. The farthest he strays from righteous behavior in *The Deerslayer* is when he shoots a bird to test his gun, and he is immediately aware of his transgression. Even when he does kill another human being, he does so in self-defense. Bumppo does not murder his Indian enemy; he is in a life and death struggle. Even then, he kills his enemy with great reluctance.

Examining the Life of the Noble Hunter

Throughout the Tales, Cooper's descriptions of Bumppo and comments about the nature of time reinforce Bumppo's role as noble hunter. In creating a past for Bumppo, Cooper was restricted by what the reader already knew about the character. Cooper re-created the historical period from 1740 to 1805 through Bumppo. To truly understand this American hunter's life at each stage of his development, and to understand Cooper's vision, we need to examine Bumppo's life chronologically. His concern with the landscape, his identity, and his attitudes toward gender and race are best studied from the perspective Cooper created or, more accurately, re-created. Cooper depicted Bumppo in a changing world. As he crosses the ever-moving borderlines between civilization and wilderness, Bumppo brings the reader with him. Examining the Tales individually and in the order of Bumppo's lifetime provides a useful framework for a comprehensive exploration of Cooper's vision.

The Deerslayer or The First Warpath
The Deerslayer establishes Bumppo's identity as the prototypical American hunter. He is simultaneously an original and a composite. His literary persona is Cooper's creation, but he is based upon the figure of Daniel Boone. The character of Bumppo develops over the course of the five Tales, culminating with The Deerslayer.

Physically, Bumppo is not handsome, but he is unconventionally attractive. He stands in sharp contrast with his companion, Hurry Harry, on both physical and spiritual planes. The surface beauties of Harry (and Judith Hutter, as well) are foils for inner flaws. As a result, Bumppo's innate goodness and talent are even more striking.

The landscape of The Deerslayer is at once Edenic and primitive, reinforcing a motif of oppositions and extremes. The capacity of the setting to be either heaven or hell depends largely upon each character's moral state. Cooper's characters frequently discuss the nature of heaven and consider the possibility of segregated heavens for those of different dispositions and races. The Happy Hunting Grounds of the Indians appeals to Bumppo, although affirmation of his white heritage and "gifts" never waivers. He leaves it to God to figure out the details. What such discussions point up is the close association of human nature and environment.

Bumppo emerges from the forest at the beginning of The Deerslayer dressed in deerskins with a guileless expression on his face; he is "between the skirts of civilized society and the boundless forests" (13). The forest and the lake are two central settings in the novel and frequently opposed to one another. When Harry and the Hutters are on land, they are in peril; when the Indians venture onto the lake they also face danger. Deerslayer is able to move between the lake and the land because he has the advantage of superior skills and a personal philosophy that allow him to adapt to changing circumstances. Cooper reinforces Bumppo's ability to adapt and survive by contrasting him with the other characters.

Harry's racial prejudice toward the Indians denies him harmony in the environment. His egotism denies him harmony in his love life. He will never be the woodsman that Deerslayer is. And although he is captivated by Judith's physical charms, he is haunted by her reputation. Judith is intelligent and good-hearted, but she is vain. She has compromised her happiness by consorting with garrison officers, and her reputation is sullied. When Deerslayer meets her, she is already lost. Even life in the woods, with its capacity for redemption, cannot recapture her lost innocence.

Hetty Hutter is another character whom Cooper contrasts with Bumppo. She is unable to adapt because of her mental flaw. This flaw also seals her fate, while it affords her certain advantages in the Indian camp. Hetty is regarded by the Indians as holy. She has the simplicity and sincerity of a child. Her failing is her lack of judgment, but her purity is never questioned. She can create a perfect world in her mind, but the other significant white characters—Harry, Judith, Hutter—cannot.

As for Chingachgook and Hist, they are in harmony with their world and with one another. Hist is the nearest thing to perfect womanhood in the book. She is simple and childlike, but is clearly intended by Cooper as a portrait of an ideal Indian maiden. Chingachgook is described as an "Apollo of the wilderness" (226). He is the ideal mate for Hist, physically and spiritually beautiful. They are a royal couple.

The world of *The Deerslayer* emphasizes "first" experiences. This is the first time Deerslayer has seen a lake. It is the first warpath for Bumppo and Chingachgook. They are looking for adventure, and they are looking to establish themselves. Cooper constantly reminds the reader of these firsts. This attention to initial experience underscores the emerging identity of the characters. Individual identity is self-consciously addressed in the novel's character portraits. Characters identify themselves and others largely through racial and gender references.

Bumppo's constant allusion to "red gifts" and "white gifts" is probably the most striking example of Cooper's sense of racial identity. Bumppo's identity as a hunter means he is an amalgamation of Indian and Euro-American characteristics. He is close to the hunter/warrior tradition of the Indians because he has lived with them. However, he is profoundly aware of his hereditary connection with the white world. His constant references to what is "white" and what is "red" are attempts to anchor an identity. The word "gift," within the shifting boundaries of the wilderness, becomes a heavily weighted term. When Bumppo explains the gory practice of scalping, for example, he rationalizes that it is acceptable for Indians to engage in the practice because it is part of their gifts, while it is unacceptable for whites because it violates theirs. Bumppo defines "gifts"

near the end of *The Deerslayer*, when he is speaking to Judith about
what constitutes someone's "nature" as opposed to his "gifts."

> "A natur' is the creatur' itself; its wishes, wants, idees, and feelin's, as all are born
> in him. This natur' never can be changed in the main, though it may undergo
> some increase or lessening. Now, gifts come of sarcumstances. Thus if you put a
> man in a town, he gets town gifts; in a settlement, settlement gifts; in a forest,
> gifts of the woods. . . . All these increase and strengthen until they get to fortify
> natur', as it might be, and excuse a thousand acts and idees. Still, the creatur' is
> the same at the bottom, just as a man who is clad in regimentals is the same as a
> man that is clad in skins. . . . Herein lies the apology for gifts, seein' that you
> expect different condict from one in silks and satins from one in homespun,
> though the Lord, who didn't make the dresses but who made the creatur's them-
> selves, looks only at his own work. (425)

Behavior based on race seems a preoccupation of Cooper's, and his
views are expressed through Bumppo. Accordingly, "nature" is what one
is born with; "gifts" are the culture's contribution to such predispositions.
How appropriate the culture's dictates are for the person, however, is
based upon the society into which one is born. Of course, one might
argue that if white and red live together, their gifts would blend.

Like race, gender references are important in *The Deerslayer* because
they define the characters' identity. When Cooper describes women, he
generally does so in a sentimental fashion. They are "the gentler sex,"
have a "meek demeanor," and are "inherently feminine." The more interesting descriptions, made without much narratorial comment, are those
where gender roles deviate from the expected norm. Two examples of
Judith's talent and strength are described but not developed. First, when
Judith and Hetty are paddling the canoe, they outmaneuver and outrun
the attacking Indian warriors. Cooper does explain that the girls have
been raised in the woods, so they have such talent. Second, we learn that
Judith can shoot a rifle and has actually killed deer.

> Judith, in the main, was a girl of great personal spirit, and her habits prevented
> her from feeling any of the terror that is apt to come over her sex at the report of
> firearms. She had discharged many a rifle and had even been known to kill a deer,
> under circumstances that were favorable to the effort. (410)

These details make Judith much more appealing and worthy of consideration than Cooper's endless bewailing of her lost innocence. Cooper
creates Judith as a flawed hunter. She is flawed for two reasons, both of
which are gender related: She is female, and she is unchaste. If we contrast her with Bumppo, who is the perfect hunter, the ideal he represents

is male and celibate. Judith cannot alter her sex or her experience; therefore, she can never hope to be the female complement to Bumppo. Cooper limits Judith's development based on the contemporary culture's mores. Cooper constructs the world of The Deerslayer so that Bumppo is the only one able to negotiate its boundaries. Judith, especially, would be a more interesting character if Cooper did not limit her. What is significant, though, is that he ascribed attributes to her that are potentially comparable with Bumppo's.

Hetty Hutter, Judith's flawed, simple-minded sister, is able to paddle about the lake in a canoe by herself and wander the woods with impunity. Cooper accounts for this capacity by noting Indian tolerance for the mentally ill. That someone so impaired is simultaneously so competent in a wild, natural setting is significant. Perhaps her ability to survive in nature indicates Cooper's romantic notion of a benevolent cosmos for the innocent. Hetty is even able to interact with the animal world with impunity, as evidenced when she encounters a family of bears. We are also told in an off-handed manner that she has raised bear cubs and wants to embrace the playful animals when she encounters them on the way to the Indian camp.

When Hist and Hetty meet in the woods, Hist does not notice that there is anything wrong with Hetty. Cooper's sentimentality, again evident here, is subverted by Hist's actions. Her role, like that of Hetty and Judith, is far from passive. She and Hetty both demonstrate great mobility in traversing the landscape. But Cooper seems most interested in her physical delicacy. Despite Cooper's chauvinistic flourishes, the three women—Judith, Hetty, and Hist—are remarkably active, especially within the context of this most talkative of the Leatherstocking Tales. In a sense, they are hunter figures themselves: Judith hunts; Hetty plays with bears; and Hist is an Indian princess. Cooper is often contradictory in his portrayals. On one hand, he has the three women running about the forest, paddling canoes, plotting to save the lives of their men; and on the other, he dwells on the physical, mental, and moral limitations of these same women. However, the unusual treatment of gender roles in the action sequences is testament to the possibility of female power.

The world of nature unites disparate forces in The Deerslayer, despite Cooper's efforts to carefully define what belongs to the natural world and to the civilized world. The Indian and white worlds are united through the friendship of Bumppo and Chingachgook. Gender roles are blurred in the forest and on the lake. Bumppo as hunter sets a standard for behavior. He represents the best aspects of both worlds, while the other characters embody negative forces in their societies. Chingachgook and Hist are the only characters who serve as models, but they are limited to the Indian world.

Bumppo is a hybrid of both Indian and white worlds; thus his identity is complicated. The one clear definition of Bumppo's identity is that of hunter. Slotkin says that "Deerslayer is portrayed as a man consciously seeking to create his own character through his deeds as a hunter" (*Regeneration Through Violence* 498). Tension exists between amalgamating and delineating cultures, with Bumppo on the borderline. He rejects marriage, he distinguishes constantly between what is "red" and what is "white," and he keeps moving. The basic nature of the American hunter is, in the final analysis, solitary.

The Last of the Mohicans: A Narrative of 1757
The trope of the hunter as solitary in the American landscape is reinforced by looking at the Tales in both chronological and publication order; *The Last of the Mohicans* is second in both. Its focus is the action, not the diction, of its characters. Bumppo is at the peak of his powers, and his Indian counterpart, Chingachgook, also enjoys the dignity of middle-age and fatherhood. Uncas, the last of the Mohican line, is in the flower of young manhood, an emblem of Indian perfection.

As the biological son of Chingachgook and the spiritual son of Hawk-eye, Uncas amalgamates the white and red races. In his relationship with Cora Munro, the mulatto daughter of Colonel Munro, he amalgamates three races. The amalgamation never comes to fruition because the culture and Cooper cannot allow anything so radical. But the possibility itself remains intriguing. Though unconsummated, their relationship is more provocative than if a resolution were attempted. The potentiality of amalgamation is attractive, while its actuality is problematic. Therefore, the suspended hope for such a resolution satisfies the desire for racial harmony, and the culturally threatening realities of interracial marriage are avoided.

There is not a great deal of time to ponder anything in *The Last of the Mohicans* because action predominates. Battles, kidnaping, and rescues come in quick succession, and Bumppo is the organizing agent for this action.

In 1757, the landscape is sublime and dangerous. In the preface, Cooper compares the setting with his day:

> In point of fact, the country which is the scene of the following tale has undergone little change, since the historical events alluded to had place [sic], as almost any other district of equal extent within the whole limits of the United States.

There are fashionable and well-attended watering places at and near the spring where Hawk-eye halted to drink, and roads traverse the forests where he and his friends were compelled to journey without even a path. Glenn's has a large village; and while William Henry, and even a fortress of later date, are only to be traced as ruins, there is another village on the shores of the Horican. But, beyond this, the enterprise and energy of a people who have done much in other places have done little here. The whole wilderness, in which the latter incidents of the legend occurred, is nearly a wilderness still, though the Red Man has entirely deserted this part of the state. Of all the tribes named in these pages, there exist only a few half-civilized beings of the Oneidas, on the reservations of their people in New York. The rest have disappeared, either from the regions in which their fathers dwelt, or altogether from the earth. (vii–viii)

Cooper dates this preface 1850, almost a hundred years from the tale's setting. The setting is the third year of the war between England and France "for the possession of a country that neither was destined to retain" (13); it is the time of Washington, "a Virginia boy, whose riper fame has since diffused itself" (14); it is the time when the Royal Americans of the 60th Regiment wear red coats.

Naming locations is important as well as naming characters. Lake George is the "Horican" for the tribe called "Les Horicans" and Lac du Saint Sacrement.

As each nation of the Indians had either its language or its dialect, they usually gave different names to the same places, though nearly all of their appellations were descriptive of the object. Thus, a literal translation of the name of this beautiful sheet of water, used by the tribe that dwelt on its banks, would be "The Tail of the Lake." Lake George, as it is vulgarly, and now indeed legally called, forms a sort of tail to Lake Champlain, when viewed on the map. Hence the name. (12)

Names reflect the nature of the object or person named. Here, Bumppo is Hawk-eye. His appellation as "hunter" has been established, but his role as warrior becomes preeminent during the course of the novel. Names also reflect the characters' histories, and the names change to reflect the condition of the characters. In reading the names (and shapes) on the map, as with Filson's map of Kentucky, the text becomes a scripture in need of explication.

The Last of the Mohicans is named for Uncas, a hunter and a warrior. Uncas is also mythically "the tortoise," a totemic sign of royalty in his tribe. When the young Uncas is to be killed by a branch of this ancestral tribe, he reveals the blue tattoo of the tortoise, signifying his claim as their leader. What such an allusion connotes is a heritage of power. But, for Cooper, such a heritage of power is limited. Uncas dies valiantly, but young. He represents the unrealized potential of the hunter to cross all borders, including race.

Identity is examined in this work largely through race. The process of racial amalgamation is addressed by the characters of Uncas and Cora. Although their relationship remains inchoate, it is, nonetheless, significant. We also find out what Bumppo and Chingachgook mean to one another as a result of the deaths of these two young people. Their relationship and identities are reinforced through their mutual grief.

Bumppo's famous description of himself as "a man without a cross" inscribes his identity and is based on his hunter status, living on the borderline between the Indian and white worlds. His insistence on his being without a cross springs from his desire to anchor his identity in a world of radical flux. He is not limited by the dictates of Christian doctrine, which rejects the pagan's natural world. Neither is his bloodline "crossed" by Indian blood. Slotkin comments on Bumppo's self-description as implying he is also "a man beyond the pale of Christianity, a man without the Cross to guide him" (*Regeneration Through Violence* 505).

Although he is "a man beyond the pale of Christianity, a man without the Cross to guide him," Bumppo does accept the basic teachings of Christianity in that he loves his fellow man. But he is not limited by restrictions of form in religious observance. He picks and chooses what form the practice of his own natural religion takes.

Uncas and Cora, and Heyward and Alice, provide the useful contrast against which Bumppo may be defined. The rescue from captivity in the wilderness has thrown the two couples together. The resolution of the book, with Uncas and Cora dying, Heyward and Alice marrying, and Bumppo and Chingachgook uniting in friendship and sorrow, reaffirms the unmoveable character of the gulf that separates nations and races. Bumppo and Chingachgook survive to hunt together and go on with their lives, but their "son" and their future is dead.

What is and what is not racially appropriate is underscored by the novel's setting. Cooper writes that white voices are inappropriate in the woods; they are "out of pitch" (*The Last of the Mohicans* 238). The ongoing comic description of David Gamut, the psalmster whose profession is absurd in the context of the wilderness, continually points up the futility of civilization's trappings. His pitch pipe, his bursting into song, and his physical clownishness are constant reminders of the conflict between European civilization and its organized religion and the primitive forces of nature and Bumppo's natural religion. The serious business of the hunter/warriors is placed in sharp contrast to the frivolous occupations of the civilized world.

Cooper explored relationships between the internal and external conditions of his characters. He pointed out how inner and outer worlds mirror one another. He also juxtaposed characters to further illuminate their natures. For example, Uncas and Magua are both fierce warriors externally; internally, Magua is degenerate in several ways. He has been banished by his tribe, flogged and humiliated by Munro for his drinking. He is the antithesis of Uncas, bent on revenge for his disgrace. He seeks to exact it through the slaughter or dishonor of Munro's daughters. Uncas, on the other hand, is spiritually pure as well as physically godlike. Cooper shows us the demonic face of the hunter/warrior to reinforce the power, danger, and potential of the figure.

Physical landscape in *The Last of the Mohicans* reflects the mental landscape of the characters. The treachery and nobility in the setting always underline action in the plot. Fog, waterfalls, and raging rivers are hazardous but sublime features of the landscape. These obstacles are features of the physical setting that must be negotiated. The hunter, with his skills to survive in the natural world, is the perfect guide. But Magua is a perversion of the hunter figure. At the beginning of the novel, he deliberately leads the party with Heyward and Munro's daughters astray. When the party links up with Bumppo, Uncas, and Chingachgook, they are going the wrong way to the fort. Magua is able to divert them because they do not know the territory, nor are they able to judge the true character of Magua until he betrays them.

Direction is a problem for the English throughout *The Last of the Mohicans*. They are strangers to the external landscape of the forest, and they cannot navigate its unfamiliar twists and turns. More importantly, they cannot judge the true nature of the inner world of other people.

Bumppo and his friends are able to assist them but only to a limited degree, since the numbers of the enemy party are superior. A sense of helplessness underlines the two major captivities in *The Last of the Mohicans* and numerous other episodes. At some point, every character is held captive at least once. The scenes of captivity and hiding take place in various locations: the forest, two Indian camps, behind falls, ruins, caves, even a beaver hut. In a sense, occupying the fort is also a type of captivity.

After the initial rescue, Bumppo's party must find their way through the fog, through the French, into the fort. Even Bumppo has difficulty navigating the deceptive landscape. It is unclear where one really is in the fog and who is near—friend or foe. The hunters' presence and absence become crucial for the well-being of the other characters and their ability to make their way through the landscape.

Who and what one really is becomes the ultimate question. According to Cooper, the answer lay in two factors, ancestry and inclination. The landscape is the place where both are explored. Cora and Uncas show who they are when confronted with life and death situations. Cora protects her sister, Alice, who is younger and less able to cope with the hardships of their adventures. Cora keeps her head while in captivity and remembers to leave a trail so they can be rescued from their captors. Cooper frequently refers to her nobility and dignity of bearing. She speaks up when she has an idea and is practical and cool, much like Bumppo in a crisis. That she is racially mixed is an insurmountable problem for Cooper because her marriage to Uncas would be too radical for cultural norms. He resolves the problem through her heroic death. While she lives, however, she influences the plot through decisive actions. The pale and fainting Alice seems far less worthy of notice.

Uncas is noble in both bearing and ancestry. His deeds speak for themselves. In the revelation scene, when he is about to be killed by Tamenund's warriors, the action rises to a dramatic pitch as the tortoise tattoo is revealed on his chest. The tattoo raises echoes of Daniel Boone, who was named "Sheltowee," or "Big Turtle," by the Shawnee.

Uncas and Cora reach a romantic resolution in death that they could not have reached in life. Cooper never allowed a racially mixed couple to be living examples of amalgamation. He had the freedom in their deaths to unite them without any negative or even uncomfortable consequences. The mourning Indian maidens romantically link the two and will tell stories of them, although we are told that the romantic notion is just the fancy of young girls. The space devoted to the funeral of Cora argues for its appeal despite any disclaimers by Cooper. The elaborate description and emotional pitch of his diction subvert protestations that linking Cora and Uncas is unimportant.

The unity of the surviving hunter/warriors, Bumppo and Chingachgook, in the aftermath of Uncas's funeral is conveyed through an emotional exchange at the end of the novel. Chingachgook speaks to the assembly of mourners:

> "Why do my brothers mourn!" he said, regarding the dark race of dejected warriors by whom he was environed. "Why do my daughters weep! That a young man has gone to the happy hunting grounds; that a chief has filled his time with honor? He was good: he was dutiful; he was brave. Who can deny it? The Manitto had need of such a warrior, and he has called him away. As for me, the son and the father of Uncas, I am a blazed pine, in a clearing of palefaces. My race has gone from the shores of the salt lake, and the hills of the Delawares. But who can say that the serpent of his tribe has forgotten his wisdom? I am alone—" (414)

To which Bumppo replies:

> "No, no," cried Hawk-eye, who had been gazing with a yearning look at the rigid features of his friend, with something like his own self-command, but whose philosophy could endure no longer. "No, Sagamore, not alone. The gifts of our colors may be different, but God has so placed us as to journey in the same path. I have no kin, and may I also say, like you, no people. He was your son, and a redskin by nature; and it may be that your blood was nearer—but if ever I forget the lad who has so often fought at my side in war, and slept at my side in peace, may He who made us all, whatever may be our color or our gifts, forget me! The boy has left us for a time; but, Sagamore, you are not alone." (414)

The two men, described as "intrepid woodsmen," then grasp hands and bow "their heads together, while scalding tears fell to their feet, watering the grave of Uncas like drops of falling rain" (414).

The two hunters, red and white, are then married in their grief. But it is a union that cannot change the essentially solitary nature of each of their lives. The impossibility of conquering such a hostile world is reinforced in this scene. The only way of living in this world or, rather, in this conflict of worlds, is by carefully walking the borderline between them, stepping into one world or the other only as necessity dictates. Those living within the two worlds are separated but learn about each other through Bumppo.

The location of Bumppo between the Indian and "civilized" worlds, and his role as a link between the two, is a partial resolution of his preoccupation with identity. The borders themselves may change, but his definition as scout and hunter remains fixed. The movement is westward since the borders move to the west over the course of his lifetime.

The Pathfinder or The Inland Sea

Bumppo as Pathfinder is a hunter and forest scout. His talents have earned him his latest name but, ironically, he is left for long periods of time on the trackless water. Bumppo is out of his element in many settings in this volume. For the first time, he falls in love. Although he is unsuccessful in his courtship, the threat that domestic influence will mitigate his status as frontiersman makes Bumppo vulnerable.

The title, The Pathfinder, becomes ironic. Correctly reading the signs in his world earned Bumppo his appellation, and he misreads many things throughout this story. The reader sees him struggle with several unknown languages. He certainly does not understand the language of love; he has great difficulty translating the seafaring jargon of Cap, Mabel's uncle; and he is removed from his beloved woods to flounder on the inland sea.

The focus in *The Pathfinder* also contributes to a diminishing of Bumppo's stature. At certain points, he is absent from the scene altogether. Even when he is in the woods, often we do not see him. The plot frequently proceeds without his physical presence.

As in the other Tales, especially *The Last of the Mohicans*, location underscores action and sheds insight on character. Much of the landscape in *The Pathfinder* is physically and emotionally strange to Bumppo. His skills as hunter do not help him on the inland sea, and his ability to read signs in the forest does not help him read the language of love. What is Cooper's purpose in letting Pathfinder lose his way? Bumppo crosses borders in *The Pathfinder* that first challenge, then reinforce who he is. He will not marry, although he comes as close as he will ever to doing so. In *The Pioneers* he continues to be displaced by civilization. For the time being (the time covered in *The Pathfinder,* that is), he struggles with forces that are alien to him: love and the "sea."

As the novel opens, four people—two men and two women—come to a break in the forest where a windstorm has piled trees 30 feet high; the trees have been broken off or completely uprooted. The party includes Mabel Dunham and her maternal uncle, Charles Cap; and the Tuscaroras, Arrowhead and his wife, Dew of June. They come upon Pathfinder and Chingachgook, whose fire they saw from the trees. As in the other Tales, Bumppo introduces himself by various names, "La Long Carabine," "Hawk-eye," and "Pathfinder." It turns out the party was in search of Pathfinder, who has been entrusted with escorting Mabel and Cap to her father, Sergeant Dunham, whom Mabel has not seen in years.

Different paths are a concern throughout the novel. The topography of the landscape and the human heart are both difficult to traverse. An atmosphere of deception is present; one does not know whom to trust. Characters seem to fit into the categories of either "deceivers" or "deceived." Self-deception or misinterpretation figure into this equation as well. How well one knows oneself becomes an important question.

Bumppo thinks he knows himself and his place in the world. Early in the book, Bumppo converses on one of his favorite subjects, the different inclinations of red and white, specifically Chingachgook and himself.

> "The Sarpent, here, has his fashions, and I have mine; yet have we fou't, side by side, these many years, without either's thinking a hard thought consarning the other's ways. I tell him there is but one heaven and one hell, notwithstanding his traditions, though there are many paths to both." (25)

Again, Cooper introduces the idea of different paths through Bumppo's discourse. The various paths in *The Pathfinder* are not all familiar to

Bumppo. Discussion ensues about the ocean and the forest, of being in nature or being in town. The purifying nature of water and the superior aspect of the water to the land is asserted by Cap, as he replies to Bumppo's observations:

> "That is rational, and he [Chingachgook] is bound to believe you, though I fancy most of the roads to the last [hell] are on dry land. The sea is what my poor sister, Bridget, used to call a 'purifying place,' and one is out of the way of temptation when out of sight of land. I doubt if as much can be said in favor of your lakes, up hereaway." (25)

Bumppo answers: "That the towns and settlements lead to sin, I will allow; but our lakes are bordered by the forests, and one is every day called upon to worship God in such a temple" (25). Bumppo is part of the forest and part of nature.

In every other volume of the series, Bumppo is in his proper place. *The Pathfinder* is an anomaly because here Bumppo is placed in situations where he is uncomfortable. Cooper defines Bumppo in this volume by what he is not. Overall, the effect is to reestablish his proper place in the natural world. No one in this book is comfortable or safe outside his or her element. Cap is suspicious of any life except that of the sailor; Mabel is uncomfortable out of the settlement; Jasper Western, the young freshwater sailor, is rendered powerless when not sailing the *Scud* on Lake Ontario; and, of course, Pathfinder is reduced to dependence upon others when not in the forest.

Other characters are dislocated as well. The numerous Scotsmen, including Dunham, are soldiers fighting for Britain, which does not hold their primary loyalty. Not only are they outside Scotland, they are fighting the French and Indians in America. Their accents pervade the garrison. Lundie, the commanding officer, longs for his fiancée and the life he could have across the sea. He foolishly trusts Mr. Muir, who is a double agent and causes the main mischief in the book. Arrowhead, as Muir's Indian counterpart in treachery, acts to sabotage the expedition on the lake, and later on the island, where the secret base of the British is located. Jasper is maligned because he speaks French. Despite his constant proofs of competence and loyalty, he is easily undermined by Muir with the acquiescence of the others, including Bumppo.

In this atmosphere of deception, the issue of identity becomes problematic, and self-deception becomes the biggest issue of all. Bumppo deceives himself when he trusts Dunham's evaluation of the real state of emotional affairs with Mabel. His wonderful heart betrays him, and he makes many mistakes. In addition, he does not see the true nature of circumstances because he is blinded by love.

Bumppo is touched by Mabel's loveliness. Her main advantage for Bumppo, and for Cooper, seems to be her flawlessness. She is one of a long line of motherless females in the Tales, but she does not have their disadvantages. Her own father is a lifelong friend and father figure to Bumppo. Dunham selects Bumppo for Mabel, even though Mabel is nineteen or twenty and Bumppo is almost forty. However, Pathfinder is described as "in the flower of his strength and activity" (35).

He is old only when contrasted with Mabel and Jasper. Bumppo's inability to see the true nature of Mabel's emotions is understandable up to the point where he actually asks her to marry him. But after her initial rejection, his renewal of hope upon the urging of Dunham seems absurd. That he does not learn by experience here is in direct opposition to his life's pattern. His talents for hunting and life in the woods have been enriched by experience. But in the realm of love, Bumppo has no "gifts" for negotiating the territory of the heart. As a hunter, he can learn about the rules of nature. This education does not transfer to the world of human emotions. He has a discussion with Mabel about the British soldiers' inability to learn from experience when it comes to warfare in America.

> "Exper'ence makes them but little wiser; and they wheel, and platoon, and battalion it about, but here in the forest, just as they did in their parks at home. . . . One redskin has more cunning in his natur' than a whole rijiment from the other side of the water—that is, what I call cunning in the woods." (49)

The British cannot learn what they need to overcome the nature of their foes. They do what they have done before. British soldiers will defeat the French and Indians, but the colonial Americans will defeat both adversaries, foreign and domestic. Unfortunately, Bumppo does not learn from the experience of Mabel's rejection either. We see how inept he is when he cannot apply to himself the lessons he sees in the mistakes of others.

Learning to read the environs of one's physical and emotional world correctly becomes an overriding consideration in *The Pathfinder*. To survive, one must find one's element and reside within it. Bumppo returns to the familiar territory of the forest and his solitude, excepting the company of Chingachgook. The other characters variously resolve their crises and find life solutions for good or ill.

In the final analysis, only Bumppo reaffirms the life he has always known and will continue to live. Even Mabel and Jasper relinquish the *Scud* and the lake upon the advice of Cap.

That the American hunter is a solitary figure when viewed by others is a cliché. The striking sense in *The Pathfinder* is that, for the first time, Bumppo experiences loneliness. At the beginning of *The Pathfinder*, Bumppo is in control of his environment. During the course of the book, he is deceived by experience and dislocation. In the end, he is more formidable because he has traversed the treacherous emotional landscape.

> Pathfinder was accustomed to solitude, but, when the Scud had actually disappeared, he was almost overcome with a sense of his loneliness. Never before had he been conscious of his isolated condition in the world, . . . particularly as the last were connected to domestic affections. Now, all had vanished, as it might be, in one moment, and he was left equally without companions and hope. Even Chingachgook had left him, though it was but temporarily; still, his presence was missed at the precise instant which might be termed the most critical of our hero's life. (422)

Bumppo takes care of June for a month while she mourns at Arrowhead's grave. He brings her to Mabel on his one and only visit to the young couple before they go to New York. They never speak with him again. He resolves to try to think of Mabel as a daughter or sister, but is left solitary with only memories of his love.

Years later, Mabel sees him at a distance when she is in the company of her own sons.

> Thrice Mabel received valuable presents of furs, at intervals of years, and her feelings told her whence they came, though no name accompanied the gift. Later in life, still, when the mother of several youths, she had occasion to visit the interior, and found herself on the banks of the Mohawk, accompanied by her sons, the eldest of whom was capable of being her protector. On that occasion she observed a man in a singular guise, watching her in the distance with an intentness that induced her to inquire into his pursuits and character. She was told he was the most renowned hunter of that portion of the State—it was after the Revolution—a being of great purity of character, and of as marked peculiarities, and he was known in that region of the country by the name of Leatherstocking. Further than this Mrs. Western could not ascertain, though the distant glimpse and singular deportment of this unknown hunter gave her a sleepless night and cast a shade of melancholy over her still lovely face that lasted many a day. (428)

The figure who so intrigues Mabel at the end of *The Pathfinder* is more familiar to the reader than the unsure, displaced Bumppo evident in the earlier pages. When she is older, Mabel seems more in tune with Bumppo at a distance than she did when she was the object of his affection in her full bloom of youth. He never desires anyone other than Mabel. At the end, Bumppo again knows himself and so do we.

He is the hunter, even more resolved that hunting is his only true path. Perhaps he has crossed one border too many and must retreat further into the world of the woods for balance.

The Pioneers: Or the Sources of the Susquehanna:
A Descriptive Tale
In *The Pioneers*, Natty Bumppo is in his seventies. As a hunter, he comes into conflict with man's law when his view of land rights differs from society's. He crosses borders not only between wilderness and civilization, between the world of the woods and that of the town, but also between nature's law and man's. He is also on the borderline between the past and the future.

Judge Temple may be the mitigating figure in the novel between the freedom of the "old day" and the potential excess of the new, but Bumppo will have to move on to a new frontier. Cooper may have portrayed the development of New York State as desirable and inevitable, but Bumppo, the hunter, can no longer stay on the land where his tenure predates that of its current owner. As with Boone, the merits of the settled life are not questioned, but Bumppo will not be able to live that life.

The Pioneers begins with Cooper's description and prediction for the area where the Tale takes place. The area "near the center of the State of New York," Cooper tells us, will become in a few years

> beautiful and thriving villages . . . interspersed along the margins of the small lakes, or situated at those points of the streams . . . most favorable to manufacturing; and neat and comfortable farms, with every indication of wealth about them . . . scattered profusely through the vales and even to the mountaintops. (13)

Although *The Pioneers* is the first novel Cooper wrote, Bumppo's lifetime is nearly at an end. Robert E. Spiller sees the subtitle, *A Descriptive Tale*, as significant because he argues that Cooper's primary intent was to create a novel whose purpose encompassed realism, description, and moral and social significance, rather than one that dealt with romance, action, and adventure (438).

In one sense, *The Pioneers* begins Cooper's vision; it constructs all the Tales. We are viewing the main character near the end of his lifetime. We cannot think that Cooper ever forgets who Bumppo becomes in time, no matter how romantically he re-creates Bumppo's youth. Slotkin sees a mythic connection between the Arthurian legend and Bumppo's character in *The Deerslayer* and *The Last of the Mohicans* (*Regeneration Through Violence* 501). Bumppo is a sacrificial hero who can be viewed simultaneously as a national representative. Furthermore, in the structure of the Tales is an interesting manipulation of time that further reinforces the connection between Arthur and Bumppo. The nature of a legend is that it may be reworked by different authors to satisfy their artistic and even mythic agendas. In one treatment of Arthur's legend, *The Once and Future King* by T.H. White, the young Arthur's mentor, Merlin the magician, lives backwards in time. He tries to help Arthur become a good king, but he has a problem since he knows what will happen to the boy, but not what has already happened. Cooper is in the same position as Merlin—he creates a figure who has lived a full life, but the author must re-create a past appropriate to what readers already know about the central character.

In the lifetime of Natty Bumppo, there are important details to keep track of regarding who, what, and where he would have been previously. Historically, culturally, and socially, Cooper must track him in the American landscape. Placing the narrative in chronological time, it is 1793. The autobiographical elements in *The Pioneers* are helpful in exploring the development and limits of character, especially in regard to Bumppo. Spiller points out:

> James Cooper . . . was four years and three months old on the frosty Christmas Eve with which *The Pioneers* opens. He was probably at home in bed when his father, Judge William Cooper (or Temple), encountered Natty and his friends, Indian John and young Oliver Edwards, and the latter suffered the accident that sets the tone and theme of the novel. . . . [T]here are two Nathaniel Shipmans who contend for the honor of being the original of Natty Bumppo; and equivalents of many of the events and places of the novel are recorded in *The Chronicles of Cooperstown*, which Cooper wrote and his neighbors the Phinneys published in 1838. (438–439)

That Cooper was working with actual people whom he then fictionalized explains the realistic quality of *The Pioneers*. Cooper develops the hunter hero Bumppo from the historical human Bumppo, which accounts for the more romantic treatment of the character in later novels.

What is true of Bumppo is not true of Chingachgook. The Indian is more removed in origin, as he is not based on someone Cooper knew. The chronological lifetime of the characters thematically underscores the poignancy of growing old in a young country. That the virulent Deerslayer becomes a toothless, humiliated Natty Bumppo and the noble young warrior Chingachgook becomes a Christianized but drunken Indian John are commentaries indeed on the price of "progress." Bumppo and

Chingachgook are old, but they still have the values and instincts of hunter/ warriors. They still regard the land in the same way they always have.

The landscape becomes civilized, tamed from the time of *The Path-finder* to *The Pioneers*. The description of "beautiful thriving villages" as appealing and proper to the order of things is juxtaposed with the price of such progress. Who owns the land and how ownership is deter-mined drives the plot in this novel. Cooper's background is significant here, too. Spiller tells us that William Cooper and the growth of Cooperstown have direct parallels with Judge Temple and Templeton. He points out that there are "three theories of the relationship of property rights to social stability—the Tory view held by young Oliver, the demo-cratic view held by Judge Temple, and the view of primitive rights held by Indian John" (440).

The characters who have power in *The Pioneers* try to displace Bumppo, all except Oliver Edwards, who we learn is really Oliver Effingham. Because he is also part of the natural world, he seems like a younger, better educated version of Bumppo. Kelly points out that, like Uncas in *The Last of the Mohicans*, in a sense Oliver is one of Bumppo's sons (6).

Nature is the ultimate proving ground for who is righteous and who is not. Oliver is aligned with the power of former British claims to land, but he is also an American amalgamation of Indian and European culture. He lives with Bumppo and Chingachgook in the forest, which proves his worthiness to inherit the land. This claim as inhabitant is as important as his claim by heredity. His relationship with Elizabeth is a romantic flourish that echoes the relationships in *The Deerslayer, The Last of the Mohicans,* and *The Pathfinder*. These relationships are yet to come in real time. However, Cooper re-creates a background that makes sense, chronologically and emotionally. *The Pioneers* is the reference point, no matter how one looks at the series. In this novel, Cooper establishes the borderlines that Bumppo as hunter will cross, physically, temporally, and metaphorically.

The Prairie: A Tale

In *The Prairie*, Natty Bumppo is an old man in his eighties. He now lives in a forest of grass, and his occupation as hunter has been modified to that of trapper. In his eighties, Daniel Boone also resorted to this hum-bler aspect of pursuit to accommodate the physical limitations of age. Cooper dwells on Bumppo's bodily decay, and we are conscious of his delicate hold on life. He seems in defiance of time, and he is as surprised as the reader and the other characters in the novel at his longevity. In one way, time has diminished him; in another it has released him from the boundaries of human existence.

Henry Nash Smith has comments that

> [a]n analysis of the structure of *The Prairie* reveals that Cooper works from one to another of a series of visual images conceived as if they were paintings lacking the dimension of time. . . . Several tableaux in *The Prairie* are among the most effective passages in Cooper. (introduction to *The Prairie* ix)

Again, time is an important component in Cooper's creation of physical and mental landscape. To be set in time and place, and yet simultaneously timeless, suspended in a series of imagistic tableaux, may seem contradictory. However, the drama and symbolism of Bumppo's life not only make such a thing possible, but appropriate. Particularly since Bumppo's experience is a reflection of the American frontiersman's experience and, as such, the country's, there is no contradiction. However, the ablest hunter, in the person of Natty Bumppo, is no longer at the peak of his powers. Bumppo's command over the landscape is diminished in one way and transcendent in another.

A striking aspect of the hunting motif in *The Prairie* is the presence of predators, both animal and human. Bumppo has always been in control of his hunting skills. He has been able to hunt for food and, when necessary, for protection. Now he can no longer control the forces of nature that have previously challenged but not overwhelmed him. Cooper makes reference to prowling wolves and bears, as if danger can never be ignored, even in the twilight of life. Bumppo is at risk as he never has been before. The change of occupation from hunter to trapper connotes his relegation to a more passive stage of life. The nature of the characters he encounters from the human world also are a threat because of his great age. Those he would have avoided or despised before are now forces to contend with, and his powers to resist them are limited.

On the first evening after Bumppo meets the Bush family, Bumppo's dog, Hector, is uneasy and growls at the unseen presence in the darkness. Bumppo urges him to indicate the nature of the visitor. Ellen Wade, the young niece of Ishmael Bush, emerges from the night and chats with Bumppo. She is there to meet Paul Hover, the bee hunter, whose subsequent appearance Hector also heralds. A third indication of Hector's vigilance reveals that Indians are about to invade, and the only recourse is hiding.

The captivity and rescue scenarios are used once again as in the other Tales, but with several differences. Previously, Bumppo was the active force for resistance to the forces of evil. Now, instead of facing evil head-on as he used to do, he must avoid or avert it. In many respects, Bumppo is beyond the struggles of other mortals in *The Prairie*. Though physically less powerful, he is spiritually more perfect than ever. And because of the symbolic nature of Cooper's tableaux, the measure of his stature moves from the physical realm to the mythic.

The opposition in the novel is between good and bad—whites and Indians both have their range of good and evil characters. This opposition reflects the state not only of Bumppo's life, but of the nation. This is Bumppo's last frontier; he has always been in the advance guard of progress (Kelly 89). However, he is still on the margins of opposing worlds and their extremes.

Bumppo crosses the ultimate border in this novel, the border between life and death. This border, when finally crossed, does not permit recrossing. Perhaps this is why Bumppo seems removed to the peripheries of Cooper's plot. Bumppo gives the work perspective, the end of his life indicates a "sense of closure" and "epitomizes the history of the American people." The novel in this context acts as a self-conscious work that reviews the Tales and surveys the variety of American experience (Kelly 90–92).

As Jane Tompkins suggests, the setting of vacant landscape provides the scene for a genesis, the creation of a world and the implied ending of that same world (70).[9] The physical setting or location also implies an accompanying mental landscape reflecting the culture's concerns. Kelly comments that

> [o]ne of Cooper's primary concerns in both *The Pioneers* and *The Last of the Mohicans* is the location of a cultural genesis. By designating points of national departure, he erects a fictive barrier against the past and validates his claims for American "originality." Cooper does not, however, simply privilege a moment in time from which the course of national development has followed but conceives beginnings which also imply endings. (85–86)

Cooper manipulates time for thematic purposes and stylistic emphasis. We are located in time, and yet it is a vehicle for reinforcing meaning. The complication arises from the contradictory nature of the meaning. According to Kelly, the struggle of America is to reconcile a yearning for legitimacy by referral to and identification with the European traditions of the past and an insistence upon originality and independence from that past. The emblematic nature of all of Cooper's characters reflects such concerns.

The conflict between characters underlines the idea of extremes and the range and margins of those extremes. Bumppo and Middleton act as mitigating forces, providing a rational alternative for the disparate forces battling for preeminence. Kelly points out that "Ishmael and his family are ideas clumsily masquerading as characters [although] Ishmael himself is one of Cooper's most memorable creations . . . [representing] the embodiment of two centuries of American anxiety about the frontier" (95).

The complexity of that anxiety can be realized only through examination of the characters and what they embody. The frontier is a place to escape from the past, but it holds dangers of its own. In one sense, Inez represents the tyranny of the Old World since she is Spanish and Catholic. However, she is carried away by the Bush clan as a prisoner to the prairie, which is part of the Louisiana Purchase, a token that the power is shifting from the Old World to America. She is the victim of independence and lawlessness, represented by the Bush family. Both forces are evil in their extremes, and both forces are active in the development of the American nation.

In their less virulent forms, tradition and independence are desirable forces. The careful balance of the two qualities is a positive attribute of character for a person or a nation. However, in their aberrations, they are forces that tend toward chaos. In his younger days, Bumppo would have been able to actively intervene by virtue of his skills as a hunter/warrior. That he is too old at this point in American time to employ his skills implies that this representation of the hunter needs to evolve to deal with the changing landscape. A border between chaos and order is always present in some form in Cooper's Tales.

It is interesting that, in this novel, tradition and independence are acting upon one another directly. The resolution through the characters in *The Prairie* is satisfactory in this sense; metaphorically, it is not quite so comfortable. Does the struggle of the two extremes, two wrongs, make one right? The swing of the pendulum ideally ends up in the middle, but at what price to both extensions of its route? Natty Bumppo, as hunter/hero and permutation of Daniel Boone, frames the Tales and the American experience in his lifetime. His liminal position on the borders of the evolving frontier is uniquely appropriate as a signification of cultural issues and concerns. He encounters the "variety of American experience" in the other characters he meets and through them explores aspects of race and gender. His interaction with the landscape and its inhabitants results in self-knowledge that further establishes his identity. The

Leatherstocking Tales may constitute a discrete unit in American literature and history, but the liminal figure of the hunter continues to evolve.

Both Daniel Boone and Natty Bumppo serve as a gauge of cultural history, and the hunter/warrior trope is significant for an understanding of early nineteenth century American culture. The hunter at this time represents the development of the nation across the continent. This emerging American hero integrates the disparate elements of Indian and Euro-American cultures within his persona. His flexible image makes him an appropriate representative of the multiple and often conflicting segments in contemporary American society.

Notes

1   Daniel Boone as a composite figure is discussed throughout John Mack Faragher's biography of Boone, and the idea of Boone as a flexible entity resolves many problems. Boone scholarship has tended to portray Boone in various positive or negative terms; Faragher includes all the Boone material he finds, especially conflicting versions of the same incidents to offer possibilities of interpretations. Faragher also postulates on the needs fulfilled by portraying Boone in particular ways by different sources.

2   See Edmund S. Morgan, *The Puritan Dilemma: The Story of John Winthrop* (Boston: Little, Brown, and Co., 1958).

3   See R. W. B. Lewis, *The American Adam: Innocence, Tragedy, and Tradition in the Nineteenth Century* (Chicago: University of Chicago Press, 1975).

4   See Henry Nash Smith, *Virgin Land: The American West as Symbol and Myth* (New York: Vintage, 1950).

5   John Mack Faragher, Richard Slotkin, and Mary Lawlor all discuss the importance of John Filson's portrayal of Boone in establishing his legend. Various reworkings of the legend yield different impressions, but "Filson's Boone" forms the foundation figure upon which the following portrayals build. Lawlor's essay in *Desert, Garden, Margin, Range: Literature on the American Frontier,* edited by Eric Heyne, points out the differences in portrayals of Boone by John Filson, James Hall, and Timothy Flint, as well as portrayals of James Fenimore Cooper's Natty Bumppo character.

6   Daniel Boone and Davy Crockett are linked most notably by the Boone and Crockett Club, founded by Theodore Roosevelt and Henry Cabot Lodge in 1887.

7   Yvor Winter discusses Bumppo's extreme reluctance to kill the Indian and the significance of this reticence in his essay, "Fenimore Cooper or the Ruins of Time," in his book *In Defense of Reason* (Denver: Alan Swallow, 1947), 185–190.

8   Mark Twain satirizes Cooper in two essays: "Fenimore Cooper's Literary Offenses" and "Fenimore Cooper's Further Literary Offenses." Both essays can be found in *Mark Twain: Collected Tales, Sketches, Speeches, & Essays, 1891–1910,* ed. Louis J. Budd (New York: Library of America, 1992), 180–200.

9   Tompkins quotes *The Virginian* by Owen Wister: "'A world of crystal light [as it says in *The Virginian*], a land without evil, a space across which Noah and Adam might come straight from Genesis.'" She discusses how the landscape of the western is used, particularly in film, to create a world appropriate for the action to unfold. She likens the literal starkness of the western landscape to the Old Testament description of creation.

Chapter 3

Teddy Roosevelt and Buffalo Bill: From Sustenance to Slaughter, From Excess to Conservation

From Hunters to International Players

The most thrilling moments of an American hunter's life are those in which, with every sense on the alert, and with nerves strung to the highest point, he is following alone into the heart of its forest fastness the fresh and bloody footprints of an angered grizzly; and no other triumph of American hunting can compare with the victory to be gained. (Roosevelt, in DiNunzio 266–267)

. . .

[L]eaving my saddle and bridle with the wagons, we rode to the windward of the buffaloes, as usual, and when within a few hundred yards of them we dashed into the herd. I soon had thirteen laid out on the ground, the last one of which I had driven down close to the wagons, where the ladies were. It frightened some of the tender creatures to see the buffalo coming at full speed directly toward them; but when he had got within fifty yards of one of the wagons, I shot him dead in his tracks. This made my sixty-ninth buffalo. (Cody 173–174)

Theodore Roosevelt's life was a grizzly hunt or, more accurately, one grizzly hunt after another. William "Buffalo Bill" Cody's life was a buffalo hunt. Roosevelt and Cody have become figures in the American imagination who suggest physical and political expansion across the continent and the globe. In their personae, the hunter becomes a metaphor for domestic and foreign power. These two figures represent the departure of the United States from nineteenth century isolationist political policies and social sentiments. They were literal hunters whose prowess made them nationally and internationally recognizable. They traveled extensively in their capacities as world leader and world entertainer, respectively, and their names became synonymous with American influence.

Both Cody and Roosevelt were hunters and cowboys, although the term *cowboy* may be problematic since, as David H. Katzive points out, Buffalo Bill was not technically a cowboy. He was never a hired hand who wrangled cattle. But this is a semantic technicality. Buffalo Bill and Teddy Roosevelt embody the essence of cowboys, encompassing a range of figures from "the hero of Wild West stories, rodeo performer, movie actor, singer, dude ranch wrangler, Wild West performer, Mexican *vaquero* in Texas, rough rider, bad man of the Plains and even Southwestern rancher. And then, of course, there is also the real cowboy who works on a ranch with real cattle" (57). Cody and Roosevelt contributed to the notion of the cowboy, endowing it with aspects of their own personalities that endure even today. They elevated the cowboy from a plebeian/ hunter/ workman to a hunter/warrior/gentleman.

Roosevelt's efforts to conserve natural resources and Cody's efforts to preserve the Indian way of life through his Wild West exhibition (it was never called a "show")[1] were attempts to mitigate the ravaging effects of American expansion and excess on the frontier. Although their efforts at conservation and preservation were imperfect, and many of their actions were directly contradictory to their supposed aims, they were motivated by good intentions.

Both Roosevelt and Cody were representative American hunters. Roosevelt traveled abroad and acquired a reputation as a prodigious big game hunter. The powerful image of the hunter/cowboy made an imprint upon the American imagination and upon the world's imagination. Roosevelt became the "cowboy president" and America the "cowboy of nations."

The Closing of the Frontier

With the closing of the frontier, the continent was no longer limitless.[2] This realization sparked concern for preserving the nation's natural resources because, after the 1850s, the hunters' prowess was redirected from wrestling nourishment from the wilderness to slaughtering the buffalo herds in order to feed the railroad workers. This reckless hunting deprived the Indians of their main source of sustenance and heritage, thus bringing about their decline and ultimate suppression. American "progress," or dominance of the continent, was the end that justified such means.

Richard Slotkin has analyzed Roosevelt's stories of his big game hunts and sees them as naturalizing force and violence. He also points out that Roosevelt's depictions of these hunts follow stages that reflect hierarchical and historical patterns, where Roosevelt stalks and kills game in a progression of increasing danger, from deer to grizzly bear and panther. By helping to exterminate the buffalo, he indirectly played a role in the warfare that would subjugate the Indians. He then moved from the world of nature to that of politics; as a deputy sheriff, Roosevelt became a man-hunter. James Fenimore Cooper established this pattern of hunting as preparation for the higher function of warrior in *The Deerslayer,* one of Roosevelt's favorite books. However, Roosevelt did not fully develop into a warrior until the Cuban war, when he finally had the chance to "get his Spaniard" (Slotkin, *Gunfighter Nation* 41).

Slaughter and excess may express the desire for power and serve as a vehicle for control over enemies. As embodied in Roosevelt, the hunter represented both domestic and foreign control. Through all the stages of his life, Roosevelt expanded his personal territory, which was literally and emblematically tied to the country's territory. After being graduated from Harvard in 1880, he served as a Republican in the New York state legislature for two years. After the shock of the deaths of his wife and mother on the same day, Roosevelt traveled to the Dakota Territory in 1884, where he ranched and became a deputy sheriff. He later returned to New York and remarried. He served as president of the Board of New York City Police Commissioners and then as assistant secretary of the Navy, where he was instrumental in the involvement of the United States in the Spanish-American War.

To be more directly involved in the action, Roosevelt formed the Rough Riders and became a hero for his charge up San Juan Hill. After the war, he ran for governor of New York and won. Roosevelt's active role in social reform and labor prompted Senator Thomas Collier "Boss" Platt of the Republican state machine to engineer Roosevelt's place on the presidential ticket with McKinley. Platt thought this would rid the Republicans of Roosevelt's efforts on behalf of the common man. McKinley's assassination in 1901 unexpectedly put Roosevelt into the position of presidential power—power he extended during his administrations.

Roosevelt's domestic policies and intervention in labor-management disputes established his leadership in the national arena. In foreign relations he was even more aggressive. He claimed the United States had the right to impose order in Latin America and he intervened in the civil war in Panama to foster construction of the Panama Canal. He acted as mediator to end the Russo-Japanese War, an effort that won him the Nobel Peace Prize in 1906.

Initially, the hunter as embodied in Cody represented domestic control, but this image expanded internationally. After Cody's Wild West completed its first European tour in 1887, Cody, too, represented American influence in the world of foreign affairs. Cody's Wild West exhibition traveled the United States and abroad for thirty years. The show was modified over the years to educate the public about the changing nature of affairs in the United States and the world.

The evolution of these public figures into conservationist and Wild West showman represented for Americans an attempt by Roosevelt and Cody, respectively, to re-create a mythic connection with the American past. Ironically, both men played a prominent role in destroying the buffalo herds and displacing the Indians, yet once the frontier life was gone forever, they became its biggest advocates. Whether this idealized reminiscence of frontier life was realistic is another matter. Their longing for the "good old days" seems paradoxical since both men were instrumental in bringing them to an end. However, what remains important is that the evocation of hunter images by Roosevelt and Cody legitimized and consolidated American claims to domestic and world power. According to Slotkin, both men advocated Manifest Destiny as a rationalization for U.S. intervention in the Spanish American War and as an idea that fostered "American confidence and optimism" (*Gunfighter Nation* 30).

This concept of Manifest Destiny is particularly relevant to the figures of Roosevelt and Cody because they literally covered the continent in their role as hunter figures. The popular press reinforced this image in its coverage of their activities throughout the period. Their particular image as hunter/cowboy ignited the imagination of Americans and Europeans alike. Roosevelt and Cody became synonymous with the popular image of the American character.

In July of 1893, Frederick Jackson Turner, an eminent American historian, presented his essay, "The Significance of the Frontier in American History," in Chicago at the American Historical Association conference, convened in conjunction with the Columbian Exposition. Cody was in attendance for this epoch-making work that gave rise to new and important areas for historical study. Although they did not meet, both men represented views of westward expansion that shaped the American national identity.

The purpose of the exposition was to celebrate the four-hundredth anniversary of Columbus's discovery of America. Although such celebrations were portrayed as educational at the time, in practice their primary function was entertainment. That two such influential figures on the nineteenth-century American imagination as Cody and Turner had come together at this greatest of American celebrations was especially significant since the event combined education and spectacle to form a marriage of cultural unity (White and Limerick 7–9).

Roosevelt's view of frontier settlement corresponded with Cody's: a violent process. Turner's view, on the other hand, was of a benign march of pioneers filling up an empty West. But Turner and Roosevelt shared "a concern that the passing of the agrarian frontier marked the beginning of crisis in American history" (Slotkin, *Gunfighter Nation* 30). Richard Slotkin rejects as premature Turner's conclusion that the frontier was closed. Slotkin cites the fact that "more public land would be taken up and brought into production between 1890 and 1920 than during the supposed heyday of the western frontier in the decades that followed passage of the Homestead Act (1862)" (*Gunfighter Nation* 30). However, development and production of land and resources represent a frontier different from the untapped expanse of continent with no limit in sight.

Slotkin's comment that the "closure of the old agrarian/artisanal/entrepreneurial frontier coincided with a crisis in American social and political history . . . and . . . were . . . causally linked" (*Gunfighter Nation* 31) certainly seems accurate. He associates Turner's vision of American development with the yeoman farmer tradition and Roosevelt with the hunter/warrior.

While Turner was seen as a man of the people, Roosevelt's persona was that of an "aristocratic character lurking under the hunter's buckskins," like those found in Cooper's works (Slotkin, *Gunfighter Nation* 35). Roosevelt's self-image emerged from an "intuitive identification with the Frontier." For two years after the unexpected deaths of his wife and mother, he escaped to the wilderness: ranching, big-game hunting, and serving as deputy sheriff. Before he re-entered politics, Roosevelt wrote several articles about the West, as well as books about his hunting and ranching adventures, expansionist Senator Thomas Hart Benton, and the seven-volume series *The Winning of the West* (36).

> Roosevelt was imaginatively engaged by the literary mythology of the Frontier, especially Cooper's *Leatherstocking Tales,* and he favored historians like Francis Parkman, who portrayed history in Cooperian terms as a real-life "romance" in which heroes representing national virtues test and vindicate the "character" of their people in "savage war." (Slotkin, *Gunfighter Nation* 33)

Roosevelt identified with hunter/pioneer figures of the past; he was committed to "the strenuous life," or a return to nature. His return to the wilderness regenerated his personal power. He linked his own experiences in the West with historical precedents, thus giving himself and his views the blessing of the past.

Roosevelt co-founded the Boone and Crockett Club with Henry Cabot Lodge. The Boone and Crockett Club was a place to enjoy the company of other "gentleman hunters" and foster conservative politics (Slotkin, *Gunfighter Nation* 36–37). This frontier image of Roosevelt's gentleman hunter is in contrast to Turner's yeoman farmer.

Turner saw the farmer as the main figure in American development. Much as Crevecoeur's farmer of colonial America embodied the ideal of progress in cultivating the land, Turner saw the farmer as the civilizing and legendary force in American expansion. Roosevelt had a very different perspective; he saw the primary agent of American expansion as the white man who knew the ways of the Indians. His heroic models, therefore, became the hunter/warriors of American fiction and history. These figures included Hawkeye of Cooper's *Leatherstocking Tales,* Daniel Boone, Davy Crockett, Robert Rogers of the Rangers, Kit Carson, Sam Houston, and Andrew Jackson. The American readership of the time preferred the romances and dime novels that popularized these figures, with the farmer as a secondary figure to these more active heroes (Slotkin, *Gunfighter Nation* 33).

The New "American Type"
Roosevelt believed the closing of the frontier was a significant national issue. His commitment to the landscape was based on personal experience and political beliefs; where he got his ideas and how he developed them into a personal philosophy is complex. Edward N. Saveth sees Roosevelt's father as his inspiration and points out that the family's money made possible Roosevelt's personal, political, and philosophical inclinations. In a country that was traditionally anti-aristocratic, Roosevelt had decidedly aristocratic associations. His family was relatively wealthy at a time when the rich and their power were coming under scrutiny. He fervently believed in a rigid family structure as the society was changing rapidly, and such rigidity could be a drawback. His education and taste for cultivation and refinement were often identified with the snobbish and feminine. Even so, Roosevelt was able to dissociate himself from what the public found suspect and create an image of masculine activism. His advocacy of the strenuous life grew out of his personal experience with childhood illness and its reversal resulting from his father's support and his own tenacity to build a strong body and mind. Roosevelt viewed his ancestry as linked inherently with the American past, his destiny as linked with the American present and future. He believed that the people had "a proprietary interest in him" (Saveth 129–131).

Although Roosevelt tried to distance himself from identification with the "snobbery"of the rich, he subscribed to a view of race and class that privileged the Anglo-Saxon race. He constructed a philosophy based on the Teutonic mythological concept of the hunter/warrior, which stressed the racial superiority of the western European, especially the German. This figure was a superior being—a physically and mentally adept super-man who assumed the active role of leader and protector of the common people.[3]

Roosevelt extended his role as a hunter to domestic and world affairs. The underlying implications of race and class distinctions also become manifest in his use and extension of hunting metaphors into his political life. In a telling anecdote from Edward N. Saveth, two very important ideas are brought together: Roosevelt's attitude toward aristocracy and how he translates this view of the hunter as an "American type."

Roosevelt visited a group of Austrian aristocrats in 1909 on his post-presidential tour of Europe. He tried to clarify his status in terms of American versus Austrian social structure and found the aristocrats' interest in him amusing since they indicated to him he was not regarded as the conventional American millionaire, but rather a new type. Although he was a Democrat (that is, a member of a democracy; his political party was Republican), he was also politically and socially a gentleman in their eyes. His reputation as a soldier, big-game hunter, and trust-buster set him apart from those who only had wealth, but no class, to recommend them. That Roosevelt combined so many disparate traits puzzled them (Saveth 144–145).

Roosevelt, in attacking the "big financial interests," was the hunter/warrior, a figure of great power. And the power to control the powerful resided in this perfect "American type." He embodied the sources of American power, power that came from his relationship with the land.

Both Roosevelt and Cody are permutations of the hunter/warrior type. To Slotkin, Roosevelt represented the aristocratic gentleman hunter, while Cody represented the "archetype of the American frontier hero" (*Gunfighter Nation* 75). Cody attained "gentleman" status through his association with the military later in his career, especially after General George Custer's demise. Eventually, Cody attempted to reintegrate the American Indian's way of life into the mythology of the frontier. The hunter as personified in the figure of Buffalo Bill became the avenue for reliving, reworking, and redefining relations with Native Americans. Reworking the relationship between Indians and cowboy/settlers was Cody's way of "preserving" the Indian way of life that he had been instrumental in destroying.

Both in America and abroad, the Wild West mirrored the political events unfolding at the end of the nineteenth and beginning of the twentieth centuries. The nation of the Wild West was a product of Cody's successful stage experience, in which he played himself in a series of melodramas. From 1872 to 1876, he starred in plays about his adventures; between engagements he scouted and guided on the Great Plains. In 1876, after Custer and his men were killed at Little Big Horn by the Sioux and Cheyenne Indians, Cody left the theater and swore he would get "the first scalp" for Custer. He killed and scalped Yellow Hand of the Cheyennes at War Bonnet Creek. He wore a theatrical Mexican outfit to the conflict, intending to later model the costume he wore when he scalped Yellow Hand. The relevance of such a connection between "show" and real life cannot be overstated. Cody was at once making history and then portraying it in an original art form.

Cody's performances on the stage provided the perfect preparation for his Wild West exhibition. Begun in 1883, Buffalo Bill's Wild West ran for more than thirty years. The exhibition evolved over the decades in response to current events in the United States and abroad. Initially, the show was mainly a rodeo, with riding and roping events, shooting displays and contests, races of various sorts, and parades. Cody then added spectacles based on reenactments from history, such as Custer's Last Stand, and Cody's killing of Yellow Hand; he also added Indian war dances and scenes from the Pony Express, the attack on the Deadwood stagecoach, a buffalo hunt, and various battle reenactments. The condensed re-creations, or "Epochs," of American history Cody portrayed caricatured and sensationalized people and the West to entertain the audience and, more importantly, to promote his own agenda. He created a personal image that grew with the show, and he created an image of America as the Wild West.

Both American and foreign audiences were "educated" about the American West through these tableaux. The impressions left on the public imagination were profound. The exhibition was a financial success and an effective vehicle for education and propaganda about the United States' growing global power. In an age when communication was mainly conveyed in written form, the Wild West provided an experience where people all over the country and the world could share a common sense of the pageant of contemporary history in the making.

In the simplest terms, Roosevelt and Cody as hunter figures were a bridge between the humble backwoodsman and the military conqueror. A number of steps in the evolution of hunting in America can be traced through their lives and careers. The first evolutionary step was from sustenance hunting to market hunting and slaughter of both the buffalo herds and Native American people who relied upon them. The next was from the excess of unrestrained capitalism on a continent with seemingly unlimited natural resources and industrial potential to a recognition of the need to preserve and conserve these resources and control the forces that would exploit them. A need to reconcile the power of conscience with the power of control may be behind Roosevelt's and Cody's actions. They affirmed their personal philosophies through crusades to save the landscape and re-create a way of life that had vanished or, some might say, had never existed.

Theodore Roosevelt: One Man's Vision

Photographs of Roosevelt in his Rough Rider outfit, and later in his hunting costume, show a vigorous and manly figure. From his autobiography, it is clear that Roosevelt struggled with his physical disabilities. His self-creation had begun in childhood when he decided to build his frail body by boxing, riding, and shooting. He recounted:

> Having been a sickly child, with no natural bodily prowess, and having lived much at home, I was at first quite unable to hold my own when thrown into contact with other boys of rougher antecedents. . . . Then an incident happened that did me real good. Having an attack of asthma, I was sent off by myself to Moosehead Lake. On the stagecoach thither I encountered a couple of other boys who were about my own age, but very much more competent and also more mischievous. I have no doubt they were good-hearted boys, but they were boys! They found that I was a foreordained and predestined victim, and industriously proceeded to make life miserable for me. The worst feature was that when I finally tried to fight them I discovered that either one singly could not only handle me with easy contempt, but handle me so as not to hurt me much and yet prevent my doing any damage whatever in return. (*Autobiography* 27–28)

Roosevelt's narrative voice reveals a certain detachment from his youthful self. He was not sentimental about his disability; he cast no blame on his tormentors, but he clearly established the need for physical development if he was not to continue to be the "foreordained and predestined victim."

> The experience taught me what probably no amount of good advice could have taught me. I made up my mind that I must try to learn so that I would not again be put in such a helpless position; and having become quickly and bitterly conscious that I did not have the natural prowess to hold my own, I decided that I would try to supply its place by training. (*Autobiography* 28)

He went on to recount how his father had approved of his plan and hired a professional fighter named John Long to train him. He then worked for about three years before he saw any improvement, but he persevered and finally won a prize in an exhibition. "I was entered in the lightweight contest, in which it happened that I was pitted in succession against a couple of reedy striplings who were even worse than I was. Equally to their surprise and to my own, and to John Long's, I won, and the pewter mug became one of my prized possessions" (*Autobiography* 28).

Roosevelt next resolved to learn to ride, and this activity was also a struggle. Poor eyesight accounted for much of his clumsiness. In trying to learn to shoot, he realized that others were hitting targets he could not even see. When he began to wear his "spectacles," he improved, but someone who wore glasses was regarded as less than virile.

These early examples of Roosevelt's stubborn resolve to succeed demonstrate his self-discipline. While he ostensibly understood the nature of an individual's struggle with personal adversity, he was less patient with others who did not persevere precisely because he had succeeded. But, of course, when Roosevelt wanted to learn to box, his father could employ an instructor for him. And when he wanted to ride and shoot, his family had the resources to provide for his training. Roosevelt's personal experience and education formed the basis for his view of the world, but he viewed life from the superior vantage point of the upper class.

Roosevelt on Race

Thomas Dyer, in his exploration of Roosevelt's attitude toward race, explains that the present-day definition of *race* is quite different from that at turn of the century. According to Dyer, at least five different aspects of race were operative in the anthropological and cultural discourse of Roosevelt's time: (1) a broad designation, any human group that possessed social, physical, or cultural traits in common; (2) a national label, "the French race"; (3) an extension of a national label, meaning those with close ties of family or nationality; (4) color; and (5) representative ethnic divisions of mankind. Roosevelt's fundamental assumptions about race were built on these definitions, which were tantamount to a belief system.[4]

Roosevelt subscribed to a combination of Lamarckianism and Teutonism. Jean Lamarck, a French naturalist, argued that species survived by adapting physically to their environments.[5] This theory was especially attractive to Roosevelt because it suited his notion of an "American race" that had been and continued to evolve, nurtured by the wilderness landscape; this is congruent with the hunter's relationship with his environment. This close connection between the American hunter, who is the perfect model of this race, and the landscape is reinforced by Roosevelt's terminology. Into his discussions on race, Roosevelt incorporated language that described nature and animal species. Such language was a kind of "jargon in which he often expressed . . . [his] ideas" (Dyer, xii).

Roosevelt argued that Americans were a different race from their European progenitors. They had evolved into a new "breed" by inhabiting the American landscape. This new land had shaped a new man and, for that matter, a new woman. The basis of this American race, however, was descended from Teutonic "stock" with "strains" of other northern and western European "blood." From boyhood through his years at Harvard and Columbia, Roosevelt was influenced by popular, literary, and "scientific" notions that the "white races" were destined to govern and rule the world. The hunter/warrior was the root of such a breed. Following Lamarck, Roosevelt refined this theory to include a process incorporating a special evolution for Americans, who were destined to rise above their European ancestors precisely because of the challenging North American landscape.

Roosevelt's taste in literature reflected his philosophy of race. By contrasting the figure of the farmer and that of the hunter in a mythological/ideological scenario, the implications for the American myth of the frontier are clear. This frontier myth emphasizes a necessary link between farmer and hunter as a basis for spiritual regeneration. The hunter/warrior must wrest the "virgin land" from the "savages" in a war between the races so that the farmer may cultivate and civilize the land. However, there are two distinct themes present in this relationship. The "free" or "virgin land" theme stresses the economic aspects of ideological concern, while the "race war" stresses political concerns like the use of force and the right of conquest. A novelist or historian almost always gives preference to one theme or figure over the other, and this breaks the harmony of the original concept. Two alternative versions of the myth exist and can be read as two different historical interpretations of the dynamics of the frontier (Slotkin, *Gunfighter Nation* 33–34).

The frontiersman was Roosevelt's ideal. The Kentucky frontier furnished an especially dramatic example of landscape spawning American character that appealed to Roosevelt. Dyer points to the influence of Nathaniel Southgate Shaler—the Harvard professor, geologist, historian, and naturalist—on Roosevelt's conception of landscape as pivotal in the development of such an American character. Shaler wrote a chronicle of the Kentucky frontier and several other works with themes that attracted Roosevelt. In these books and scientific treatises, Shaler connected the "character" and "social evolution." He saw the development of an American "race" and believed that the best example of such an evolutionary figure emerged specifically from Kentucky and New England (Dyer 6).

Dyer argues that "Shaler's personal background, as well as his intellectual interests, bore sharp similarities to Roosevelt's. He was a dedicated Unionist with deep ties to the South, whose mother, like Roosevelt's, had come from a prominent southern family." Also like Roosevelt, Shaler "developed interests in paleontology and zoology and became a disciple of Jean Lamarck" (6). Unlike Shaler, however, Roosevelt was not an apologist for slavery. Dyer also points out that the biggest difference between Shaler and Roosevelt was that Roosevelt lacked the overt hostility toward blacks; Roosevelt rejected any justification of lynching as a method of social control, and Shaler did not condemn lynching outright (7).

Clearly Roosevelt believed that "the English Speaking peoples" were superior, although his view of race evolved over his lifetime. His initial model for the American hunter/warrior was the Teutonic hunter/warrior, a primitive and highly mythological white hunter/warrior figure. A metaphor for power, he saw the evolution of the hunter/warrior in racial terms.

Progress implied that, as civilization became more complex, primitive races and classes were superseded by superior ones. In the United States, the Indian gave way to the hunter/trapper and Indian fighter. These men were replaced with the cowboy, rancher, and farmer. Roosevelt saw the cowboy as nearest in spirit to the hunter and, as such, a cut above the farmer or agricultural laborer and the mechanic and workman of the city. He failed to acknowledge the racial diversity of the cowboy of this era, however. The cowboy is not a pure archetype of freedom, though, because he is a hired hand (Slotkin, *Gunfighter Nation* 39).

In *African Game Trails,* Roosevelt recounted his extensive hunting trips on safari in the year preceding his 1910 Oxford address. During his hunts, Roosevelt found validation for his theories on race, gender roles, and political power. The hunting experience and the metaphor of the hunt provided a framework for his personal philosophy.

> The house at which we were staying stood on the beautiful Kitanga hills. . . . It is a dry country, and we saw it in the second year of a drought; yet I believe it to be a country of high promise for settlers of the white race. In many ways it reminds one rather curiously of the great plains of the West, where they slope upward to the foot-hills of the Rockies. It is a white man's country. (38, 46)

Roosevelt went on to explain that he had encountered several Boers hunting and he then listed several of their names, which he characterized as honorable. He observed that there were probably those who had gone backward (though he hadn't met any on this journey) through experiencing "the stress of a hard and semi-savage life," just as in America there were "poor whites" and "mean whites" who were shiftless; but these were exceptions in both countries. Most important, "they fulfilled the three prime requisites for any race: they worked hard, they could fight hard at need, and they had plenty of children" (47–48).

Later in his life, Roosevelt admired the warrior figures of other cultures. He especially admired the Japanese, an admiration that transcended his racial views, although he was never able to shed the effects of his "racial education" (Dyer 6–7, 9).

Roosevelt also closely associated class with race. In fact, he defined *race* largely in terms of class. He saw the competition of race-like classes as a driving force of civilization, where several stages are present in an upward movement. Each stage fosters a distinctive social type or character in the course of history. Each type possesses distinctive social attributes, and these attributes suggest the type's identity as a class or cultural entity. Roosevelt believed that differences among these classes were contained in the "blood," or heredity, and were therefore genetically transmitted to future generations (Dyer 38).

When Roosevelt wrote about "Frontier Types" in *Ranch Life and the Hunting Trail,* he used the term *race* in a broad sense, although he did refer to nationality and ethnic background as well.

> The Old race of Rocky Mountain hunters and trappers, of reckless, dauntless Indian fighters, is now fast dying out. Yet here and there these restless wanderers of the untrodden wilderness still linger. . . . To this day many of them wear the fringed tunic or hunting-shirt, made of buckskin or homespun, and belted in at the waist—the most picturesque and distinctively national dress ever worn in America. It was the dress in which Daniel Boone was clad when he first passed through the trackless forests of the Alleghenies and penetrated the heart of Kentucky, . . . it was the dress worn by grim old Davy Crockett when he fell at the Alamo. The wild soldiery of the backwoods wore it when they marched to victory over Ferguson and Parkenham, at King's Mountain and New Orleans; when they conquered the French towns of the Illinois; and when they won at the cost of Red Eagle's warriors the bloody triumph of the horseshoe Bend. (qtd. in Dyer 81)

Roosevelt's tone is reverent and inspirational in this passage. It is a history lesson, history according to Roosevelt, initiated ostensibly by a discussion of the hunters' dress. "These old-time hunters have been the forerunners of the white advance throughout all our Western land," he continued (qtd. in Dyer 81). He moved from the old-time hunters to the trappers to the cowboys. An evolution then took place when the "best of the cowboys" succeeded and became the upper-class ranchers, who then evolved into political movers and shakers. Class evolution is simply a refinement of this process. Dyer describes Roosevelt's West as a "Darwinian arena" and likens races to different phases or principles of social organization that are vying for mastery. Indians are displaced by Mexicans and White hunters, who are themselves displaced by Texan cowboys. The most efficient Texans subordinate the cowboys, and the Texans are in turn outdone by eastern capitalists. Even these supplanters will be supplanted, much as Boone and Crockett were when yet another stage of progress was evolving. Roosevelt saw a lesson in his conception of progress as a historical fable. No one can stop the march of history or seek to do so because progress should not be stopped. He saw his own role as rancher and gentleman as akin to the vanished Indians of Cooper's romances (Dyer 39).

Thus, Dyer distinguishes between Roosevelt's conception of evolution and Darwinism, insisting that Roosevelt was not taken with the theory of Social Darwinism, or what he called the "tooth and claw" aspects of natural selection. Although it was a key element in popular Darwinism, Roosevelt did not find competition of the tooth-and-claw variety a satisfactory explanation of progress. He believed that a certain amount of stress and strain was needed but, if it became too severe, the race would be debilitated, not strengthened (32).

Roosevelt believed that evolution did not "necessarily ensure progress." Rather, he believed in a "general forward movement." He would not take for granted that everyone was bound to progress or that evolutionary advancement was "foreordained" (Dyer 33). According to Dyer, just as Roosevelt questioned the Darwinian notion of progress, he doubted other aspects of Darwin's theory. Roosevelt distinguished between Darwinism and evolution, and rightly observed that the two were often confused. He was skeptical of natural selection's application to society and the validity of the scientific concept itself (33).

Roosevelt saw parallels between human society and nature. In his lecture at Oxford in 1910, "Biological Analogies in History," he drew an analogy between conflict in nature and conflict between North American whites with European roots and South American indigenous peoples who had been isolated from European influence. Roosevelt stressed the weakness of these peoples and further reinforced the popular idea that northerners could not endure the unhealthy conditions of the tropics. Even more significantly, he used the organic analogy to illustrate his theory of the progress of civilization by what he considered the higher races (Dyer 35–36).

Roosevelt became obsessed with the idea that the decadence of the white race would contribute to its extinction. Since racial superiority could be developed, so could it be diminished. The love of luxury, loss of the fighting instinct, and refusal to "breed" warned of race suicide. Roosevelt saw examples of what he considered this tendency in the French and in the "old stock" New Englanders, whose birth rates were greatly reduced. The census of 1890 provided evidence of this decline, according to Roosevelt, and he preached that the future of the "American race" depended upon doing one's duty to "work, fight, and breed" (Dyer 151). In the domestic arena, the primary responsibility of women became to produce offspring. Birth control, working outside the home, refusal to marry, or having fewer than four children were acts tantamount to treason. The development of the new American "race" of hunter/warrior aristocrats would be threatened if women did not do their part.

Roosevelt on Gender Roles

Roosevelt's views on the role of women in society can be traced to his Harvard days. His concept of womanhood was a romantic middle- and upper-class view. He stressed that as keeper of the family and preserver of the race, women were invaluable and deserved recognition. His undergraduate thesis of 1880 on "Practicability of Equalizing Men and Women Before the Law" presaged his later concerns about feminism. As Dyer argues, Roosevelt believed that woman's role as childbearer was a great injustice because of her physical fragility. Man should be grateful to her for this function and out of this gratitude consider her an equal partner. According to Roosevelt, the "higher and nobler the race is, the more nearly the marriage relation becomes a partnership on equal terms. . . . [E]quality consisting not in performance of the same duties but in admirable performance of utterly different duties . . . in mutual forbearance and respect" (qtd. in Dyer 151). Mutual respect and dignity belong within the marriage relationship, but the responsibility for bearing and raising children is the woman's domain.

Issues such as marriage, birth control, and health were not matters of individual conscience and choice, but potential threats to the perpetuation of the "English-speaking race." Roosevelt saw the reluctance of the "best people" to breed as race suicide. The traits of the hunter/warrior were dissipated when the race became overly civilized. Thus it was important for society to engage in the "strenuous life" and reproduce.

Dyer characterizes Roosevelt's language in his speech and writing as "heavily sexual and stress[ing] potency, virility, need for healthy and vigorous sexual instinct. . . . [It was] plausible that an awareness of his own advancing age and debilitated condition may have led him to translate personal physical concerns into an obsession about the possible loss of national and racial potency" (167). Preservation of the family was a paramount concern, and Roosevelt wanted to bring the "whole question of marriage and divorce under federal authority to safeguard the nation's home life" (Dyer 154).

In his books, Roosevelt reflected on his experiences in the West and saw in his own life a connection to historical antecedents. He saw himself as representing his class and embodying its virtues. His personality was inextricably tied to his stance in public affairs; in particular, he saw his struggle with poor health early in life and his subsequent efforts to increase his vigor as a metaphor for the country's rise to power. His identification with the myth of the frontier further advanced this vision. His own ranching and hunting activities were a model for regenerating what he considered the loss of manliness and vigor of his class (Slotkin, *Gunfighter Nation* 37).

Obsessed with manliness, vigor, and fertility, Roosevelt identified with the Teutonic tribes of his ancestors, which predisposed such a "strain" as his own to succeed in the challenging landscape. Heredity and environment fostered development of this "race." Although today such notions of race suicide may seem absurd, Roosevelt was profoundly affected by the idea of racial self-destruction—and he was not alone in his obsession with race and its implications in the Progressive Era (Dyer 168).

The special role of women as "perpetuators of the race" (Dyer 150) places them in the untenable position of responsibility for the future of the "race" with no recourse but acquiescence. Roosevelt exhorted both men and women to marry early and raise large families. Hamlin Garland, an American author who wrote about the difficulties of life on the prairie, suggested that multiple childbearing could physically destroy women. Although Roosevelt gave lip service to not wanting "to see a woman worn down and perhaps killed by too much maternity," he remained fixed on the notion of a woman's role as analogous to that of a soldier's. "If the women flinch from breeding . . . the deserved death of the race takes place even quicker" (qtd. in Dyer 153). He saw a woman who flinched at childbearing much as he would a soldier who fled in the face of enemy fire: Both were contemptible.

In a sense, the woman had to be a passive hunter/warrior, facing the trials of physical danger without access to the weapons afforded a man. By extrapolation, the more children a woman had, the more worthy she was. The woman who could not have children was to be pitied; the woman who did not want to bear children was a "race criminal." Roosevelt said:

The man or woman who deliberately avoids marriage and has a heart so cold as
to know no passion and a brain so shallow and selfish as to dislike having children, is in effect a criminal against the race and should be an object of contemp-
tuous abhorrence by all healthy people. (qtd. in Dyer 152)

"Domestic control" became a loaded term with a double meaning.
The center of domestic power is the home and, by implication, is reflected in the nation. At the end of the nineteenth and beginning of the
twentieth centuries, the United States was an emerging world power.
Roosevelt's personality and philosophy were emblematic of the nation's
developing role in world affairs.

For Roosevelt, the home was the bedrock of national greatness. During his 1905 address to the National Congress of Mothers in Washington, he lectured on the duties of men and, especially, women. He revealed the intensity of his feelings about the role of women in the society.

[T]he nation is in a bad way if there is no real home, if the family is not of the right
kind; if the man is not a good husband and father, if he is brutal or cowardly or
selfish, if the woman has lost her sense of duty. . . . [T]he average woman is a
good wife, a good mother, able and willing to bear, and to bring up as they should
be brought up, healthy children, sound in body, mind, and character, and numerous enough so that the race shall increase and not decrease. (qtd. in DiNunzio
314)

Although Roosevelt believed that marriage could be a full partnership
between a man and a woman, he nonetheless believed that a woman's
primary duty was motherhood. Despite this position, his acknowledg-
ment that women could actually follow careers and hold positions traditionally held by men was relatively progressive for his day. In "The Para-
site Woman: The Only Indispensable Citizen," Roosevelt admitted a wide
range of careers that women might wish to pursue.

Some of the best farmers are women, just as some of the best exploring work and
scientific work has been done by women. There is a real need for a certain number of women doctors and women lawyers. Whether a writer or a painter or a
singer is a man or a woman makes not the slightest difference, provided that the
work he or she does is good. (qtd. in DiNunzio 324)

Roosevelt continued that not only does he admit all this, he "insists
upon it" as long as the "primary work" of the "average" or the "exceptional" man or woman is "home-making" and "home-keeping" (DiNunzio
324).

He elaborated on that "primary work" of men and women. The "average" man needs to earn a livelihood that will support a wife and family.

The basic jobs necessary for the advancement of a country and a society must be done well. The exceptional individual then has an arena in which to excel. If an individual wishes to devote himself to public service and does nonremunerative work, that person should be able to finance these activities. Roosevelt had the luxury of a family fortune to underwrite his own political career, for example. He fully realized that public service was exceptional. Roosevelt added:

> Now, this also applies to women. Exceptional women—like Julia Ward Howe or Harriet Beecher Stowe or Mrs. Homer—are admirable wives and mothers, admirable keepers of the home, and yet workers of genius outside the home. Such types, of course, are rare whether among men or women. (qtd. in DiNunzio 325)

That Roosevelt could stress the importance of woman's role in society and at the same time deny her the status of his ideal hunter/warrior is ironic. He likened her to a soldier who must suffer for her race, as he pointed out in his views on the rigors of childbirth, yet he assigned her additional restrictions when working outside what he considered her pro-scribed role.

Roosevelt addressed the responsibility of men in this scheme, but his implicit message was women may be afforded the opportunity to work outside the home, based upon a theoretical right to equality. Exercising this right was—with a few exceptions—impossible. The need for health and caretaking are present throughout Roosevelt's writing and speeches. The health of the individual, the family, and the nation are interrelated and dependent on the woman's energies. Physical health is connected to moral health; this is nowhere as evident as in Roosevelt's speeches and writing, which stress strength, vigor, aggressiveness. His obsession with the "breeding" of the "right type" of American "stock" is tied in with his attitudes toward women and their crucial roles as wives and mothers of the hunter/warrior figure.

Cowboys and Conservation

For Roosevelt, the hunting metaphor applied to domestic and foreign affairs. The hunter/warrior/cowboy became an emblem of expanding power and influence under Roosevelt's presidential administration. His idea of a new American "type" exuded individuality, masculinity, robust-ness, and bravado. And Roosevelt illustrated this type himself, most nota-bly as a Rough Rider. As president, Roosevelt did not have time to hunt as he did in his youth. But his time with the Rough Riders illustrates his consistent attachment to the hunter/warrior figure. When he temporarily took leave from politics to fight the "Spaniard," the hunter/warrior represented his personal ideal on an intellectual and mythic level. The bravado of the hunter/warrior/cowboy showed a "superior" American coercing the landscape of the American continent and, by extension, the world. He believed the American nation deserved a place in international affairs because it was destined to rule lesser peoples and nations. The American landscape had made the man; now, the man could remake the landscape.

Both Roosevelt and Cody were profoundly influenced by Frederick Jackson Turner's essay, "The Significance of the Frontier in American History." In their book, *The Frontier in American Culture,* Richard White and Patricia Nelson Limerick address the impact of Cody's Wild West and Frederick Jackson Turner's essay on the frontier in American history. In his introduction to the White and Limerick essays, James R. Grossman comments: "Cowboys, Indians, log cabins, wagon trains. These and other images associated with stories of the frontier maintain a constant presence in our lives." He added that the Colombian Exposition held in 1893 in Chicago was an important occasion that saw the figures of two men, historian Frederick Jackson Turner and Buffalo Bill Cody, present two opposing views of the American West and the frontier. There's no indication that they met, but their influence pervaded our culture thereafter (1).

Turner's story was "presented in the form of historical scholarship," and for all its later influence, attracted little attention at the Chicago exhibition. Its substance was a "sweeping explanation" of settlement of "free" land which "framed . . . the evolution of a uniquely democratic, individualistic, and progressive American character." Turner's version was appealing and spread "through . . . classroom, . . . journalism, and . . . popular histories" as a notion that the "West was something we settled, rather than conquered." Cody's story emphasized the violent nature of wrestling the land from the Indians, portraying vast scenes of conflict and slaughter. Both versions of the frontier have become part of American culture. There is "agreement on the fact of [its] significance but not of its content," making the story, or rather stories, of the frontier replete with implications (Grossman 1). Roosevelt's view of the frontier is more closely aligned with Cody's version, especially in terms of tribal displacement. While Turner marginalized Indians and stressed the settlement of "vacant land," the frontier of Cody and Roosevelt was a battlefield filled with warring tribes to be conquered. And the conquest ultimately was tied to hunting the buffalo.

The buffalo is emblematic of the Indian way of life. Buffalo provided food, clothing, and various other practical and symbolic necessities for Indian life on the Plains. The destruction of the buffalo signaled the transformation of the frontier into "civilized" space. The mixed emotions accompanying this transformation are reflected in Roosevelt's essay, "The Lordly Buffalo."

> Gone forever are the mighty herds of the lordly buffalo. A few solitary individuals and small bands are still to be found scattered here and there in the wilder parts of the plains; and, though most of these will be very soon destroyed, others will for some years fight off their doom and lead a precarious existence either in remote and almost desert portions of the country near the Mexican frontier, or else in the wildest and most inaccessible fastnesses of the Rocky Mountains; but the great herds, that for the first three-quarters of this century formed the distinguishing and characteristic feature of the Western plains, have vanished forever. (*Theodore Roosevelt: An American Mind* 242)

Roosevelt's admiration for the animal is obvious, but equally apparent and more important for gauging the temper of the time is his tone of resolution and certainty of the buffalo's demise. Later in the same essay, the extermination of the buffalo is justified as prerequisite for national development. "From the standpoint of humanity at large, the extermination of the buffalo has been a blessing" (245).

Today, we might well ask, a blessing for whom? Certainly not the Indians. The desire to preserve the buffalo was characterized as selfish. Roosevelt applied the epithet to himself, as if he needed to purge such sentimentality and stress the more noble motives of development and progress. His practical tone when advocating extermination of the buffalo to displace the Indians emphasizes the foregone conclusion that the Indians must be displaced. There is some regret about the buffalo, but none for the Native Americans.

Roosevelt described his buffalo hunt with excitement. He emphasized that the wilderness and its species must be conserved mainly to preserve the hunting lands. These hunting lands are for the sportsman, not the sustenance of the Indian. The relationship between hunter and land changed in the process and benefited the aristocratic hunter/sportsman over the native inhabitant's need for food and clothing. The formation of hunting and sporting clubs gave the hunter/sportsman places to pursue game. These clubs also bridged the American landscape and the European aristocratic tradition. For example, the Boone and Crockett Club represented several things simultaneously. Roosevelt and his fellow club members revered Boone and Crockett, much as the gentlemen of Victorian England practiced medieval chivalry. However, their choice of heroes and the ways in which they reinforced their connections to such frontier figures reflected their needs as Americans. Although they could be viewed as new aristocrats, Roosevelt and company identified with plebeian ancestors, the effect of which was to legitimize a connection between their level of wealth, education, and power and the origins of American democracy, where such distinctions were unknown (Slotkin, *Gunfighter Nation* 37–38). The hunter figure evolved from provider to sportsman, integrating the plebeian frontiersman/warrior with the privileged and powerful ruling class.

Roosevelt did not simply found the Boone and Crockett Club; he also created its myths of origin in his own writings. Especially in *Hunting Trips of a Ranchman* (1885) and *Ranch Life and the Hunting Trail* (1888), he linked his rediscovery of the frontier and his reaction to it with a recapitulation of American history and the stages of world civilization. Here again, he emphasized the superiority of the Anglo-Saxon race and its association with progress. He argued that his personal development was illustrative of larger historical processes (Slotkin, *Gunfighter Nation* 38).

Roosevelt avidly enjoyed and pursued hunting as a physical activity. Hunting also served as a paradigm for his beliefs about race, politics, and power. Under Roosevelt's presidential administration, conservation became a domestic blessing, while serving as a boon to the American upper class.

Roosevelt distinguished his hunting by class; he did not hunt for food or profit as the "game butchers" did. Like Cooper's character Hawkeye, he believed he was at odds with the sordid aspects of trade, and he killed only out of self-defense or in the ritual test of his manhood. This attitude emphasizes hunting as an activity of the aristocrat or sportsman. According to Roosevelt's definition of *game-butcher,* Boone or Crockett would be such plebeian hunters. However, Roosevelt saw them only in the role of ancestors for his own persona as hero of a new aristocracy; he, of course, was the prime representative of such a hunter-aristocrat. Roosevelt saw history as a series of hunts in which hunter-heroes and political leaders lead the country from British colony to independent world power. He put forth this view in his last book, *The Wilderness Hunter* (1893). He treated Boone, Crockett, Houston, Cody, Custer, and General Philip H. Sheridan as archetypes in a succession of stages of exploratory, military, and political development. As hunter-presidents, George Washington, Andrew Jackson, and Abraham Lincoln symbolized the political stages of development. Furthermore, Roosevelt made it clear through descriptions of his own adventures that he belonged with these figures in their arenas (Slotkin, *Gunfighter Nation* 41–42).

Roosevelt and Cody were American hunters who embodied American exceptionality. Like the frontier, they represent a flexible construct that accommodates individual needs while remaining capable of expansion, even to a mythic level. Especially in his writing, Roosevelt linked himself to the forces of history and nature at work in the frontier. *The Winning of the West* is a systematic study of his "myth of origins" to justify the predominance of the new elite. As in Francis Parkman's histories, Roosevelt's work focuses on the Indian wars as the crucial issue in American history (Slotkin, *Gunfighter Nation* 42).

In *The Winning of the West,* the word *West* denoted the American frontier, but *West* is a relative term, depending upon the stage of development of the nation at any given time. Within the lifetimes and spheres of influence of Roosevelt and Cody, the end of the West was the end of an era and the end of expansion across the continent.

Buffalo Bill and the Wild West

William "Buffalo Bill" Cody was primarily responsible for creating the image of the American hunter/cowboy. His Wild West exhibition disseminated images of the cowboy and the American West throughout the world. Many versions of the cowboy appeared, but the sustained presence of Buffalo Bill—especially in his three decades as Wild West showman—overshadowed other figures.

William Frederick Cody was born February 26, 1846, in Scott County, Iowa. He died on January 10, 1917, in Denver, Colorado. The family had moved to Kansas in 1854, where the young Cody attended several sessions of the country schools his father had organized. His father, Isaac Cody, died in 1857, when William was eleven years old. Sometime afterward, William Cody went to work as a mounted messenger for a wagon-freight firm. This firm, later known as Russell, Majors, and Waddell, backed the Pony Express. By his late teens, Cody had become a talented hunter, horse wrangler, and Indian fighter.

He served in the Civil War in the 7th Kansas Cavalry and, after the war, worked for the U.S. Army as a civilian scout and dispatch bearer out of Fort Ellsworth in Kansas. Cody acquired his nickname, *Buffalo Bill,* during 1867–68 when he hunted buffalo to feed the workers constructing the Kansas Pacific Railroad. He carried dispatches through hostile Indian territory for General Sheridan. Afterward, he became chief of scouts for the 5th U.S. Cavalry, where he served for more than four years. During his career as a scout, Cody engaged in sixteen Indian fights. In 1872, he was awarded the Medal of Honor, but it was revoked in 1916 on the grounds that scouts were technically civilians. In 1989, the medal was posthumously restored by the U.S. Army.

In 1869, Ned Buntline, the pen name for E.Z.C. Judson, wrote the dime novel that launched Cody's career as folk hero. The novel was later dramatized, and Buntline convinced Cody to star in the production. Cody left Buntline after a year, but continued to act for eleven seasons. This acting experience led to his final career as a showman. In 1883, Cody organized his Wild West exhibition. Over the years, it included riding; roping; sharpshooting; reenactments of a buffalo hunt, the capture of the Deadwood stagecoach, and a Pony Express ride; and other action-packed entertainment. The "cowboy fun" portion of the show was the basis for the rodeo. The "Rough Riders of the World" were horsemen from other countries who displayed their riding skills in national costume. The show also reflected domestic and world events. The charge up San Juan Hill was reenacted, as was Custer's Last Stand. Cody took the Wild West show to London in 1887 for Queen Victoria's Jubilee celebration; the queen saw the four-hour spectacle three times. It became an international success. Stars of the show included Annie Oakley, Buck Taylor, Johnny Baker, and Sitting Bull. The show's greatest success in the United States was in 1893 at the Chicago World's Fair.

Buffalo Bill's Image
Before Buffalo Bill's Wild West, Cody led a truly adventurous life. In explaining Cody's tremendous appeal, it becomes important to look at the accounts of his life. Like Daniel Boone, the stories about Cody range from the factual to pure fancy. Also like Boone, Cody's image is flexible and encompasses contradictory elements. For example, his relationship with the Indians was adversarial in his scouting days, yet benevolent in his showman days. Although some of the most popular attractions of his show were reenactments of battles between Indians and settlers or soldiers, Cody also featured Indian ceremonies and vignettes from daily life.

The best source of details about Cody's early life is his autobiography, published in 1879 when he was just thirty-four years old. The credibility of this volume has been challenged for many reasons, among them its true authorship. Another problem concerns several inaccuracies, including Cody's citing the wrong year for his own birth (Russell, in Cody xi). In a foreword to the reissued edition (1978), Don Russell argues for both its accuracy and Cody's authorship.

> Strange as it may seem to the skeptical, internal evidence suggests . . . [Cody's] *Autobiography,* was actually written by William F. Cody. Who but Cody would have mentioned his brief and unrecorded involvement with Chandler's jayhawkers and horse thieves? Who but Cody would have admitted that he volunteered for Civil War service while so drunk that he didn't know what he was doing? What ghostwriter would have omitted so many of Cody's real claims to distinction while including less credible episodes? (Russell, in Cody vii)

It has been established that, contrary to popular belief, Cody was not illiterate. Although his skills were by no means polished, he could tell a story and write it well enough for a copy editor to prepare it for publication (Russell, in Cody viii). There were more elaborate editions of the autobiography, but the first edition is as close to the truth as one is likely to get. As for criticism that the prose style varies in different parts of the book, this is easily resolved. Many stories about Cody's adventures had already been published, and Cody simply incorporated them as written rather than correcting them (Russell, in Cody xviii). Passages where the tone becomes melodramatic usually are the work of others. Another problem is Cody's imperfect memory of dates, such as the confusion surrounding the story of Cody killing his first Indian. If the date could be determined, a newspaper account of it might be located (Russell, in Cody xv).

Again, what is important here is the flexibility of Cody's image. What he wrote and what was written about him testifies to the power of this image. And the source of this power is his role as hunter. Cody's accuracy about his life and exploits points to some revealing characteristics. Cody recounted numerous exploits in his capacity as Indian fighter or hunter that may seem exaggerated but, in most cases, records bear out their truth. According to Russell:

> Cody is credited with fourteen expeditions against Indians and fifteen Indian fights. That might not seem many to those exposed to the ideas of Indian fighting sponsored by movies and television, but a computer applied to the Indian wars shows that the average soldier of the period could expect one fight for each five-year enlistment. Buffalo Bill did not exaggerate in telling of his services as scout; on the contrary, he leaves out much that is to his credit. (in Cody xvi)

Cody was not unduly modest, but he was probably too busy living his life to bother about all the details. In his storytelling, he might have made mistakes. If these erroneous details turned out to be more interesting than the true ones, he was apt to leave them in for entertainment value.

Becoming Buffalo Bill

However, external evidence points to the veracity of Cody's autobiography. For example, Cody's career as army scout may seem sensationalized, but monthly records were kept by the quartermaster and the scouts were named in these reports. Scouts were civilians hired by the Army; their knowledge of the terrain, trails, and Indians was invaluable. Cody was employed from September 1868 through November 1872 in such a capacity (Russell, in Cody xv–xvi).

Another point of contention in the Buffalo Bill legend stems from his name. According to Russell, "It might be pointed out that all the buffalo he killed were eaten; he had no part in the hide hunting that threatened the animal with extinction" (in Cody xvii). However, the pattern of excess is more damning in itself than the explanation of actual events is vindicating. James B. Trefethen describes the buffalo hunting in clearly accusatory terms for all involved:

> The most common method of procuring buffalo was to intercept an approaching herd from a strategic position and kill all animals that came within range of their powerful single-shot Sharps, Remington, or Springfield rifles. . . .
>
> Other hunters preferred the more strenuous and exciting method of coursing, in which the animals were killed at close range with pistols or carbines. This was the favorite technique of the most famous of the buffalo killers, William F. "Buffalo Bill" Cody.
>
> Cody obtained a contract in 1867 to supply the Kansas Pacific Railway with fresh meat. In the next eighteen months, by his own account, he killed 4,280 buffalo. Competing on a wager with another hunter, he slaughtered sixty-nine in a single day; his adversary managed a score of only forty-six. (14)

The facts of the slaughter are undeniably brutal, underscored by the emotionally charged language. That Cody is referred to as the "most famous of all the buffalo killers"—"killer," not "hunter"—and he "slaughtered"—not "shot"—expresses Trefethen's view very clearly.

Cody related the same information himself, but his narrative conveyed excitement, not bloodthirstiness. The actions are appalling, especially to late twentieth-century sensibilities. But the perspective for viewing Cody should be adjusted to accommodate his position as a man of his time. His autobiography recounted the same information, but in a considerably different tone.

> It was about this time that the end of the Kansas Pacific track was in the heart of buffalo country, . . . As the Indians were very troublesome, it was difficult to obtain fresh meat for the workmen, and the company therefore concluded to engage the services of hunters to kill buffaloes. . . . It was at this time that the very appropriate name of "Buffalo Bill," was conferred upon me by the road-hands. It has stuck to me ever since, and I have never been ashamed of it.
>
> During my engagement as hunter for the company—a period of less than eighteen months—I killed 4,280 buffaloes; and I had many exciting adventures with the Indians, as well as hair-breadth escapes, some of which are well worth relating. (161–162)

Cody's power as a hunter ensured that the workers building the railroad would be fed. Therefore, the railroad would be built; the country would grow; and so Cody would build the United States. Cody's occupation was hunter, and his job was dangerous. He had to hunt with one eye always watching for Indian attacks. This meant that volume was important when shooting buffalo. He had to kill quickly and get the game back to camp to feed the waiting hungry workers.

Even when Cody recounted the contest between himself and Billy Comstock, during which they killed sixty-nine and forty-six buffalo in one day, respectively, the emphasis was not on the slaughter but on the ceremonies accompanying the event. The details of the scene are important because they provide the context within which Cody acted. Many borders are apparent: the borders between the vast plains and civilized space, and the borders between the people and animals that inhabit them. Cody's skill allowed him to cross these borders.

> I had my celebrated buffalo hunt with Billy Comstock, a noted scout, guide, and interpreter, who was then chief of scouts at Fort Wallace, Kansas. Comstock had the reputation, for a long time, of being a most successful buffalo hunter, and the officers in particular, who had seen him kill buffaloes, were desirous of backing him in a match against me. . . . We were to hunt one day of eight hours, beginning at eight o'clock in the morning, and closing at four o'clock in the afternoon. The wager was five hundred dollars a side, and the man who should kill the greater number of buffaloes from on horseback was to be declared the winner. (171)

This was no random killing spree, but a command performance—commanded, that is, by other influential people. It is as if the event had been organized and Cody was drafted to perform; he complied, it seems, almost out of politeness. Details of the circumstances leading to the contest are elaborate. Public interest in the event and participation by a large number of people forced Cody to comply. He agreed to do the thing he always does—hunt—but with more restrictions, for the edification of his audience. For once, the spectators who watched the contest crossed the border that the hunter crosses, from the civilized world to the edge of the frontier. This performance illustrated the hunter's importance in providing enormous quantities of food. Cody, as the best of the hunters, embodied the most powerful symbol of control over the landscape and, therefore, the nation.

The hunt included referees and three different chases; the description could just as well be one of a fox hunt or a football game. Cody did not gloss over the graphic details. If anything, he was scrupulously objective.

> At last the time came to begin the match. Comstock and I dashed into a herd, followed by the referees. The buffaloes separated; Comstock took the left bunch and I the right. My great forte in killing buffaloes from horseback was to get them circling by riding my horse at the head of the herd, shooting the leaders, thus crowding their followers to the left, till they would finally circle round and round.
>
> On this morning the buffaloes were very accommodating, and I soon had them running in a beautiful circle, when I dropped them thick and fast, until I had killed thirty-eight; which finished my run.
>
> Comstock began shooting at the right of the herd, which he was chasing, and they kept straight on. He succeeded, however, in killing twenty-three, but they were scattered over a distance of three miles, while mine lay close together. I had "nursed" my buffaloes, as a billiard-player does the balls when he makes a big run. (172–173)

Cody had studied the behavior of the buffalo and used this knowledge to predict how they would act. He then dispatched them efficiently. He wrote of how "accommodating" they are. Of course, he deployed a strategy he had used before. He was the consummate professional.

Cody described each of the three runs of the contest. Between the forays, the spectators provided champagne; by the third run, when it was clear he would win, he proposed riding bareback for the final sortie to entertain the crowd. He finished spectacularly by driving the last buffalo near the crowd and, as the women screamed, he dropped his sixty-ninth animal (173–174). Cody's account of the contest emphasizes specific hunting tactics, the detailed action in each run, and self-deprecating humor suggesting his bravado in bareback riding may have had something to do with the champagne.

Cody's buffalo hunting exploits can be portrayed as exciting adventure or senseless slaughter. He represents power over life and death on many levels. The chord that he strikes has to do with an image of authority. As hunter, he killed to provide food that would sustain life. He was a scout who knew the Indians and their habits, and could negotiate space where others were lost. He survived and ensured the survival of others.

Cody's exploits as hunter and Indian fighter raise questions about his actual relationship with the Indians. In his essay, "The Indians," Vine Deloria identifies three different stages of Cody's career. Cody was a scout and hunting guide first, then a showman, and finally a legend: "he might not have approved had he been able to choose how he would be remembered" (47). Cody's early experiences were similar to those of other young men who grew up on the frontier and learned to survive. Cody was a successful Pony Express rider who covered dangerous routes that were outside U.S. territory. The Indians mainly targeted telegraph poles and railroad tracks, but they often attacked and killed Pony Express riders. However, the riders were not subject to a concerted effort by the Indians to destroy them. A surprising lack of personal animosity existed between rider and Indian; possibly these young men showed the courage and determination prized by the Indian warriors (47–48).

Cody also was a civilian scout for the army. Apparently, he displayed none of the racism and arrogance of many regular army officers. Although he did not deny his role as Indian fighter, he would not say how many Indians he had killed. He further insisted that he never killed an Indian who was not trying to kill him (Deloria 56). He never participated in treaty negotiations between the government and the Indians.

Cody understood government policy regarding the Indians, and his absence at any of the treaty negotiations indicated his reluctance to align himself with the forces that ultimately sought to displace the Indians. He had ample opportunity to be instrumental in such affairs, and it is to his credit that he never put himself into a position where he had to lie to the Indians (Deloria 51).

Becoming a Legend

As a hunter, Cody respected the Indians' skills as hunters. Later, in his Wild West exhibition, Cody attempted to portray various scenes from Indian life. He respected the Native Americans' way of life—their relationship with the land and the animals that inhabited it. Inherently, he believed it was important to educate the public and preserve such pieces of the vanishing frontier. These "scenes" were more accurate portrayals of the reality than the wildly sensationalized battles and reenactments of daring exploits. They included firebuilding and other domestic crafts of the tribes.

As a legend, Cody is difficult to analyze. The literary Buffalo Bill was someone penned by Easterners, most of whom had never visited the West and who constructed fantasies and stereotypes that no true Westerner would have believed, let alone created. Cody's inability to uproot this image was due to its powerful grasp on the public imagination. "Frightened at the changes that large industry was making in their lives, Americans sought in Buffalo Bill . . . assurance that frontier virtues were capable of transcending the determinism of historical and natural processes" (Deloria 55).

It is difficult to evaluate Cody and his relationship with the Indians because of the influence of the dime novels and movies that have so pervaded his image. However, what does comes through clearly is that Cody was a man of his times. He knew what stirred the public and was able to translate his ideas into actions. He had adventures that others only read about, so he could speak with authority about them. He was a hero in tangible form, much like Daniel Boone. The later denunciations of Cody are another testament to the strong feelings he aroused.

Howard R. Lamar claims that it has become the fashion to deride Cody as a talented showman who exploited his featured players (57). However, this view does not do justice to Cody's career as hunter, scout, and guide. It also does not show an appreciation for Cody's ability to read popular American culture. The cowboy's evolution paralleled that of the nation. The hunter who became the mounted frontiersman or ranger is the basis for the cowboy figure. The cowboy's image is multifaceted as well. Lamar identifies three types of cowboy: the historical, the fictional, and the folklore cowboy. The historical cowboy, the one based on the ranger, emerged after the Civil War. Along with the range of cowboy types who emerged were cowboys from various ethnic groups. Black Americans, many of whom were ex-slaves, comprised one-seventh of the cowboy population (58).

The cowboys in Cody's Wild West crossed the borders of race and nationality. Bill Pickett, a black rodeo star, was known for biting a steer's lips to immobilize him. Also in the show were Mexican horsemen, Argentine gauchos, and Russian cossacks. The significance of the Wild West cowboy was that anyone could identify with his image. In 1887, when Cody took his show and his cowboys to London, this figure became an international symbol of America (Lamar 61).

To be a cowboy required skills celebrated in the rodeo and later in Cody's Wild West exhibition. Although plebeian in origin, the cowboy evolved into a figure elevated by association and metaphor. Dime novels and stage shows used a figurative language that illustrates how the cowboy figure became American royalty.

Ned Buntline wrote "an exaggerated story, entitled *Buffalo Bill, the King of Bordermen,* that appeared in New York in December 1869" (Lamar 59). The title "King" at once places special emphasis on Cody's talents and worth. Juxtaposing the plebeian cowboy/borderman image with royalty is a seeming oxymoron, but the special context of the American western landscape makes possible the amalgamation of two opposing terms. The word "borderman" itself is synonymous with the idea of the cowboy who may have literally crossed borders between state and territory in his job herding cattle or in moving from ranch to ranch for work. The literal borders crossed by the borderman are only part of his significance, however, since other more figurative and symbolic borders of the American experience are also represented in this figure. The borderman may have been racially mixed, thus crossing a normally impenetrable social border.

The border between fantasy and reality, between real life and show business is emblematic of Cody's life and career. Cody's eleven successful years acting in melodramas, starting in 1872, gave him the wherewithal to purchase his own ranch at North Platte, Nebraska. For the first time, the king of the cowboys lived on a ranch. The technical definition of *cowboy*—a hired hand employed to wrangle cattle—is less important than the concept of *cowboy,* which embraces many images.

In fact, the plurality of definitions is essential when dealing with the powerful forces that shaped the contemporary popular imagination. For example, Annie Oakley, who joined the Wild West show in 1884, was automatically considered a Westerner even though she was from Ohio because of her impressive skills as a horseback rider and sharpshooter (Lamar 60). "Little Miss Sure Shot" provided meat for the family stewpot since she was a youngster. That she was from Ohio was less important than her shooting skills and her association with the American West.

The confusion between the reality and the myth of the West came to a head in the persona of Cody. The Wild West exhibition echoed real life, and real life was then influenced by the "show" of the West. One example provided by Leslie A Fiedler is the case of Sitting Bull's horse. Sitting Bull was part of the show for only one season. However, Cody gave him a Stetson and a dancing horse that Sitting Bull was fond of. In a "tragicomedy of errors," Sitting Bull was shot by one of his tribesmen who was trying to prevent his arrest. When the horse heard the shot, he took it "for his customary cue, [and] went into his customary dance. And who was to say that he was wrong, that what happened was not, in some sense, a part of Buffalo Bill's ongoing mythological show" (87–88).

The overlapping of show and reality illustrates a crossing of borders. The borders delineate worlds simultaneously joined and divided by common circumstances, events, and people. Cody and Roosevelt traversed many borders as hunter/cowboys. According to Lamar, it "is not too farfetched to say that just as Cody used the cowboy to rescue the beleaguered stagecoach, Roosevelt used him to rescue Cuba from supposed Spanish tyranny" (65). Interestingly, Cody readily incorporated Roosevelt's Rough Riders into an episode in his show, and even went so far as to hire veterans from Roosevelt's troop. The connection between show and reality is underscored here: The hunter/cowboy who dominated the landscape embodied the country's emerging military dominance.

The Meaning of Buffalo Bill

In *West of Everything* (1992), Jane Tompkins recounts her experience visiting the Buffalo Bill Museum:

> The video at the entrance to the Buffalo Bill Historical Center says that Buffalo Bill was the most famous American of his time, that by 1900 more than a billion words had been written about him, and that he had a progressive vision of the West. . . . Strangely enough, it was as a progressive civic leader that Bill Cody wanted to be remembered. . . . "The best of civilization." This was the phrase that rang in my head as I moved through the museum, which is one of the most disturbing places I have ever visited. It is also a wonderful place. . . . Among other things, the museum is admirable for its effort to combat prevailing stereotypes about the "winning of the West," a phrase it self-consciously places in quotation marks. There are placards declaring that all history is a matter of interpretation, and that the American West is a source of myth. (179–180)

Tompkins' account capsulizes how portrayals in westerns have shaped American attitudes toward "death, women, the use of language, the landscape, cattle and horses" (Hallgarth 17). The western genre, whether rendered in print or film, derives many elements directly from Cody and his Wild West show. Cody himself is an icon of the West. And the basis of his image is that of hunter; after all, hunting buffalo is how he got his name.

Tompkins stresses the integral relationship between the buffalo as prey and the hunter. Cody is renowned for shooting the buffalo, but once the species was in danger of extinction, he used them in large numbers in his Wild West show, thereby preserving them. Forty million buffalo roamed the North American continent in the 1600s, but their number had diminished to one wild herd in northern Alberta by 1900. That Cody, the greatest buffalo slayer, was among the foremost in their conservation is just one of the anomalies that characterized late nineteenth-century America (186–187).

Cody was very much a man of this period. Movement westward represented the growing power of the nation, and development changed the landscape in the name of "progress." And Cody was largely responsible for changing the West that he loved. His roles as hunter, guide, scout, and Indian fighter were instrumental in bringing about such change. Once he and others had "succeeded" in slaughtering the buffalo herds and displacing the Indians, the West became a romantic remnant of itself. But, like Roosevelt, Cody did not question the necessity of this transformation. What mattered to Cody was capturing the experience of the West, its essence, and presenting it to the public. Even though the Wild West was a sensationalized representation of Cody's experience, it deeply touched audiences over its thirty-year run, leaving a legacy of images of the West that linger today. If in fact Cody preserved buffalo by using them in his show after he and his imitators nearly brought about their extinction, it is perfectly logical to believe that hunters did the most for conservation. Whether hunting for sustenance or sport, the hunters' need to conserve game is crucial. Once the railroads were built, the buffalo diminished, and the Indians displaced, the hunter evolved into the sportsman. The sportsman is the aristocrat of hunters, a status mirrored in Europe. Once land is limited, game is limited. Once game is limited, only the privileged pursue it.

The men who worked hardest to conserve the America wilderness were the big-game hunters. Roosevelt, Lodge, George Bird Grinnell, and Owen Wister founded the Boone and Crockett Club, which was a preeminent player in the conservation movement. It could be argued that such sportsmen were only preserving their own future hunting pleasure, but such a view seems overly cynical. The hunter and the animal he hunts have a relationship, and any true hunter loves and admires the animals he pursues, as well as the setting—the environment—in which he hunts. According to Tompkins, "the desire to kill animals was in some way related to a desire to see them live. It is not an accident . . . that Roosevelt, Wister, and Remington all went west originally for their health. Their devotion to the West, their connection to it, their love for it are rooted in their need to reanimate their own lives. The preservation of nature, in other words, becomes for them symbolic of their own survival" (187).

To love the animal you kill is not a strange idea for a hunter; it is inherent in the experience. This was true for the Native American hunter, and it was equally true for Cody. However, the Indian saw man as part of nature and, as part of nature, the hunting and killing of game was a sacred and necessary ritual. The hunter had a respect for the prey, and was grateful when the prey was sacrificed to ensure the life of the hunter and his tribe. The hunter was responsible for maintaining a balance between his own needs and the lives of his prey. This relationship was violated by the market hunters who killed indiscriminately to supply food for large numbers of railroad workers. Ironically, Cody's career links him to both the Native American tradition and the market hunters.

Trophy collecting also demonstrates the relationship between hunter and prey, as well as preserving the animal in other ways. Tompkins observes that we are not really different from Roosevelt, Remington, or Cody. Like the hunter who absorbs the life of his prey and enriches his own, and in the taking of another life realizes the bond of mortality all creatures share, the visitor in a museum connects himself with the past and gains perspective on his role in the scheme of things by appreciating the artifacts—only he does so through a safer form of the same enterprise (188–189).

Here, the relationship between the visitor and the museum parallels the relationship between the hunter and his prey. Cody and Roosevelt both "absorbed" the lives of their prey in a sense because their personae were inextricably linked to their prowess as hunters, best illustrated by their nicknames. Cody is "Buffalo Bill," and the "Teddy" bear is named for Roosevelt. That hunters reaffirm their lives by absorbing others' (in one form or another) was and is a belief in many cultures. The point can be expanded: Aren't we all partly a result of what we "take in"? What we see, what we do, and what we think about?

Tompkins cites some of the phrases used to describe Cody. She starts with those describing his physical looks and skill, his handsomeness, grace, demeanor. She describes his generosity, his flamboyance, his bravery. She mentions his negative traits, but not pejoratively: "He liked people, drank a lot, gave big parties, gave lots of presents, and is reputed to have been a womanizer" (196). She discusses his hair and his uncanny resemblance to General Custer, a likeness Cody fostered and capitalized upon. Finally, she tries to pin down the quality that connected him to others.

Tompkins searches for an explanation of Cody's seemingly timeless appeal. She finds it in a poster for one of his shows during his travels in France. In the foreground is an immense buffalo at full gallop across vast plains. The prominent hump of the animal immediately draws the viewer's attention not only because of its enormity, but also because it features a cutout framing a likeness of Cody—mustache, famous white hat, and all—above the words "Je viens" (I come) (197).

"Je viens," Tompkins notes, are the words of a savior. Cody becomes associated with a religious figure within the Christian tradition—the savior who will be able to help us and do something for us that we cannot do for ourselves. This, she suggests, stems from childish desires for "glamour, fame, bigness, adventure, romance" (198).

More than this, Cody appeals to the child in us, the part of us that we would like to experience again without the strictures of the adult world that were imposed upon us in our "real" childhood—fun without boundaries, discipline, or limits. The "childlike" American cowboy/hunter has both positive and negative connotations. The cowboy/hunter is appropriate as the young country's emblem. This figure suggests strength, daring, adventure. The same figure also symbolizes wildness, bravado, and danger. Fascination with the West was stirred by Cody's Wild West tours in America and abroad. Cody crossed and recrossed the borders of reality within the context of his show. He was a symbol himself of the multivalent entity that was the American West.

Notes

1   Buffalo Bill's Wild West was called an "exhibition" rather than a "show" by those associated with it. The Wild West ran from 1883 to 1916, touring both the United States and Europe. It was a financial success. Although Cody stressed the educational character of the endeavor by re-creating the frontier in scenes, showmanship was evident in all aspects of the production. Cody exploited the commercial aspects of his enterprise by adapting portions of his performance to current affairs, yet he sought to educate the public about places and people from the Old West—especially Indians—that could be visited only through his presentations.

2   See Frederick Jackson Turner, *The Frontier in American History* (New York: Holt, Rinehart and Winston, 1962). Turner introduced the concept of the "closing of the frontier," which gained popularity as westward expansion brought about the near-extinction of the buffalo herds, the concomitant decline of the Indians as they were displaced from their lands, and the settlement by white pioneers when railroads linked East and West within a thirty-year period.

3   The relationship between Roosevelt's racial beliefs and his public and private life will be examined in the following section, "Roosevelt on Race."

4   For a discussion of Roosevelt's theories of race, see Thomas G. Dyer, *Theodore Roosevelt and the Idea of Race* (Baton Rouge, LA: Louisiana State University Press, 1980), 21–44 (especially 29–30).

5   For a discussion of Jean Lamarck and Lamarckianism, see Dyer, 6–7, 37–44.

Chapter 4

Ike McCaslin and Ernest Hemingway: Nostalgia and Degeneration

It was . . . the men, not white nor black nor red, but men, hunters with the will and hardihood to endure and the humility and skill to survive, . . . only hunters [who] drank, drinking not of the blood they had spilled but some condensation of the wild immortal spirit, drinking it moderately, humbly even, not with the pagan's base hope of acquiring the virtues and cunning and strength and speed, but in salute to them. (Faulkner, "The Bear," qtd. in Utley, Bloom, and Kinney 162–163)

. . .

I was beginning to feel strong again . . . and it was a pleasure to walk in the easy rolling country, . . . to hunt, not knowing what we might see and free to shoot the meat we needed. . . . I loved the country so that I was happy as you are after you have been with a woman that you really love. . . . Now, being in Africa, I was hungry for more of it. (Hemingway, *Green Hills of Africa* 51, 72–73)

After World War I, figures of the hunter and the hunt represent attempts to recapture a simpler, more pristine world. Hunter figures like William Faulkner's Ike McCaslin in "The Bear" and Ernest Hemingway in his life and his fiction seek personal definition and a system of values that can only be found away from the modern world. The wild worlds of the woods and the jungle are sites where moments of clarity and self-realization take place. Between World War I and World War II, the hunter as deployed by both Faulkner and Hemingway is a nostalgic figure who bridges the gap between the troubled present and an idealized past.

Faulkner's Ike McCaslin suggests the possibility of reconciling the wrongs of the past through immersion in nature and participation in the hunting ritual. He relies on Sam Fathers, who acts as Ike's spiritual father, to advise him in the ways of the wilderness. Part Native American and part black, Fathers amalgamates the marginalized elements of American culture in his character. He is a dignified and uncorrupted man who steers Ike toward self-knowledge.

Miscegenation and incest permeate Faulkner's work through several generations, as if these issues were not the idiosyncrasies of a particular family, but rather an integral aspect of American history. In such an atmosphere, establishing identity becomes crucial. Faulkner's world is marked by a sense of overwhelming doubt because the conventional paths to self-knowledge, even such simple information as family history, have been obscured. Ike does not know that his family, too, is racially mixed. The key to identity shifts from one's relationship to others to one's sense of self. The test for Ike, which takes place in pristine nature, and which yields genuine self-knowledge, is the hunt.

Ike's test takes several years. The truth of the hunt is perhaps the closest thing to an antidote for the corruption with which Ike lives. The hunting trips into the woods as a boy, then an adolescent, and, finally, a young man, is a journey into the simpler world of the American past. Irving Howe has commented that:

> "The Bear" [is] both a beautiful account of a hunt and a symbolic fable concerning . . . moral growth . . . It turns to a vision of American life not yet soiled . . ., nor tainted . . . [I]t records the secret voice of a society yearning for its innocent past and regretting its very existence. (1017)

Isaac McCaslin is an ideal figure who offsets the web of corruption and dissolution so prevalent in Faulkner's work. He suggests the possibility of negotiating worlds that hold both promise and peril.

In the life and work of Ernest Hemingway, a similar motif is apparent. Hemingway's self-representation as a hunter, as well as his fictional portrayal of hunters and sportsmen, including Nick Adams in "Big Two-Hearted River," are set against a larger world whose values are corrupt and unreliable. Like "The Bear," *Green Hills of Africa* effects moral judgments through its descriptions of hunting. "The Short Happy Life of Francis Macomber" and "The Snows of Kilimanjaro" rework Hemingway's African experience to interrogate questions of identity.

Hemingway was concerned with a "code" for living in a world wounded by "the war to end all wars." Mark Schorer comments that Hemingway used the imagery of "wounding" to describe the effects of the war (951), much as Faulkner drew on the Civil War and World War I to provide a syntax for his work (Howe 1009–1024). Hunting bridged the grim reality of both authors' personal worlds and a nostalgic ideal world. Hunting was more than an enjoyable activity; it was a ceremony of purification. Howe points out that American literature emphasizes the recurrent theme of the pastoral retreat to Eden and the wilderness as a regenerating force. He points to the Leatherstocking Tales of Cooper and the Hemingway stories (1024).

"The Bear," *Green Hills of Africa,* Hemingway's short stories, and *The Old Man and the Sea* use the hunt as a test of the individual's worth. Modern society suffers by comparison with the wilderness, and the hunter figure who crosses the border between the two rarely finds peace.

Faulkner and "The Bear"

The search for identity underscores Ike's hunt, and Faulkner uses nature as the setting for this search. In *William Faulkner and Southern History,* Joel Williamson examines the family history of the Falkners and pursues their relation to Southern history in general (180).[1] He traces the family from the "Colonel," writer William Faulkner's great-grandfather, and draws parallels between fictional characters and Faulkner family members. Such correlations have been made previously, but the degree to which such parallels exist is more clearly established in Williamson's work than in previous analyses. What is especially relevant is Faulkner's grandfather's shadow family. According to Williamson, great grandfather William Falkner had inherited five slaves through his first wife, Holland, who "probably died of tuberculosis" in 1849 (22). He remarried in 1851, but he and his second wife, Elizabeth Houston Vance, had a troubled household. Williamson comments:

> The Falkner household in Ripley in the decade after 1851 was slightly unusual in that the mother and father at first conceived and then bore children less frequently than was common. But the household was very unusual in another respect. In 1850 all of the slaves in the yard were black; in 1860 they were all mulatto. . . . The circumstances suggest that William Falkner . . . reared a mulatto family . . . at the very same time that he maintained a white family. . . . Ironically, the mulatto family sometimes mirrored the white family not only woman for woman, but child for child, and, because it lived in the very shadow of the white family, might well be called the "shadow family." (23–25)

This history is important because its fictional reflection in Ike's family underscores the action Ike takes at the end of the story, when he rejects his legacy. Ike rejects his inheritance because he finds that the black members of his family have been denied their heritage. He spurns white privilege because he has discovered who he is through the hunt for the bear. He has established his identity and understands the importance of integrity.

The hunt in "The Bear" illustrates how landscape, identity, and race contribute to Ike's journey to self-knowledge. The plot unfolds over the course of several years. The much shorter, earlier version of the story, published in *The Saturday Evening Post* in 1942, is organized chronologically.[2] The longer, later version begins when Ike is sixteen and unfolds through flashbacks. These two versions give vastly different impressions of Ike's experience. In the shorter version, the action develops in a straightforward fashion. Ike joins the hunt when he is ten, although he has felt connected to it for years by the stories of his elders. The story ends with his decision not to shoot the bear, Old Ben, and his discussion of that choice with his father, who reads to him from Keats's "Ode on a Grecian Urn."[3]

The longer version introduces Ike at sixteen, with flashbacks to earlier times. The disorienting effect of Faulkner's temporal manipulation underscores Ike's feelings and his situation. He must learn who he is through the semiannual hunting trips, but these are excursions into the unknown. Ike must learn to navigate the morass of the forest, which he does with increasing ease and skill. He must also navigate the emotional morass of familial deceit. Both lessons are learned through his pursuit of Old Ben. Ike faces many dangers in his hunt, but he overcomes them and discovers his place in the world.

Ironically, neither Ike nor Sam Fathers, the two most skillful hunters, kills Old Ben. Instead, Ben's throat is slit by the simple Boon Hogganbeck in a gory fray, leaving bear, dogs, and men dead, wounded, and dying. Ike comes close enough to the old bear to kill him, but chooses not to. Faulkner emphasizes the hunt's larger context by stressing Ike's affinity to the bear. Hunting is not just about killing; it is about the balance between life and death. Further, it is about the way one lives and dies. That Ike does not kill the bear becomes the subject of discussion when he and his cousin meet to clear up family affairs after his father's death.

Ike inherits his father's estate. As Ike and his cousin, McCaslin Carothers, are discussing the family business, McCaslin refers to Keats. This reference, cited by Ike's father in the earlier version of the story, now comes from the mouth of Ike's cousin.[4] The setting is the old office, where they have been looking into the ledgers kept by their fathers, ledgers chronicling decades of miscegenation, incest, and despair. Ike rejects his father's legacy of wealth and guilt, and he tries to explain his feelings to McCaslin. In Ike's view, his family has usurped the land and the labor of others, first from the Indians who owned it, then from the blacks whose labor paid for it.

Faulkner's style in the fourth section of "The Bear" is reminiscent of James Joyce. The section is difficult to read because so many things are unclear. The histories of Ike's family and the South in general are interwoven with references to people and events through which the reader must sort. Faulkner uses a combination of voices—Ike's, McCaslin's, and the narrator's—to comment on fragments of the ledgers. Although kept as business records, these ledgers chronicle the travesties of the past in their accounts of goods and people, bought and sold. The passages purposefully begin with small letters, not capital letters, with minimal indication of who is speaking in the exchange between Ike and his cousin.[5] The details are too complex to catalog without more information and a clearer explanation of what has occurred in the family history. What becomes clear is that Ike cannot undo the injustice of the past; he can only reject profiting from it.

Faulkner powerfully conveys Ike's frustration at his inability to articulate his feelings to McCaslin, who cannot comprehend Ike's views. McCaslin would have cherished the inheritance that Ike rejects. What McCaslin can understand is Ike's relationship to the bear and why Ike didn't shoot him. Both actions, not killing the bear and not accepting a corrupt legacy, reflect Ike's personal code of behavior.

In the earlier, *Saturday Evening Post* version, the emphasis is on Ike as a character who fits into a larger framework.

> He was ten. But it had already begun, long before . . . he saw for the first time the camp where his father and Major de Spain and old General Compson and the others spent two weeks each November and two weeks again each June. He had already inherited then, without ever having seen it, the tremendous bear with one trap-ruined foot which, in an area almost a hundred miles deep, had earned itself a name, a definite designation like a living man. (52)

Faulkner accomplishes several things in this paragraph. "He was ten" points up the youth of the boy who has inherited an overwhelming, spiritual legacy in the bear. The setting, hunting season, is framed as a repetitive cycle. The different episodes in the story reflect the seasons, the corporeal time of men. The bear itself, or rather himself (we are immediately told he has a specific identity), is flawed with a "trap-ruined" foot. The creature of nature is still at large, but he has been marked by a mechanical device that continues to identify him. The idea that he has been marred by man makes the bear an object of both sympathy and admiration. He seems magical in his ability to elude capture. But he is not imaginary; there is tangible proof of his existence.

Ike is tied to the bear because he has heard stories about him from his earliest moments. The bear's reputation has become part of Ike's legacy.

> He had listened to it for years: the long legend of corncribs rifled, of shotes and grown pigs and even calves carried bodily into the woods and devoured, of traps and deadfalls overthrown and dogs mangled and slain, and shotgun and even rifle charges delivered at point-blank range and with no more effect than so many peas blown through a tube by a boy a corridor of wreckage and destruction beginning back before he was born. (52)

This catalog of destruction and power, the very concreteness of Faulkner's images, contrast with the ten-year-old boy. That such an inheritance comes to a small boy suggests that, on one level, we are dealing with a fairy tale or parable. Juxtaposing Ike and Old Ben also suggests a David and Goliath relationship. The religious association underscores Ike's experience in the natural world. Although the meetings between Ike and Old Ben occur within the framework of the hunt, their relationship is not simply a case of hunter and hunted.

The longer version of "The Bear" begins not with the simple statement of Ike's age, but rather with a summary of the story's background. This history builds to the point where the action begins.

> There was a man and a dog too this time. Two beasts, counting Old Ben, the bear, and two men, counting Boon Hogganbeck, in whom some of the same blood ran which ran in Sam Fathers, even though Boon's was a plebeian strain of it and only Sam and Old Ben and the mongrel Lion were taintless and incorruptible. (qtd. in Utley, Bloom, and Kinney 5)

Ike develops his skill as a hunter over the course of the story. The second paragraph of this version tells us that Ike is sixteen and that he has been a man's hunter for six years. The longer story is more difficult to understand initially, but it is a richer yet darker account of Ike's development and the world he lives in. Both versions emphasize several legacies from the other hunters. Most notably, Ike receives guidance from Sam Fathers, an Indian hunter. Like Fathers, Ike is spiritually joined to his prey. Ike's relationship with the bear links him to Old Ben personally and mythically through this special knowledge.

There is a long passage where the omniscient narrator dips into Ike's unconscious and establishes this mythic connection between the boy and the bear. We are told the child has dreamed of the animal in his habitat before men started axing the trees and invading the territory where he lives. The violation of the landscape and the life it contains is emphasized through the exemplar of the bear and the pursuit of it by countless men.

That Ike dreams of the bear long before he ever sees it emphasizes his infantile foreknowledge, which Faulkner uses to create a psychological landscape that parallels the actual one. Also, emphasizing this dream-like state, which pervades much of the story, reverses the expected order of things. In the descriptions, humans are diminished to insect-like status. The bear and the wilderness loom as great forces but, ironically, they are threatened by the "gnawing" of the "puny" attackers.

The relationship between Ike and Old Ben is noble; the encroaching progress of those who cut down the "unaxed" portions of the remaining wilderness is venial by contrast. The onslaught of "myriad and nameless" men with axes are "pygmies about the ankles of . . . [an] elephant." Faulkner compares Old Ben to Priam, "an anachronism, indomitable and invincible, out of an old dead time, . . . epitome and apotheosis of the old wild life." The bear is magnificent and ancient.

Faulkner's references to the bear and to Sam Fathers as figures of royalty are also indicative of their worth. What is good and what is true are illustrated through Ike's experiences and his perspective. Ike questions the expected order of things. *What is nobility? What is an inheritance?* These questions are most often answered in negative terms. Faulkner illustrates for the reader what nobility and inheritance are *not*.

By emphasizing Ike's age throughout the story, Faulkner foregrounds each stage of Ike's physical and spiritual development. Before the age of ten, Ike did not expect to see the bear brought back in the wagon after the hunt. When he finally joins the hunt, Ike's connection to the bear becomes more concrete. He hears the dogs twice in the first two weeks he is in camp. He has a sense of something going by, but it is unseen and undefinable. At one point when Ike is in the woods he senses a presence but Sam tells him it was just a deer. This experience prepares Ike to understand what is going on around him, the first step toward self-knowledge. With Sam's help, Ike comes to realize that he is part of the bear's world and, by extrapolation, nature. Each foray into the woods reveals more clearly the connection between Ike and the bear.

Then, on the tenth morning, he hears the dogs again. He readies the gun, which is too long and too heavy for his size, just as Sam has taught him to do. But this time it is no deer. Sam shares the revelation that the bear has come to check on who is in camp this year and identify any newcomers. The bear has come to see Ike and to test him. Sam indicates to Ike that the bear has come to see him, and the boy once again feels another link forged to the chain of experience that connects him and the bear.

When they return to camp after another foray into the woods, the hunting dogs are under the kitchen and there is a peculiar smell hanging in the air. The last hound comes in at noon and has a torn ear and claw marks. In the afternoon, Sam takes Ike deep into the woods. They do not follow any path that Ike can see; they see claw marks on a dead log and the two-toed paw print. Ike suddenly realizes that what he smelled under the porch was the scent of bear. Sam explains that Old Ben will pick someone to run over if he gets cornered and that it will be Ike. Ike now sees the connection between the bear's earlier visit to camp to see who was there, who was new, and who would be the most vulnerable.

Ike is placed on stand by Sam Fathers and he waits, seeing and hearing nothing, but tasting something brass-like in his saliva, and realizing that the woodpecker's tapping has ceased and begun again while he stood motionless. When Sam returns, he knows Ike has not seen the bear but the bear has been near.

Ike realizes that he must see the bear or the standoff will go on forever as it had with the other men. This is a defining moment for the boy. He knows that he is linked to the other men of the camp by the experience of hunting the bear and that he will establish his own identity by seeing Old Ben. This event must happen to confirm the reality of what he feels. Ike cannot picture himself and the bear within a framework of real time and experience. Although Ike has seen the clawed log, the two-toed paw print, the evidence of a wounded dog, he has not yet seen Old Ben himself. Once Ike is able to see Old Ben, he will begin to know himself.

The next year passes, and it is again June. Ike is eleven. He pretends he is hunting squirrels. Coming back into camp, Ike passes Sam Fathers. Sam is not fooled by the ruse, and he tells Ike that the gun is what prevents him from seeing Old Ben. He also reassures Ike that being "scared" is natural and inevitable. He cautions Ike not to be "afraid" because the bear can smell fear. To be "scared" shows the appropriate respect for the bear and the danger that meeting him will entail. "Scared" indicates the excitement natural to the occasion. Conversely, to be "afraid" connotes the inability to function in the situation. Old Ben can "smell fear."

Ike leaves the camp before daylight, long before the others are awake. He takes only a compass and a stick for snakes. We are told he can go almost a mile before he needs a compass; he has become better as a woodsman without realizing it. Ike has improved his skill in the woods; he is willing to accept nature on her own terms and grows more adept within her precincts. Part of the hunter's skill lies in being intimately attuned with nature to such a degree that he can set aside the tools of hunting and learn from the hunted.

Ike travels far into the woods, and by noon he is farther than he has ever been. He uses the compass and the silver watch which had belonged to his grandfather. After nine hours, he knows he has traveled "far enough." He makes two circles and finally sees the fresh paw print that fills with water even as he watches.

> As he looked up the wilderness coalesced, solidified the glade, the tree he sought, the bush, the watch and the compass glinting where the ray of sunshine touched them. Then he saw the bear. It did not emerge, appear; it was just there, immobile, solid, fixed in the hot dappling of the green and windless noon, not as big as he had dreamed it, but as big as he had expected it, bigger, dimensionless, against the dappled obscurity, looking at him where he sat on the log and looked back at it. (qtd. in Utley, Bloom, and Kinney 158–159)

Ike's journey toward the bear has taken years. To see the bear, he has learned to understand his relationship with nature. The bear is also a part of Ike. It has pervaded his psyche since his early childhood. At the onset of Faulkner's tale, Ike heard the stories and dreamed about the bear. Then he hunted the bear and sensed him but did not see him. Now he sees the bear.

When Ike actually sees the bear, the encounter is a simple one; Ike remains seated on the log where he has stopped, and the bear and he look at one another "while his quiet breathing inhaled and exhaled three times." The bear moves across the glade and stops to regard him over his shoulder. Then the bear simply fades as quickly as it appeared and Faulkner describes the departure as a comparison with the way a fish sinks out of sight below the surface of the water. This meeting, so long anticipated, is remarkable for its lack of incident. Ike seeking the bear without a gun, compass, watch, or stick is beyond "catch and release" in fishing; it is going to the pond without a pole. Faulkner's comparison of the bear to an old bass makes the bear seem benign. The bear and the fish are old, admirable, and mysterious. They reenter their respective worlds of woods and water seemingly without movement or effort; they both "sink" into their environments and disappear.

In the later version of the story, Faulkner introduces several new incidents, most notably the episode with Lion. Lion is a huge, wild dog, trapped and tamed by Sam Fathers and assigned to the care of Boon. When Ike is thirteen and has truly joined the hunters, he can comprehend the importance and significance of Lion. Lion is the dog that Sam has been waiting for to pursue and bring down Old Ben.

Ike is near the end of his novitiate in the wilderness. He has killed his first buck with a rifle and has felt the hunter's humility, a sense of his own fragility in the timeless woods. He has had blood from his kill smeared on his face by Sam Fathers in recognition of his accomplishment and as a mark of connection to his prey. He has eaten meat cooked by men who were more hunters than cooks, and he has slept the sleep of a true hunter.

The sequence of time in the next part of the story is foggy and purposely fragmented. The following November Ike kills a bear, although it is not Old Ben. In a single paragraph we learn that Ike has been given his own gun and that he'll have it until he's seventy. Here Faulkner looks ahead to the end of Ike's life to frame what he does as a young man. Showing us that Ike, too, will grow old is a way of connecting him to Old Ben and the mortality of the other characters and animals in the story. This is not simply an account of a bear hunt.

This time Lion jumps and holds Old Ben at bay and Ike hears the commotion. He runs as fast as he can to the scene but his lungs are on the verge of bursting and, despite his strong will, he can go no farther. Faulkner emphasizes the inexorable quality of the hunt and makes it a touchstone for man's experience. Every hunt ends, whether the hunter kills his prey or not. The mortality of human beings is reinforced by the mortality of animals. No animal lives forever; no man lives forever. It is part of the same cycle of nature, inescapable no matter how any one hunt may resolve itself. It is foolish to mourn because mourning is useless. The best one can do, according to Faulkner (who attributes the sentiment to Ike), is to feel privileged to have participated in the experience.

The resolution of the story should come with the death of Old Ben, and it does in *The Saturday Evening Post* version. But in the longer version, Ben's death occurs at the midpoint. The change in structure between the two versions of the story serves a thematic purpose. The later, more developed version stresses Ike's goodness as a young adult. In an attempt to break the cycle of duplicity that enslaves him and his "shadow" relatives, Ike renounces his legacy. The ways in which landscape, identity, and race are entwined become clear to Ike precisely because of this legacy as hunter and child of nature. He rejects the idea of perpetrating more injustices to keep the land.

We learn Ike is now twenty-one. He and his cousin discuss the family legacy and the corruption and greed of their ancestors is revealed as a convoluted history of numerous violations of the law and common decency. The land was the habitat of the Native Americans, where they hunted and conducted their lives. With the coming of the white men the land became corrupted. Slaves were forced to clear land and plant crops.

The McCaslins' black relatives were defined in terms of ownership and profit. Ike's renunciation of land and money is particularly significant since he alone carries the McCaslin surname. He is the surviving white male heir. His cousin cannot fathom why Ike would refuse something so precious.

Ike replies to his cousin in one of the more straightforward exchanges of this section that he cannot repudiate what was never really his. His father and uncle never had the right to bequeath what they had in fact stolen from others, who themselves had stolen. In his denunciation of the sins of the past, Ike repeats the word "repudiate," and this repetition has two effects. It clarifies the McCaslin genealogy and establishes his own innocence. His inheritance is worth nothing, at least in his view. Ike's is the moral voice that contrasts with the corrupt voices of the past and the deceived voices of the present. However, his cousin McCaslin questions Ike's conclusion.

The argument goes on, and Faulkner uses biblical references, as well as comparisons between the Old World and the new. The history of the American South is, of course, the larger part of Faulkner's vision of the McCaslins' history; his works are peopled with endless variations of the South's fall from Eden. The exchange between Ike and his cousin progresses from discussion of the land's violation to the violation of humanity.

Ike has difficulty articulating his feelings, and this difficulty, as well as the web of deceit in which his family is tangled, is reflected in Faulkner's style in section four. It is often hard to know exactly who is speaking, but the more passionate and repetitive speeches seem to be Ike's.

"What is truth?" becomes the ultimate question for Ike and for Faulkner. McCaslin questions the nature of personal truth—if it is one thing to one person and another to someone else, how does one judge? Ike's simple but insightful answer is that the heart is the judge; in the end the individual heart knows. The truth has been obscured for generations in the family ledgers, which pose an almost demonic contrast to the Book of Truth. The ledgers reveal a truth that compels Ike to refuse the inheritance they record. Ike discovers that his revered grandfather raped his own child— the daughter of his shadow black wife—and this daughter had a child. Reflecting on the outcomes of the past, Ike realizes that none of them has been free, slave or owner. As the cousins look at each other, staring into each other's eyes, the narration draws a parallel between the pride of liberty and freedom in the example of the bear and his fight for survival and the struggles of the humans in a changing world.

Faulkner contrasts the simple purity of the bear and Sam Fathers with the complex corruption of the McCaslin family. These contrasts underscore Ike's position since he must live in both worlds. He rejects his hereditary family and turns to Old Ben and Sam, his chosen "family" from whom he learns the important lesson of how to live his life. Furthermore, the bear and Sam Fathers are like one another. The bear is compared to Priam, ancient and childless, and Sam is an old man who is the son of a Negro slave and an Indian king. His double legacy of pride and suffering of being both Indian and black underscores his nobility. He is wild and free in spirit like the bear. Ike has sought the qualities of humility and pride which will make him worthy of the knowledge of the woods. However, he fears he cannot simultaneously be properly humble and proud of his skill because he learns so well and so fast. Ike has seen the abuses of power and, while he appreciates the power his hunting and woodcraft give him, he realizes the necessity of controlling himself. Sam Fathers teaches Ike to follow the examples of the old bear and a little mongrel dog, even though Sam cannot articulate concepts like humility and pride. Yet McCaslin, who quotes Keats and understands why Ike doesn't shoot Old Ben, cannot understand why Ike rejects the family legacy.

That Faulkner has Ike's cousin, McCaslin Carothers, quote the passage from Keats's "Grecian Urn" provides an unexpected twist. McCaslin recalls Ike's chance to kill the great bear and questions the reason Ike did not shoot when he had the chance. Ike is not literary, but McCaslin seizes upon the volume of Keats and reads the pertinent passages from the poem which articulate the lasting nature of beauty. Ike misunderstands and sees only a poet talking about love and a woman. This moment is especially poignant because Ike does not need to draw the connection between his respect for the bear and for life and the poet's cry for truth as the preservation of beauty.

The defining moment for Ike has taken place during the hunt. As a hunter Ike chooses not to kill. Hunting is not about killing, just as living is not about dying. However, both hunting and living are sometimes about managing death. In "The Bear," the rites of passage from childhood to adulthood involve Ike's symbolic death and rebirth, and these rites use hunting as a metaphor for the experience. Ike lays to rest one phase of life for another. Sam Fathers smearing blood on Ike's face after his first kill symbolizes this process. That Ike will lose his wife, never have a child, and never have more than a few possessions in a long life does not matter. He has broken the McCaslin family's inheritance of deceit and despair.

Hemingway and the Aesthetic Hunt

The American Hunter in Africa

Hemingway uses hunting episodes in his work as both a framework for his personal reflections and a vehicle for developing his characters. As with Faulkner, Hemingway's hunter figure internalizes the landscape that he traverses, and the natural world becomes inextricably linked to his identity. Hemingway treats many forms of natural landscape in *Green Hills of Africa,* his short stories, and *The Old Man and the Sea.* In the Foreword to *Green Hills of Africa,* he writes:

> Unlike many novels, none of the characters or incidents in this book is imaginary. Any one not finding sufficient love interest is at liberty, while reading it, to insert whatever love interest he or she may have at the time. The writer has attempted to write an absolutely true book to see whether the shape of a country and the pattern of a month's action can, if truly presented, compete with a work of the imagination. (n. pag.)

Green Hills of Africa

In his biography of Hemingway, James Mellow points out that *Green Hills of Africa*

> was indeed a book about landscape, though Hemingway referred to it in more magical or mystical terms as "country," equating it with the love of a woman. . . . But Hemingway took it further, making it a trope for sexual intercourse. He described it in passionate terms. (437)

Hemingway speaks of being happy, but this happiness is fleeting because things change so quickly. He may be submerged in the world of the jungle, but the threat of the outside world is barely kept at bay.

In *Green Hills of Africa,* the notion of possessing, owning the land is juxtaposed with the visiting hunter's temporary affair with the landscape. Hemingway's attention to the setting, the beauty of the land and its animals, the passing of precious time, stresses the corporeal and temporal nature of life. The human hunter's vulnerability also comes through in his emphasis on time and place.

In *Green Hills of Africa,* Hemingway downplays his recurrent amebic dysentery, although he does discuss physical suffering. He relates to his prey, and he has made the commitment to a clean kill so that he will not wound an animal to suffer and die.

> I had been shot and I had been crippled and gotten away. I expected, always, to be killed by one thing or another and I, truly, did not mind that anymore. Since I

still loved to hunt I resolved that I would only shoot as long as I could kill cleanly
and as soon as I lost that ability I would stop. (147–148)

Accidents in hunting are part of the danger of the activity. Wounding
an animal, another hunter, or oneself can happen even when exercising
the greatest care. Hemingway's preoccupation with wounding is generally attributed to his experience as an ambulance driver in Italy; however,
as a hunter he was throughout his life subject to accidents, a circumstance
that may account for his portrayal of suffering as the malignant joke of
fate.

"The Snows of Kilimanjaro"

In "The Snows of Kilimanjaro," a slight scratch ultimately kills the story's
protagonist, Harry. The scratch blossoms hellishly into gangrene, which
finally takes his life. Harry and his wife, Helen, are on safari in Africa.
Harry hopes to regenerate his dissipating powers by hunting. The scratch,
an absurdly insignificant injury, combined with other seemingly innocu-
ous circumstances proves devastating. At first Harry doesn't treat the
scratch at all. When he does treat it, the carbolic is diluted. Then the lorry
breaks down. Next, the plane is late. None of these events by itself would
be particularly important, but each exacerbates his condition. The combination of circumstances proves inevitably fatal. Hemingway uses the setting of Africa, the summit of Kilimanjaro, to underscore the operations of
a malignant fate.

> Close to the western summit there is the dried and frozen carcass of a leopard. No
> one has explained what the leopard was seeking at that altitude. (*Short Stories of
> Ernest Hemingway* 52)

The meaning of the leopard is never addressed in the story. It simply
acts as the exemplar of fickle destiny. It signifies the powerlessness of
mortal creatures in the wake of nature's sweeping force. In the most general sense, Hemingway suggests we are not masters of our fate.

Harry blames his wife, Helen, for his downfall, for making things too
comfortable for him with her money. He also acknowledges the unfair-
ness of this view. He vacillates between accepting responsibility for his
own failings and holding her accountable for his problems. Their marriage is adversarial at its heart. Harry cannot draw strength from his relationship with his wife, and he cannot draw strength from satisfaction in
his professional life.

In his dying hours, Harry regrets wasting his writing talent. He has
come to Africa to put his life and art into perspective and to start anew.

But he has found only death. Harry was supposed to "work the fat off his soul" and regain spiritual purity. But he never gets the chance to reform. He is a writer who hasn't written and now will never be able to write. He is a hunter on safari, but it is his wife who hunts and who survives.

That Hemingway's life and career in some ways parallel Harry's is no coincidence, although by no means is he Harry. Perhaps Hemingway feared he could be Harry and exorcised such a demon in writing the story. Harry's continuing reflection might be Hemingway's. He ponders his talent and how he has used it, which leads to thoughts about his wives. He realizes each woman has been richer than the last and that he has performed better for women even as he has loved them less.

In the story, Helen's characteristics are also Hemingway's. The reversal of conventional male/female roles is significant. According to Mellow, Hemingway was fascinated by role reversals. In the human hunting world, the male predominates; in the animal world, females are often the dominant predators. Hemingway reverses the expected order of things in his African stories. Predatory females in his fiction are cited by Mellow and others as evidence that Hemingway deeply resented domineering women. His mother was such a woman, and he felt he had to rebel against her. In her biography of Hadley Richardson (Hemingway's first wife), Gioia Diliberto describes Hemingway's attraction to Hadley as evidence of this rebellion. Hadley's passivity was the opposite of Hemingway's mother's aggressiveness.

> That Ernest all his life feared domination by women and that this fear was a powerful motivation have long been recognized by Hemingway readers. Ernest was determined not to marry a woman like his mother, Grace, that "bitch, who had to rule everything, have it all her own way," as he put it. (Diliberto xi)

"The Short Happy Life of Francis Macomber"

Hemingway expresses his fascination with and fear of strong women in another hunting story, "The Short Happy Life of Francis Macomber." Here, too, Hemingway stresses the vulnerability of the hunter. Macomber is on safari with his wife, Margot. They have hired a white hunter named Wilson to guide them. Francis is a well-known sportsman and has accumulated many trophies. He is anxious to hunt lion, buffalo, and rhino but, when he hears the roar of a lion close to camp, it disturbs and unnerves him. The following day he wounds a lion and reluctantly follows it into the bush and only after Wilson convinces him of the necessity of finishing the lion. Wilson does offer to take care of the lion and let Macomber off the hook, but Macomber feels he must deal with his fear. However, he bolts when the lion charges. Wilson and, what is worse, Margot see him run. Wilson is willing to let it go, but Margot is relentless about his cowardice.

When Macomber subsequently wounds a buffalo, he has an opportunity to redeem himself. He is anxious to pursue the beast because he has overcome his fear and is elated by the "rebirth" of his courage. But as Macomber faces down the charging buffalo, he is shot by Margot, who claims to have been shooting at the animal to save her husband's life. Although it is debatable whether Margot's shot is accidental or not, she proves to be the more deadly hunter. Macomber is in danger not when he loses his courage but when he finds it: "For the first time in his life he really felt wholly without fear. . . . Instead of fear, he had a feeling of definite elation" (*Short Stories of Ernest Hemingway* 31).

Macomber has gone after the buffalo because he needs to reclaim his pride. Wilson is moved by Macomber and wryly remarks, "Worst one can do is kill you." He then quotes Shakespeare, expressing the thought that a man can die only once. The narrative then reveals Wilson's inner feelings. Francis Macomber is thirty-five, but in Wilson's eyes, he has just become a man. Wilson is a professional hunter with a code that is unspoken but nonetheless his guide.

The setting for Macomber's revelation is Africa, and the occasion is the hunt. Again, it is Wilson's perspective that provides the framework for examination. Hemingway uses the hunt as the test of Macomber's manhood. Macomber is stripped of his title as sportsman when he faces the lion and runs. He agonizes over his fear, and the other characters react to his struggle in ways that are self-revelatory. Of course, the irony is that Francis Macomber loses his life as a result of losing his fear. "The Short Happy Life of Francis Macomber" is an ironic title.

Perhaps the greatest irony is Macomber's ignorance of the Somali proverb, "a brave man is frightened three times by a lion; when he first sees his track, when he first hears him roar and when he first confronts him" (11). Fear of the lion is a crisis for Macomber, and he triumphs over his fear, a fear he does not understand. That this fear is somehow universal is pointed out by the citing of the proverb after all, the proverb is about "a brave man," not a coward. But bravery is not enough. Indeed, bravery is finally Macomber's undoing.

Hemingway's portrayal of Margot as a deadly hunter who kills her husband reveals his own fears regarding the danger in human alliances. The hunter-prey relationship between man and animal is benign in contrast to the malignant human male-female relationship. Man and nature seem in accord. Macomber finds his identity in the hunt, and its danger is surmountable and ennobling. What Macomber and Hemingway cannot overcome is the danger of "love."

The Writer as Hunter

Both "The Snows of Kilimanjaro" and "The Short Happy Life of Francis Macomber" use Hemingway's experiences in Africa. The stories parallel settings and incidents in *Green Hills of Africa.* Hemingway says that if one serves "society, democracy, and the other things quite young, and declining any further enlistment make yourself responsible only to yourself, you exchange the pleasant, comforting stench of comrades for something you can never feel in any other way than by yourself" (Hemingway, *Green Hills of Africa* 148). He maintains that writing well transcends worldly recognition or compensation. He equates this feeling of satisfaction with that of an explorer who discovers new lands.

In *Green Hills of Africa,* Hemingway is searching for an original aesthetic accomplishment. He wants to create prose that is more poetic than poetry. His removal from the literary, "civilized" world is an attempt to see his art more clearly from a distance. His safari in Africa might seem the farthest thing from the life he led in Spain, Italy, and France, but he constantly reflects on other times and places from his African perspective. He is at once totally involved in the hunt and aware of the greater world and its limitations.

Nick Adams and "Big Two-hearted River," Parts I and II

Green Hills of Africa, "The Snows of Kilimanjaro," and "The Short Happy Life of Francis Macomber" are the Hemingway works most obviously associated with hunting. They are also evidence of the creative genius that Hemingway possessed and harbingers of the degenerate forces to which he eventually succumbed. The Nick Adams stories, written earlier in his life and career, however, offer more compelling evidence of Hemingway's search for personal redemption through aesthetic achievement. Here again the figures of the hunter and the hunt enact a crucial metaphoric function.

For Hemingway, hunting and fishing expeditions were a release from the tensions in the rest of his life. He immersed himself in nature to escape family pressures and reinforce his personal worth. He constantly needed to reaffirm the power he had over his life. The whole drama of life and death fascinated him. His passion for bullfighting shows a need to formalize the ritual aspects of death in order to cope with them. Ritual itself becomes a motif, traceable throughout his work.

In "Big Two-Hearted River," Hemingway develops the main character, Nick Adams, largely by narrating Nick's ritualistic actions. Nick's actions give rise to reflections that reveal the inner life of his character. Mellow discusses Hemingway's use of ritual in this story.

> Out of the country near Seney, with his ritual need for order and the mundane details of bait and gear, the lore of fishing, Hemingway would create the setting and the action for one of his most famous and audacious stories, "Big Two-Hearted River." . . . Nick goes off into the woods, sets up camp, and, in solitude, fishes the stream. . . . It was a story in which Hemingway deliberately set out to test his mettle as a writer and one in which he proved a critical theory that the best stories were those in which what the writer omitted was as important as what the writer put in. (101–102)

Hemingway's use of ritual connects his own aesthetic and natural worlds. He was already at ease in nature, but he was still developing his writing. What he knew so well from his hunting and fishing experiences were portrayed in "Big Two-Hearted River." Repetition and ritual are inherent in the world of the woods, which is based upon cycles. Man in nature must pay attention to details to survive. One way to assure that important details will be observed is through rituals that imbue repetitive acts with meaning. Although "Big Two-Hearted River" is a fishing story, not a hunting story, it includes all the elements of the hunt. In a larger sense, of course, fishing is hunting.

Nick Adams' relation to Hemingway parallels Ike McCaslin's relation to Faulkner. Nick and Ike are young, skillful, well intentioned; they represent the idealistic aspect of both authors' youthful natures. They struggle with corrupt forces around them in the civilized world and are more at home in the natural world, where they regain their lost strength. The natural world also provides the setting for their physical and emotional growth. They are linked inextricably to nature, which never fails them.

As "Big Two-Hearted River" opens, Nick sees the ruin of the town of Seney. The town is gone, its houses scattered, but the river remains. Nick peers into its waters and sees the trout keeping themselves steady in the current. "As he watched them they changed their positions by quick angles, only to hold steady in the fast water again. Nick watched them a long time" (209).

In Part I of the story, Nick arrives at the charred town of Seney, walks to where the country is not burned, and camps for the night. In Part II, he awakens the next morning, catches grasshoppers for bait, makes his breakfast, cleans up camp, and fishes. He takes comfort in the rituals he performs. Through these rituals, he is able to feel happy, to experience and reaffirm what is "good."

Nick's feelings are reflected in the landscape. All is dead and burned when he disembarks from the train, an objective correlate for his inner state. The first signs of life are in the river, the trout. "Nick's heart tightened as the trout moved. He felt all the old feeling." Hemingway implies that Nick has not been able, or allowed himself, to feel anything for a long time. It does not matter what the "old feeling" was as long as he is able to feel it again. Even though his pack is heavy and his muscles ache, he is happy. He leaves behind all his former needs.

Nick is determined to get as far as he can before dark, and he is constantly looking for signs that will tell him the country ahead of him is as it should be. He looks into the distance. Like hope, the great hills are elusive if one focuses on them too intently. Nick must have faith that they are there, but must concentrate on more immediate concerns. From the distant hills, he turns his attention to the ground and sees a grasshopper, black from living in the charred earth. All the hoppers are black. He has stopped to rest and smoke a cigarette.

But he cannot rest until he leaves behind the ruins. He is finally able to rest and falls asleep once he reaches the country that is not burned, but he wakes stiff and cramped. The dew sets in quickly after the heat of the day. He looks down the river and sees the trout rising to catch insects on the surface of the water; some jump into the air.

Nick then sets up his camp, his methodical motions underscoring the ritual aspect of his actions. Unpacking and rearranging his gear, setting up his tent, making his supper, eating, reflecting upon friendships of the past, cleaning up, and finally sleeping are all described in detail. One task after another, one stage after another, must be completed in precise order before the next stage begins. Nick is hungry, but he will not, cannot prepare dinner until his camp is made.

Hemingway captures Nick's mental state by recounting the minute details of setting up camp. His repetition of the word "done" after every task is completed is like a checklist Nick needs to go through to establish his security. The very simplicity of the mundane, the ordinary, the matter-of-fact provides a kind of stability unattainable in the outside world. Even the detail with which Hemingway describes canned goods takes on significance. Nick brings cans of pork and beans and spaghetti to cook for supper, which he mixes together in the frying pan and sops up with four slices of bread. The details are simple, yet idiosyncratic. Hemingway focuses on each step Nick performs, and this intensity of focus transports the reader to the campsite. The site's atmosphere is ripe for reflection, and Nick falls into a reverie.

Two things contribute to his mood. The hot food reminds Nick of his friend Hopkins and the old crowd with whom he used to fish. He is now alone with his rituals and his thoughts, or rather his lack of thought. He concentrates on the moment and the next task. The odd meal serves to point up Nick's independence and competence. He is able to camp alone, having planned each stage of his trip, even to the canned food. Once his practical needs are met, his emotional needs can be addressed. He has chosen to make this journey of spiritual renewal. The emphasis on the "the good place," "the good smell," reinforces the consciousness of his actions as positive steps toward healing we know not what sort of wound. Hemingway emphasizes nature's power to heal Nick; at the same time, he uses the physical landscape as a reflection of Nick's inner world.

Nick's ability to sleep once he approaches the untouched part of the river is significant. First, he sleeps in the afternoon once he is above the fire line. Then he is able to sleep at the end of Part I after dinner and the recollection of his former friends. For Nick, sleep is the test of genuine healing. Nick sleeps at the close of Part I and awakens in Part II to a new day in which he will continue his ritualized healing process and pursue the hunt. Nick crawls out of the tent with its mosquito netting to dress and start the morning rituals before his pursuit of game.

The river is Nick's anchor throughout the story. He first goes to it when he debarks the train. He looks for it as he makes his way across the burned terrain into the "good" area. He camps by it, and he goes to it in the morning even before fishing.

> A river, for instance, runs through many of Hemingway's major stories and his most important novels. Generally, in such Hemingway fictions, the river serves as a cleansing baptism, an absolution for past sins, a healing experience, a rite of escape from the outside world as the Big Two-Hearted is for Nick in the story of that name. (Mellow 125)

Nick goes in search of bait and finds grasshoppers. In contrast to the ones he saw earlier, these hoppers are not sooty. Nick is glad that he has caught the hoppers early because once the grass dries they will be hard to catch. He has gone to the same log every morning and turned it over to look for bait. The implication is that he will be camping there for some time. The grasshoppers are an emblem of a lost innocence; children catch grasshoppers. Only a child, a professional fisherman, or a naturalist would be so aware of the insects and their habits.

Nick next makes his breakfast of buckwheat cakes; he makes an extra flapjack with apple butter and two onion sandwiches to take for his lunch; he drinks his coffee and cleans up camp. "It was a good camp." He then starts to organize his fishing gear. Again he has planned ahead, preparing his gut leaders by wrapping them in damp cloth that he had wet from the watercooler on the train. The tough gut is softened and ready to use. He prepares his fly rod, leader, hook. His practicality and attention to detail stress his determination. He works with nature and brings to the world of the woods those things that allow him autonomy; he plans to spend a long time fishing the river because he needs this time for his recovery.

He starts down to the stream with his rod, a bottle of grasshoppers, and a flour sack for the fish. The healing process has begun already; Nick's meticulous preparations coalesce in the portrait he presents. He is happy with all his fishing gear. He has bulging pockets and various pieces of equipment fastened to him. He steps into the stream and the cold water is a shock. The current sucks against his legs; he loses a grasshopper in the water, and it is immediately eaten by a trout. He baits his hook, lets out his line, and gets a bite. Nick releases the small trout he catches, being careful to wet his hand first before touching it so the delicate mucus will not be disturbed. The fisherman/hunter cooperates with nature by knowing about his prey and respecting its life, not taking what is too small or too young.

Nick does not like to fish with other men on the river if they are not of his party. He has seen the destructive ways of the ignorant fishermen. He recalls seeing dead fish covered in white fungus, the result of careless handling as they were thrown back.

Next, he manages to hook a big trout, which escapes after a long struggle. The majesty of the escaped trout is evident in the reverent tone of the story. Hemingway's descriptions of animals in the hunter-prey relationship emphasize man's vulnerable position in the scheme of things. Nick projects his own reaction onto the fish. Once again, Hemingway shows Nick's close relationship with nature and its creatures. Whether or not fish feel emotion is beside the point; that Nick believes they do is important. Nick's identification with the trout describes his spiritual life. He draws solace from placing himself within the life of the woods. Envisioning the struggles of other creatures gives him a sense of perspective, of being part of the larger world. The larger world of nature is also an ordered world. And Nick has dedicated himself to order.

When Nick loses the big trout, it takes a while for him to recover, but slowly he is able to overcome his disappointment. He rebaits and catches a good trout. He does not need to catch many fish.

Nick's knowledge of the habits of the fish at different times of day further illustrates his intimate knowledge of his environment. The river narrows and becomes a swamp, and Nick reflects on the possibility of fishing there after he catches his second trout. His hesitance to proceed is based upon a disturbing association. It is sinister precisely because it is amorphous. "In the swamp fishing was a tragic adventure. Nick did not want it" (231). Hemingway's use of the word "tragic" is another indication that Nick's mental state is precarious. Although we are not told why, the charged language of Hemingway's descriptions of the swamp point to unnamed dangers for Nick. The reference to tragedy also points to forces beyond human control in the greater scheme of things.

The metaphor of the swamp in "Big Two-Hearted River" connotes a mysterious place, physically and emotionally dangerous to negotiate, unlike the river that Nick seems to know and understand completely. The river leads into the swamp, but Nick will choose to stay where he is.

The swamp is the place that Nick will not go at this point in his life, although there is an indication that he will face it one day: We are told there would be other days when he could fish the swamp.

James Mellow discusses the contrast between the earlier and published versions of the story. Mellow sees the point where Nick loses the big trout as the climax of the story.

In early versions of "Big Two-Hearted River," the parallels between Nick and Hemingway are striking. Mellow comments that "in the earliest manuscript fragment, Hemingway had begun the story as a first-person narrative in which he was traveling with two companions, Jock and Al Pentecast and Al Walker, who had made the expedition with him to the Fox River in the summer of 1919. In another manuscript version, Helen, Nick's wife, was originally Hadley" (274). Mellow also points out that the eleven pages of reflection were deleted after Gertrude Stein "read his fishing story and what she referred to as his 'little story of meditations' on writers and writing, and told him, 'Hemingway, remarks are not literature'" (276). The changes Hemingway made are significant. Nick is a solitary figure in the published story; he only reflects on the immediate environment. The narration offers no insights into personal matters. Everything is suggested; nothing is stated.

In both story and personal account, Hemingway shows himself negotiating the borderline between nature's world and man's world. Although Nick and Hemingway have functioned in society, they need the healing power of nature to regain perspective. The activities of fishing or hunting are essential; they do not just take walks in the woods. Although nature provides the setting for renewal, hunting and fishing are the vehicles for physical action and spiritual reflection.

The Old Man and the Sea

While "Big Two-Hearted River" and *Green Hills of Africa* emphasize immersion in nature as a source of solace and renewal, *The Old Man and the Sea* uses nature as a touchstone for judging character. Santiago is an old man negotiating the borderline at life's end. He is alone in his everyday struggle to live except for the loyalty of a boy, Manolin, who cares for him.

Lately Santiago considers himself unlucky. A malignant fate has beset him. The boy remains loyal to the old man because "the old man had taught him to fish and the boy loved him" (10). Hemingway stresses the old man's humility, which is reminiscent of Ike McCaslin's. Humility and skill grow out of Ike's and Santiago's harmony with their environment. Santiago "was too simple to wonder when he had attained humility. But he knew he had attained it and he knew it was not disgraceful and it carried no loss of true pride" (13–14). Santiago's age and Ike's youth provide a contrasting range of experience. But both characters are humble in the natural world.

For Santiago, the sea is feminine in much the same way as the country is for Hemingway in *Green Hills of Africa*. Santiago "always thought of the sea as la mar which is what people call her in Spanish when they love her" (29). Santiago does not desire sexual love because of his advanced age. His wife is dead and he no longer dreams of women. He only dreams about lions.

The lions in Santiago's dreams are benign. They come from Santiago's past. He tells the boy that he used to sail on a square rigged ship that ran to Africa and he used to see lions on the beach. The boy has heard about the old man's adventures before. Baseball is another love of Santiago's; he asks the boy if they should talk about Africa or baseball. This is the night before the old man catches his great fish. Santiago's discussion with the boy is about bait, about whether his eighty-fifth day will be lucky, about great ball players and managers, and about youth and age. The simple conversation between Santiago and the boy contrasts with the extraordinary struggle that will take place the next day. As in "Big Two-Hearted River," the attention to mundane details creates a sense of the ordinary, while reinforcing the ritual aspect of preparing for the hunt.

When the old man falls asleep, he travels back to Africa. Before the old man falls asleep, however, he and the boy also discuss Santiago's strength.

In the morning the old man wakes, looks at the moon that is still shining and puts on his trousers. He then goes to wake the boy.

Hemingway stresses the subsistence level of the old man's life. He may lean on the boy to walk, yet he carries his mast with its furled sail to his skiff. The image of man carrying his cross is inescapably etched. Hemingway's iconography contrasts with Cooper's. Natty Bumppo insists that he is a man "without a cross," while Santiago is a man unaware he carries one. These hunters, however, are more similar than different. The common bond among all hunters is their relationship with their environment. The heart of this relationship is their identification with the creatures they hunt. Another feature common to all hunters is their solitary life.

Other fishermen surround Santiago as he sails out alone before dawn. Each boat goes its own way. Santiago has fresh bait; he knows that this is a special day, and he will go far out to sea.

Hemingway emphasizes the connection between hunter and hunted as a symbiotic, and even egalitarian, relationship. The old man sees the flying fish and the birds. He feels himself part of the cycle of nature, of hunters and hunted. He empathizes with the other creatures around him. Even the small birds are hunters. They have a hard lot in life, and Santiago is especially in tune with them because he is a small hunter among larger predators. He and the small birds hunt on the vast ocean to survive, again reinforcing the hunter's union with other creatures.

Hemingway accomplishes two things in the passage about small birds. The great depths in which the old man fishes are another, a measure of his worth. By going far out to sea and fishing bottomless waters, he crosses the borders between the ordinary and the exceptional. He goes beyond his normal range, certainly beyond the normal expectations for his age and delicate physical condition. He reaches beyond the border for the other fishermen as well, all of whom are younger and stronger than he. The numerous references to depth reinforce a burial motif, a motif remarkable for its intensity.

> Before it was really light he had his baits out and was drifting with the current. One bait was down forty fathoms. [A fathom is six feet.] The second was at seventy-five and the third and fourth were down in the blue water at one hundred and one hundred and twenty-five fathoms. (30–31)

The depth of the water dramatizes the old man's struggle, and he is physically diminished by the grand scale of nature, yet he possesses spirit and simple courage. He watches the rising sun, the birds, and the flying fish, and he thinks, "My big fish must be somewhere" (35). He seems aware that some extraordinary thing will soon happen.

That this is a special day is reinforced several times before Santiago hooks the great fish. The action begins subtly at first, and Hemingway builds upon the moment with simple, but detailed description and then a stream of consciousness of Santiago's thoughts.

Santiago can sense the fish far below him in the depths of the ocean because he is attuned to his prey; he has spent a lifetime on the sea studying the creatures he hunts. As he pictures the action taking place below the surface, he urges fate to take a hand and bend to his will. He utters this forceful request and prayer.

"Come on," the old man said aloud. "Make another turn. Just smell them. Aren't they lovely? Eat them good now and then there is the tuna. Hard and cold and lovely. Don't be shy, fish. Eat them." (42–43)

We are privy to the old man's thoughts and wishes and moment-to-moment experience. Santiago has strived all his life to catch a great fish.

Much like Ike in "The Bear," Santiago wants to see the force that he is pitted against and with which he is strangely united. Also, like Ike, the old man wants to see his prey to make it real. To truly understand the prey, the hunter has to see it to experience it and join it as part of the cycle of nature. "I wish I could see him. I wish I could see him only once to know what I have against me" (46).

The fish drags him on into the night, farther out to sea. He wishes once again that he had the boy with him. He wonders how the baseball teams did, and he wishes he had a radio. But, he is alone except for the pair of porpoises that swim around his boat while it is still night. "No one should be alone in their old age, he thought. But it is unavoidable. . . . During the night two porpoises came around the boat and he could hear them rolling and blowing" (48).

Hemingway repeatedly draws connections between the old man and the other creatures. Santiago is human but not the ruler of the beasts, just another creature who admires his "brothers." He even pities the prey he must capture and harvest to live himself. His humanity makes him an excellent fisherman, and his humility makes him admirable.

Santiago wonders about the great fish he has hooked.

He is wonderful and strange and who knows how old he is, he thought. Never have I had such a strong fish nor one who acted so strangely. Perhaps he is too wise to jump. He could ruin me by jumping or by a wild rush. But perhaps he has been hooked many times before and knows that this is how he should make his fight. . . . He took the bait like a male and he pulls like a male and his fight has no panic in it. I wonder if he has any plans or if he is just as desperate as I am? (48–49)

Sex and age transcend species here. Santiago feels a kinship with his prey based on age, "who knows how old he is."

He recalls a time when he caught a female fish and the male stayed with her to try to help her. The recollection is poignant. Although he experienced the sadness of the female marlin's fight and the loyalty of the male, releasing her was never an option. "[W]e begged her pardon and butchered her promptly" (50). Santiago, like other fishermen, is part of the food chain and sympathy for his prey never dissolves into sentiment.

Santiago never asks nature to be different from the way it is. His spirituality grows from the immutability of nature. His humility does not allow him to question; life and death are inevitable, and so is the struggle between the two. The only choice in the matter is how best to pursue the struggle.

As the struggle goes on, Santiago talks to the fish. Speaking softly but aloud, he tells the fish he will stay with him until he—Santiago—dies. He tells the fish he loves and respects him but, nonetheless, he will kill him before day's end. He wants to see the fish jump but cannot induce him to do so.

Santiago speaks to the things around him, the act underscoring his loneliness. He even talks to his own hand. "'How do you feel, hand?' he asked the cramped hand that was almost as stiff as rigor mortis. 'I'll eat some more for you'" (58–59). He wishes the boy were there, frequently and aloud. In a strange way, his loneliness links him to the other creatures in his world. The fish is alone, the bird is alone. Their loneliness is a powerful bond.

Santiago's desire to both conquer the fish and feed him is a contradiction only in the modern world. Kinship with one's prey is an ancient concept in the hunting world and has mythic overtones. The motif of eating and devouring to gain or retain power is present in many ancient cultures. Chronos swallows his children whole, and Grendal gruesomely devours warriors in *Beowulf*. Various cannibalistic practices involve eating all or parts of one's enemies to imbibe their strength and valor. Eating connotes both honoring and conquering one's opponents. Initiation rites of passage for hunters and warriors often involve smearing the blood of the prey or enemy on the conqueror. This act signifies a communion between conqueror and conquered. Additionally, it signifies incorporation of the conquered's physical and spiritual self. Although usually associated with the young hunter/warrior's experience, Santiago's situation echoes such an initiation ceremony. He is undergoing the battle of his life, yet he approaches it from the standpoint of age, not youth.

The old man's simplicity is one of the most complex aspects of the novel. The "wise old man" is a familiar type, the natural philosopher in tune with nature and with himself. Despite his sagacity, however, Santiago's physical body constantly reminds him of his dangerous situation. His body may betray him because he is old. His hand is cramped from the abuse it has taken tending the lines. As he desperately tries to relax the cramp, the great fish decides to jump.

This is Santiago's first sight of the fish. This fish is beyond anything he has ever seen. Comparing the marlin's size with the skiff points up the size of the task ahead. He hopes that being a man will help him because other creatures "are not as intelligent as we who kill them; although they are more noble and more able" (63). He reflects on the other great fish he has seen, but he was never alone when he'd seen them, and they were not as big as this one. However, he still has a cramped hand that betrays him. "There are three things that are brothers: the fish and my two hands" (64). He evaluates the situation once more and tries to understand what is happening and what is likely to happen.

Hemingway uses simple, concrete details in his physical descriptions that then revolve the philosophical thoughts of Santiago. Once again, Santiago reflects on how he loves the fish, but must kill it.

Hemingway deals with the limits of time and space, the organization of the universe and man's place in it. Santiago is a primitive man. His life is like the hunter/gatherer leading a subsistence living. He practices a primitive natural religion where his food source, the animals, are his brothers. He is grateful to his brothers for feeding him and realizes the creatures are more noble than those they feed. At the same time, the whimsical thought that man might challenge the heavenly bodies has mythic echoes. Associating mythic elements and instances of natural religion with Santiago seems more in tune with his world than the intermittent Catholicism he mechanically observes.

Santiago's philosophical thoughts then yield to practical considerations. He hasn't slept since he put out to sea two days before. He prepares to eat the fish he caught earlier, and then plans to sleep a little. He dreams of the lions, and then the line runs out quickly, badly cutting his hand as he awakens. Santiago cannot see the fish, but he hears him jump more than a dozen times.

For much of the story, the fish is an unseen, unknown force, and the old man can only guess at his size. When Santiago finally sees the fish, his first impression is one of disbelief. 'No,' he said. 'He can't be that big'" (90). The perspective is reinforced by the companion fish swimming with the giant marlin.

The sucking fish are portrayed as parasitic courtiers to the noble marlin. They live in his shadow, deriving sustenance for their lives from his. They are like eels, serpentine echoes of evil, the worms of the sea. The degenerate forces challenging the great fish and Santiago are gross and ugly compared to the nobility of the fish and the fisherman. The marlin and Santiago are brother adversaries, and there is an inherent dignity in their struggle. The old man can see the great fish's eye, further personalizing the battle. Santiago sweats from the sun and the effort he must exert as he looks to place the harpoon and finish the big fish.

Both Santiago and the fish are ready to expire; however, Santiago is able to move the fish onto his side for a moment, and it is a victory to feel him move. The old man feels faint and fears he will not be able to endure. "'Fish,' the old man said. 'Fish, you are going to have to die anyway. Do you have to kill me too?'" (92). (These last words are strangely reminiscent of Helen's in "The Snows of Kilimanjaro." Harry is dying and they quarrel even as his life expires.)

Like Faulkner, Hemingway contrasts valiant men and creatures and the forces that seek to destroy them. It is perfectly sensible to see the old man as more closely related to the great fish than he is to many venial human beings. Especially in the environment where they contend, their kinship transcends their enmity.

The killing blow, when it comes, is sure and strong. Hemingway does not gloss over the details of Santiago's kill. The result of the struggle is death in all its raw reality. The blow from the harpoon kills the fish, and the old man sees him floating on the waves, discoloring the water with red blood. And Santiago is still in danger of joining the marlin in death. "'Keep my head clear,' he said against the wood of the bow. 'I am a tired old man. But I have killed the fish that was my brother and now I must do the slave work'" (95). The fish is too big to get into the skiff, so he has to lash him securely alongside. He wants to feel and touch the fish because he thinks he felt its heart beat when he harpooned it. The eye that he looked into before has now turned into an unresponsive mirror. The color of the fish has changed with death.

Ironically, now the old man and his great marlin are hunted by other fish. It is an hour before the first huge shark hits them. The sharks represent fickle, senseless destruction. The old man tries to defend the fish, but it is a losing battle. The mutilation of the marlin is brutal, and the helplessness of the old man to combat the army of sharks is particularly poignant. He fights valiantly, but he cannot stop their onslaught. He regrets subjecting the great fish to this terrible ignominy. He feels responsible, but he is proud that he is able to kill the first gigantic shark that attacks.

He knows there will be more assaults and that, without his harpoon, they will be impossible to fight off. His only solace is to think about baseball and the great Joe DiMaggio; he wonders if Joe would have approved of his swing when he hit the shark in the head.

The old man thinks that perhaps killing the fish was a sin. He feels confused when he contemplates the intricacies of sin and nature. He feels certain that he was meant to be a fisherman. He feels comforted that DiMaggio's father was a fisherman, that there is an order to things. "Besides, he thought, everything kills everything else in some way. Fishing kills me exactly as it keeps me alive. The boy keeps me alive, he thought. I must not deceive myself too much" (106). Santiago is an ideal man in a corrupt universe. He mitigates some of the evil in a degenerate world by living in it. Perhaps he is as much a hero as DiMaggio.

He resolves to struggle with the sharks, "'fight them until I die'" (115). He finally sails into the harbor when everyone is asleep, and there is no one to help him. The great fish is little more than bone in places, a skeleton of what it was. He unsteps the mast and prepares to carry it on his shoulder. He carries the mast up the hill and stumbles, having to sit down at least five times before he reaches his shack. When he reaches home, he leans the mast against the wall and sleeps "face down on the newspapers with his arms out straight and the palms of his hands up" (122). His hands are wounded, and when the boy comes into the shack and sees the old man, he is moved to tears. The boy tells the people in the village not to disturb Santiago; he brings the old man coffee and tells him he will care for him and that when he is well he will fish with him again. His great fish is a pile of bones on the beach that the tourists mistake for a shark.

Manolin cries without shame for the old man. Clearly, he shares Santiago's moral strength. Santiago's regret is that he went "too far out" to bring in the great fish successfully. But his venturing was the very thing that allowed him to catch the fish. The hunter always tries to assess what he did wrong and to relive the hunt to learn and plan for the future.

When Santiago sleeps, he dreams as he did at the beginning of the lions on the beach of the African coast. The novel ends as it begins, completing a cycle of experience. The important difference at the end, though, is that Santiago has achieved his life's work and confirmed his place in his world.

In *The Old Man and the Sea,* Hemingway casts the weakest of men as among the strongest. When Santiago hunts and slays the great fish, he crosses the border between the possible and the impossible. The act itself is what matters. That the great fish is ravaged by the sharks is a brutal metaphor of modern life. The fish may be nothing but a skeleton at the end of the novel, but this does not negate Santiago's feat. The old man accomplishes the impossible through his practical skills and indomitable spirit. He is a good man, the perfect hunter, who overcomes his own limitations to pursue and harvest his prey.

Both Faulkner and Hemingway portray the hunter figure confronting degenerate forces in his life and in the culture. The hunter's strength to brave such forces stems from knowing his place in his environment. Through immersion in nature, he gains this knowledge, and thus, is able to overcome his own flaws that might limit or destroy him. Negotiating the borders of his opposing worlds, the hunter not only battles the darkness in himself and society, but he finds the power to transcend them.

Notes

1. Williamson discusses Faulkner's possible motives for adding a "u" to the Falkner family name when he enlisted in the Royal Air Force in Canada.

   Rejected by the American military, William Falkner in the spring of 1918 was maturing a plan to get into the war by enlisting in the flying service of an allied nation. He succeeded. On June 27, 1918, the Oxford Eagle ran a notice in its "Personal and Local" column: "Mr. William Falkner who has been spending a few months in New York is visiting his parents Mr. and Mrs. Murry Falkner. He has joined the English Royal Flying Corps and leaves the eighth of July for Toronto, Canada, where he will train."
   Actually, Billy had enlisted in the Royal Air Force, not the Royal Flying Corps. The name had recently been changed, but Billy preferred to give out the earlier, more romantic sounding version. Also, he had not spent a few months in New York. Apparently, he had gone to New Haven in early April. Thirty years later Phil recalled that he got Bill a job in a Winchester arms factory while they both attempted, futilely, to join the allied armies by passing themselves off as Canadians. Then an English friend who dined with them at the Commons at Yale taught them to "talk like Englishmen" while they plotted to pass as citizens of that nation. In late June, Bill went down to New York and succeeded in enlisting in the Royal Air Force. Probably it was this phase in his life that Bill began to develop for himself a full-blown British, perhaps even an Oxonian persona. He somehow managed to convey the impression to some people that he was an Englishman who had been studying in the United States and now wanted to enlist in the cause of his country. He was in the process of creating that character, perhaps, when he first added a "u" to the spelling of his family name. Later, he would insist that the alteration meant nothing, but rather clearly the "u" gave him a significant distance from his family and from his own previous self. Certainly he used it while in the service in Canada. . . . With the life expectancy of a novice British flyer on the Western Front at about three weeks, Billy apparently had no real difficulty getting into the military as a pilot candidate.

2. See Frances Lee Utley, Lynn Z. Bloom, and Arthur F. Kinney, eds., *Bear, Man, and God: Seven Approaches to William Faulkner's "The Bear"* (New York: Random House, 1964); also see Stephen B. Oates, *William Faulkner, The Man and the Artist* (New York: Harper & Row, 1987), 184. Oates comments that Faulkner's writing of *The Saturday Evening Post* version of the story was driven by a need for money.

   With the summer came a creative breakthrough. Never mind how terrible things were in the outside world (the Germans launched a massive invasion of Russia, relations between Japan and the United States were increasingly tense). His recent retreat into the big woods, and his memories of Old Reel

Foot, inspired a chorus of Yoknapatawpha voices, some of which he had heard before and written down in previous stories. But now they came together in a long and magnificent new tale called "The Bear." Because of his accursed need for money, he wrote a version for the magazines, entreating Ober to sell it anywhere for anything he could get; Ober finally got $1,000 for it from the *Post*. Meanwhile Faulkner wrote a much longer version of "The Bear," which he incorporated into *Go Down, Moses* as its showpiece story and one of the triumphs of his art.

3   The scene between Ike and his father in the version published in *The Saturday Evening Post* depicts Ike not shooting Old Ben as an affirmation of life and the bond between Ike and the bear. It is a "neat" ending to the story when Ike's father reads the passage from Keats's "Ode on a Grecian Urn" to frame the episode and put it into perspective. This discussion takes place immediately after Ike's encounter with the bear, which gives the impression of a timely resolution and interpretation of Ike's actions.

4   Williamson ascribes the quoting of Keats to Ike, but examination of the passage— confusing because it ambiguously ascribes "he said" until the pronoun reference has no hope of finding the antecedent—indicates that McCaslin has the intellectual prowess to quote the poet, while Ike is not so well read.

5   The use of small letters immediately alerts the reader that something unconventional is taking place. The style reinforces the confusion of the situation and reflects the state of Ike's mind as he searches for the truth, which proves to be painful and disorienting. Ike's struggle is shared by the reader, who must also struggle for understanding in a world dimmed with corruption and deceit.

Chapter 5

Thomas McGuane and Ayla: The Cowboy and the Cave Girl

Olson came in. Thin, intelligent Jack Olson, native of this Northern country. . . .
Olson was a serious sportsman, with rigid and admirable ideas of sporting demeanor. . . . For Olson, hunting and fishing were forms of husbandry because he
guaranteed the life of the country himself. (McGuane, *Sporting Club* 55–62)

· · ·

She looked at the dead animal at her feet and let the club fall from her hand. . . .
I killed a hyena, she said to herself as the impact hit her. I killed a hyena with my
sling. Not a small animal, a hyena, an animal that could kill me. Does that mean
I'm a hunter now? . . . It wasn't exultation she felt, not the excitement of a first kill
or even the satisfaction of overcoming a powerful beast. It was something deeper,
more humbling. It was the knowledge that she had overcome herself. (Auel, *Clan
of the Cave Bear* 208)

Two late twentieth-century permutations of the hunter figure are writer
Thomas McGuane and Jean Auel's Ayla, a character from *The Clan of
the Cave Bear*. They illustrate the power to reinvent oneself and move
freely within American society. Landscape and identity, as well as gender
and race, remain intricately connected with this evolving figure. As in
previous epochs, the hunter negotiates chasms between civilization and
wilderness, achieves self-knowledge, and transcends bias through immersion in nature. McGuane uses hunting as a touchstone for developing a
personal moral code. Auel expresses concerns with gender and racial
empowerment through Ayla's development as a hunter. Ayla's life is a
metaphor for female and minority empowerment over the last two decades.

Both McGuane and Ayla are outcasts who struggle to find a place
where creativity and personal growth are possible. This territory is at
once literal space and mental landscape. One figure inhabits the twentieth-century American West; the other, prehistoric Europe. Although it
may seem strange that a woman from prehistoric Europe represents an

American hunter figure, author Jean Auel creates Ayla's character as a composite of ancient hunter goddess, romantic fiction heroine, and modern American feminist. The differences in setting make Auel's and McGuane's figures' parallel experiences even more compelling. Both seek and find their true selves through hunting.

That Thomas McGuane is an author and a hunter inevitably provides comparisons with Faulkner and Hemingway but, as Dexter Westrum suggests, such comparisons are "perhaps-too-facile" (3). However, Westrum does admit that McGuane is inextricably linked with these writers.

> His work follows a direct line from the great writers of our past, his romantic protagonists continually embodying the American frontier and transcendental traditions as they confront the often-frustrating realities of modern-day existence in quest of life's infinite possibilities. (ix)

Westrum sees McGuane expanding a "code" that becomes a personal model for life.

McGuane's life on his Montana ranch echoes Teddy Roosevelt's life on his Dakota ranch. Roosevelt first found refuge there from the problems of the world and then a way of life that he adopted and extended into a personal metaphor. The Dakota period revitalized Roosevelt's self-confidence and sparked a return to New York and politics. McGuane escaped from the financially rewarding but spiritually debilitating world of Hollywood to find renewal in ranching and hunting. He now writes screenplays for movies, mainly to finance his literary career.

The Sporting Club and other works, such as *The Bushwhacked Piano, Ninety-two in the Shade,* and *Panama* mirror McGuane's personal experience. His protagonists are reflections of McGuane's own persona. How to live a meaningful life in a chaotic and corrupt world is the subject of his art; his writing is therapeutic and echoes Nick Adams's position in Hemingway's story, "Fathers and Sons." Nick thinks that if he can write about his father, he will be able to exorcise the bad memories and put things into balance again. It is as if the ability to represent life carries the power to fully live it.

Like our other hunter figures, McGuane is a man on the border. He lives between the corruptions of Hollywood, where he must earn a living as a writer, and the spiritually pristine but stark Montana wilderness, where he hunts and ranches and lives his cowboy life. As a hunter he reaffirms his identity and the personal code of integrity he lives by.

McGuane's use of the picaresque to convey his message and his treatment of stereotypical and unreal characters are decidedly unsentimental.

His use of stereotypes, and characters Joyce Carol Oates has dubbed "unreal," opens space for social critique.

Ayla, the female protagonist of Jean Auel's Earth's Children series, suggests much the same dynamic as McGuane. She too is searching for a place in her society where she can claim an identity. Since Ayla lives in prehistoric times, the concern of the books is in a sense "unreal." But, her position in society inscribes serious racial and gender issues of the 1970s–1990s.

In the first book of Auel's series, *The Clan of the Cave Bear,* Ayla is a female of a different species, adopted by a tribe that cannot appreciate her unique gifts. She is ostracized for her differences, but she manages to teach herself to hunt, an act that has both practical and symbolic implications. She ensures her own physical survival and gains a sense of self-worth. Her ability to live through and then escape the beatings and rape of her childhood testifies to her strength of will, a strength she gains from hunting.

Ayla exemplifies the "new" woman of twentieth-century America, while McGuane continues the tradition of the hunter/cowboy epitomized by figures like Cody and Roosevelt. McGuane incorporates elements of Faulkner's and Hemingway's hunter figures because, like them, he finds an antidote to the corruptions of the modern world through hunting.

Thomas McGuane as the American Hunter/Cowboy

Like Ernest Hemingway, Thomas McGuane is both an author and a hunter figure. The rugged life he leads on his Montana ranch helps him cope with the modern world. Like Hemingway and Faulkner, he uses the hunting metaphor to develop characters in his fiction. Westrum comments that McGuane "maintains his vision of life and writes with a secure knowledge of the American canon" (ix).

McGuane's sense of alienation makes him identify with his Irish forebears in their struggle with the English. The American predisposition to resist authority and sympathize with the downtrodden comes out clearly here. But the concept of "outsider" goes far beyond any specific, identifiable difference. In his novels, McGuane's commentary on modern life employs biting satire; his characters and plots are designed to stimulate and viscerally arrest. His message is conventional, stressing moral values that transcend the cynicism of the age.

McGuane's first novel, *The Sporting Club,* illustrates McGuane's "style as message" at an early stage of his work. An anomaly in his repertoire,

The Sporting Club was written in six weeks; his other novels took long periods of time to write and required massive revisions.

McGuane desperately wanted to publish since his graduate school days. His friendship with writers who published before him put him at a great disadvantage, at least in his own mind. He wanted to devote his life to his art but did not receive the recognition he needed to be taken seriously. Westrum describes the circumstances surrounding the publication *The Sporting Club.*

"After Yale, the McGuanes spent roughly a year in Italy and Spain. Ostensibly McGuane was tracing Hemingway's footsteps. . . . In 1966 McGuane returned to the United States to accept a Wallace Stegner Fellowship for a year at Stanford . . . [which] came to an end with McGuane still unpublished" (6–8). At this low point, and with no other option, he wrote the draft for *The Sporting Club* in a short six weeks. He left for Mexico after putting the manuscript in the mail to his friend, Jim Harrison. The story continues with McGuane being camped on a beach. One morning he's awakened by a man he takes to be a policeman who is wearing a gun. McGuane has the passing thought that he's about to be shot when, instead, the fellow is "the local telegraph operator" who has been looking for him to announce that his book was accepted and the telegraph operator wanted to congratulate him. They end up celebrating together and having a good laugh over the incident (6–8).

Stylistically, many passages in *The Sporting Club* echo Hemingway, but with a twist. One striking example is McGuane's attention to detail and to graphic images. The connection is especially apparent when James Quinn, one of the main characters of *The Sporting Club,* is fishing.

> When the mayfly hatch was finished and the fish had quit feeding, he had five good trout. On the way back to his cottage, he paused four times to open the wicker creel and look in at the trout he had put in wet ferns and arranged in a hierarchy of magnitude. (qtd. in Westrum 26)

* * *

> He liked to see trout in a porcelain sink. He liked to see them on a newspaper almost as well, though not as much as the sink. . . . Quinn picked up the largest fish, gripped it under the gill plates and opened it with his pen knife. . . . In the middle was the whitish translucent stomach and its dark contents showed through. Quinn split it carefully, spreading the insides with the blade of his knife on the porcelain: hundreds of undigested nymphs. The second, smaller trout contained the same plus a bright minnow and a few red ants, some of which had eaten into the stomach lining. There was one brown honeybee in the third. (qtd. in Westrum 47–48)

If there is any doubt about McGuane's satiric intent in the first passage—where Quinn looks at the "five good trout" "four times" and arranges them "in wet ferns . . . in a hierarchy of magnitude"—there's no mistaking the fun he has with Hemingway's style in the second passage, as he describes the fish's stomach contents. Quinn's idiosyncrasies parody the rituals of Nick Adams, where the details of catching and cleaning fish are described in sacramental tones. At the same time, however, McGuane demonstrates Quinn's genuine respect for nature. The style may ridicule Hemingway's flourishes, or it may ridicule those who think that Hemingway's style is flawless. But, it does not ridicule the feeling for nature that Hemingway evinces.

James Quinn contrasts sharply with the other characters in *The Sporting Club*. Yet he also contains aspects of their personalities, and he is the character closest to a protagonist in the novel. Most notably, Quinn identifies with Jack Olson, the sporting club's manager. Olson is the ideal hunter and sportsman. The club took property from his family, but he cares about the club's preservation. He has the land and its animals' welfare at heart, and he respects nature and its gifts. Olson is skillful and sensitive, the perfect hunter and fisherman, taking only what he needs. McGuane places Quinn and Olson in opposition to the Centennial Club members with their pathetic skills and inflated egos. McGuane contrasts these two characters with the spoiled, perpetually juvenile Vernor Stanton, whose self-destructive impulses affect all those around him.

Quinn and Stanton are old friends/adversaries. Since boyhood they have had a relationship that is difficult to characterize as friendship. Quinn has been victimized by Stanton throughout his life. They have been bad boys together or, rather, Stanton has brought out Quinn's bad boy tendencies since childhood. But they are no longer boys, and Stanton refuses to grow up. Quinn has taken over his father's factory and made a success of it, to everyone's surprise. He likes to work and feels responsible to the company and its employees. He has his mail forwarded to the club and telephones the office to supervise the factory as best he can while he's away. Quinn identifies with Stanton's rebellious streak, which he admires because Stanton defies the hypocritical status quo. Quinn still feels bound to Stanton on several fronts, but he realizes Stanton's shortcomings. Stanton no longer attracts Quinn and others because he cannot accept change.

The title, *The Sporting Club,* connotes upper middle class American decency and tradition, as well as an acceptable level of New World snobbishness. Picaresque characters and situations provide a picture of the darker aspects of contemporary American society. At the same time, McGuane longs for meaning and fulfillment. Ethics involving work, love, and respect for the environment are juxtaposed with the inherent corruption of accumulated and hereditary wealth and power. McGuane uses the hunting metaphor to explore these areas.

The book treats the destruction of the Centennial Club, the oldest sporting club in Michigan. The club's location in Michigan adds another Hemingwayesque touch. Hemingway was born and grew up in Michigan, where he had his first hunting and fishing experiences.

The Michigan setting suits plot development as well as character development. Hunting and fishing are stressed as manly pursuits. On the other hand, dressing for dinner and the club's other socially elite practices overlap with country club standards. McGuane stresses the dichotomy between the club's ostensible ideals and its corrupt practices. More important, he historicizes that gap.

At the climax of the novel, a time capsule is unearthed. Inside is a photograph of the founding fathers engaged in an orgy. The club members are engaged in sex not only with each other, but with animals as well. The caption at the top of the picture reads, "Dearest Children of the Twentieth Century, Do you Take Such Pleasures as Your Ancestors?" (202). As if the discovery of the photo isn't bad enough, the club members cast off all sense of decorum and begin their own orgy. In this scene McGuane breaks down the last of the club's pretensions, reverence for the past. The literal destruction of the club takes place simultaneously. Earl Olive, the leader of a degenerate motorcycle gang, is busy tearing things down and blowing things up, with assistance from his buddies and Stanton.

Olive is captured and tied up, and Quinn tries to save him because he sees the members have become as crazed as Olive in their efforts to subdue him. Quinn is also captured and tied up. Stanton takes to his machine gun to rescue Olive and Quinn. Finally, the police arrive and Quinn is cooperative in explaining what has happened as the police pore over the photograph.

Such outrageous action eliminates any semblance of verisimilitude. This isn't a "real" story. However, it does illustrate McGuane's real concern with living a moral life. His portrayal of those who abuse their power is merciless and bespeaks his depth of feeling. He uses the metaphor of sport to express his passion.

For McGuane, hunting is sport, not a subsistence activity. But he plays endlessly with the concept of hunting as searching. Every important character in the novel is searching, hunting for something. In the broadest sense, each of them is searching for meaning. *Who* one is and *what* one is are the underlying questions McGuane explores in *The Sporting Club*.

The reviews of *The Sporting Club* are mixed. Some critics see reflections of Fitzgerald and *The Great Gatsby*.[1] Others find the plot and characters uninteresting and McGuane's style unsuccessful.[2] All of them point up McGuane's stylistic and thematic links to Hemingway and Faulkner. These reviews center largely on McGuane's character development, with references to "class" as a key ingredient. Class and heredity are preoccupations of the club's members, but class and heredity do not guarantee their claim to the title "hunter."

Class is used as a way to treat the hierarchical range of characters in the novel, and several critics focus on this idea. The terms *aristocrat* and *class* are often used interchangeably, and both are applied to the work and to its author. In one *Best Sellers* review, Stanton is referred to as "the wealthy aristocrat [who] invites his rich co-members to annihilate everything" (O'Hara 28). A review by Andre Deutsch asserts that "this is a novel about the American ruling class" (927). The same review raises other points about the type of hunting that requires the lower class to beat the bushes for game, while the ruling class shoots, often to the peril of the beaters.

Deutsch's remarks reinforce how McGuane portrays corruption in America and the language he employs. Like Faulkner in "The Bear," McGuane defines what is genuine by showing what is not genuine. Inherited wealth and power are the least reliable ways of judging who is moral. One is reminded of Ike's legacy from his father, which he rejects when he finds out the truth of his ancestors' crimes. In *The Sporting Club*, the telling photograph reveals the degenerate nature of the club's founders. In both instances, the past speaks to the present and deflates any pretense that tradition or inheritance can imply moral authority.

Like Faulkner, McGuane uses language to create an appropriate tone for his message. Deutsch points out that McGuane's choices of character names have significant literary and historical allusions, but that understanding the novel does not depend on decoding McGuane's references. "Since 'Spengler' is so direct a literary reference, the same may be true of other characters. 'Stanton' is a name well known in American history. Possibly some kind of cryptogram is in operation" (927).

McGuane's education and reading rule out any coincidence in his use of these names. Deutsch uses the term "Joycean" to characterize McGuane's language, which reinforces comparisons with Faulkner. That McGuane makes "many kinds of sense without the reader needing to know the author's key" seems accurate. But the reader must have his or her own key.

McGuane's concept of "sportsman" is the key to reading character in the novel. He draws on the style of other American authors, including Faulkner and Hemingway, to provide resonance for his themes. Again, the good hunter/sportsman is the good man. The hunter/sportsman who violates the order in nature reveals his own degeneracy.

Other reviews draw comparisons with Faulkner, Hemingway, and Fitzgerald. Sara Blackburn writes:

> [T]his . . . aristocratic novel reminds one of *The Great Gatsby*. Set at an upper-class hunting and fishing club . . . , it describes the close and sadistic friendship between two rich young men . . . [who have] contempt for their marvelously stuffy club members. . . . Contained within this hard, wry, thoughtful tale, is beautiful writing about hunting and fishing. (475)

Blackburn focuses on the nature of McGuane's characters, particularly the relationship between Quinn and Stanton. She characterizes the novel itself as aristocratic. But McGuane's treatment of the socially pretentious is quite different from Fitzgerald's in *The Great Gatsby*. McGuane's broad strokes in *The Sporting Club* made it a target for being termed a "para-novel, the put-on novel, the sub- or pseudo-novel" by Joyce Carol Oates (4).

Oates characterizes Stanton as "the American aristocrat." She also refers to Snopes-like characters present in *The Sporting Club,* which is yet another connection between Faulkner and McGuane. Earl Olive is the most Snopesean of the novel's characters. He is antithetical to any notion of aristocracy. Faulkner's Snopes clan is not only repulsive on a personal level, they are destructive to the community they prey upon. In "Barn Burning," for instance, the father's inevitable tool of revenge is setting barns afire. He does this in retaliation for wrongs real or imagined committed toward him and his family. Yet the horror of the act remains indefensible no matter what the provocation. Olive and his entourage are a less grim but no less destructive bunch. Christopher Lehmann-Haupt refers to Earl Olive as "a low-life Snopesian redneck" and characterizes the conflict between Olive's crew and the club's members as "class warfare." He also comments that "Thomas McGuane writes about men in wildlife nearly as well as Hemingway did. He can also stage the interplay of obscure symbolism as intricately as Thomas Pynchon can" (35).

Other critics such as Granville Hicks were far more negative about McGuane and his novel. "McGuane writes well, though not so well as some of his admirers think, but much of the book is the sort of thing that, in the old days, bad boys wrote for private circulation among their class-mates. It will probably succeed in paperback" (31). *The Booklist and Subscription Books Bulletin* begins its review thusly: "A deteriorating plot centers on the fiasco created by a half-insane, bored-with-life million-aire bent on destruction who incites tensions among the membership of an exclusive sporting club during the summer of their centennial celebra-tion" (1060). *Publishers' Weekly* is not quite so harsh when it pronounces the novel "not completely satisfactory," but it does declare that McGuane is someone to watch. It also comments: "On one level it's [*The Sporting Club*] a bizarre treatment of the ribald rivalry between two wealthy sports-men. On another it is an oddly interesting allegory about civilization's lack of progress, a fantastic parable about a world run amok that ends with a scene of almost Breughel-like horror" (267).

Quinn is the protagonist of *The Sporting Club,* or the character clos-est to a protagonist that McGuane allows. The critics differ on the pro-tagonist of the novel. Some see Stanton as the central figure; others, Quinn; still others, Stanton and Quinn. Olson is also central, but he exits the action early when he is fired as manager of the club. Lehmann-Haupt stresses Olson's importance as a figure, important for his mitigation of bloodlust to the balance of nature. Olson is all that stands between civili-zation and holocaust since sports and sporting clubs are "ritualizations" of competition in American and Western civilization (35).

The novel begins with a description of the club from "Blucher's *An-nals of the North* (Grand Rapids, Michigan, 1919)," which tells us that the Centennial Club's former name was the Shiawasee Rod and Gun Club. Founded by lumber barons, it was the grandest of the clubs in the area, and its operations are shrouded in mystery. Membership is heredi-tary and the club is politically powerful. Then the grounds are described and various buildings such as the main lodge, a gazebo, and a toolshed are pointed out. There is also an offhand remark that tours may be con-ducted in winter.

The narrator then comments on the entry in Blucher's, indicating that it is misleading because there was never a tour. He also notes that the actual view of the club would be disappointing because the members are "in favor of roughing it" (12). The wry comment, "Even the tool-shed disappoints," unmistakably sets McGuane's satiric tone.

After this rather cryptic beginning, we see Olson and Quinn driving from the front gate of the club toward the buildings, and the topic of conversation is Stanton. Quinn's dread of Stanton is the first thing communicated to the reader, and Olson reinforces this emotion. Olson tells Quinn that Stanton has a wife and that he has built a dueling gallery in the basement of his cottage.

Once Quinn arrives at his own cottage, he decides to visit Stanton. After a few preliminaries, Quinn and Stanton duel in the basement. Quinn loses and discovers that Stanton uses wax bullets. He has a painful red spot over his heart, but he isn't otherwise injured. He is shaken, however. He's also angry but relieved and braces himself for future duels with Stanton, who has taunted him since childhood. The duel is a dangerous game, and it's unclear why Quinn feels compelled to participate. This world of upper class American sportsmen is alien and bizarre. Dueling, the ultimate gentlemen's contest, occurs early in the novel, setting the scene for increasingly bizarre behavior and events.

Quinn likes his business and is doing well with it. It probably wouldn't matter if he weren't doing well because he and Stanton and other club members are millionaires. However, Quinn has very little self-confidence. He does not have Stanton's ruthless disregard for others. Quinn hates his secretary, Mary Beth, but he can't fire her because of his compassion for a fellow human being. He knows this is a "failing" of his in the business world.

The one place where Quinn excels is in sport, which is evident when he goes fly fishing.

> Quinn held the rod high. He felt the curve of its loose rigidity. The fish broke and so began to lose ground. When it broke again it was splashy and without violence and came slowly to the net. At the net, it bolted once more and swung around behind but a moment later was in hand, a trout of two pounds that Quinn, with his thumb securely under the gill covers, held first against the trees and then against the sky before he put it in his creel. He rinsed the crushed fly in the water to rid it of slime which would sink it, blew hard on it until its hackles were upright and the false wings of feather stood out from the hook. He began his casting once again. He shortened the timing of his first cast so that the line cracked very slightly like a whip and there was a small cloud of vapor in the air where the fly had been. The fly was now absolutely dry and when it landed on the water it stood high on its sharp hackles and floated the way an insect does.
>
> When the mayfly hatch was finished and the fish had quit feeding, he had five good trout. On the way back to his cottage, he paused four times to open the wicker creel and look at the trout he had put in wet ferns and arranged in a hierarchy of magnitude. (25–26)

The extended description is detailed in the Hemingway manner. The passage is also a serious description until the very end, just before Quinn encounters Stanton again. The genuine quality of this and other portions of the narrative dealing with true sport provoke the reader as much as the glib and overtly satirical portions. The lack of irreverence, rather than the presence of reverence, conveys McGuane's attitude toward man in nature. Man in nature is truly man at his best.

Another serious subject is Quinn's feelings for Janey, who is supposedly Stanton's wife. However, Quinn discovers that she and Stanton are not legally married. Janey loves—but will not marry—Stanton. Quinn asks Stanton, "'Why won't she marry you?'" to which Stanton replies, "'Says I'm too mean and crazy. She says she's sorry she loves me and I don't blame her. I think it's bad luck for her too. I'm not domestic'" (46). Quinn feels chivalrous toward Janey. He admires her because she is loyal to Stanton, who treats her poorly in public and lovingly in private. She realizes Stanton's gaping flaws and accepts him anyway. Quinn would like such a woman but realizes she will not leave Stanton for him. If she did, she would not be the paragon he loves.

Quinn is noble in that he aspires to do the right thing, but he is weak when it comes to Stanton. He has always been bullied by Stanton, and he can't seem to shake Stanton's influence. Quinn admires the way Stanton defies the hypocritical club members, and serves as his stooge in most of the annoying pranks that Stanton dreams up to aggravate the members.

Quinn suspects Stanton may self-destruct, and this fear is reinforced by Janey in a conversation early in the novel. Quinn empathizes with Janey because, underneath the layers of resentment, he too is devoted to Stanton. "Quinn thought of Janey trying to contain this corrosive silliness and she seemed so much in danger that he thought of himself as the rescuer. . . . 'Well, I hope you still like him,' she said. 'Can't you tell I do?'" (51).

In a strange way, Quinn is bound to Stanton and in conflict with him. Janey's presence clarifies the line that Quinn must walk between friendship and personal interest. Quinn would like to court Janey and reject Stanton and Stanton's hold on him. He would like to act in his own selfish interest, but he can't. What stops him is his inherent nobility, although he is far from a conventional hero. Quinn is not larger than life, he does not perform miraculous deeds. His appeal is that he enjoys work and has a sense of honor in matters of friendship and love. And no matter how picaresque the situation, he behaves well. Quinn demonstrates his inherent decency in his behavior toward Janey and Stanton, but he best demonstrates his goodness in the natural world.

Quinn balks when he learns that Stanton wants to totally destroy the club. The first step Stanton wants to take is firing Jack Olson. The resentment toward Olson by the members is based on their jealousy and snobbishness. Olson leaves, but he has the vengeful satisfaction of appointing his successor, Earl Olive, who is Olson's demonic opposite. Olson sought to preserve the club and its lands; Olive seeks to destroy it in the most perverse way he can. Olive seems a cartoon character in a cast of already exaggerated personalities. However, this dehumanizing of characters allows for interpretive freedom. The characters become representatives rather than individuals. Thus, the novel has allegorical possibilities, which can be examined at the story's conclusion.

The action builds to the Founders' Day ceremony when the time capsule is opened and the photograph revealed. Little is left of the club because of the havoc Stanton and Olive have created. In the last scene of the novel Quinn visits Stanton, who has purchased the defunct club lands and now resides there with Janey and his young male caretakers. Stanton is still rich, but he is completely crazed. His "features had clarified impressively under madness and loss of weight. He seemed heroic and at one with his illusions" (218). When Quinn and Stanton duel once again, they do not use real pistols but pace off and turn and say "bang, bang."

After this last contest, Quinn retires and is left alone in his bed listening to the silence of the house. This moment is at once poignant and absurd. It is perhaps more frightening than the violence that has preceded it because Quinn is left to ponder what a sane, moral person can do in a totally skewed and immoral world.

The quotation preceding the opening of the novel is "Whirl is King" from Aristophanes, which asserts that chaos rules when all order is absent or has been destroyed. McGuane provokes us to step back and think about the outlandish goings-on and the characters who perpetrate the action. If Stanton were completely powerless at the end of the novel, it might lead to a neater interpretation of the whole. But Stanton buys the club and its grounds and makes sure that Quinn retains his cottage. Stanton's money ensures his power; Quinn's business diminishes after cooperating with the police.

When the police arrive, Quinn cooperates with them, answers their questions, watches as they examine the evidence, and feels a sense of relief that the hypocrisy of the club has been exposed. After the revelation, however, Quinn's business declines and he is viewed as someone who has sold his own kind down the river.

Of course, "his own kind" were not the club members or other businessmen, or even his "friend" Stanton. Quinn is alone. Olson, his only possible ally, is long gone; Janey is forever attached to Stanton. Quinn begins and ends the novel in the middle of conflicting forces. He will be able to continue his beloved hunting and fishing, but he will be caught between the worlds of commerce and nature.

Like Quinn, McGuane's life has been spent in conflicting worlds. In his book of essays, *An Outside Chance* (1990), he discusses his liminal position. His essay, "The Heart of the Game," particularly demonstrates his position on the edge.

> The snow whirled in the window light and puffed the smoke down the chimney around the cedar flames. I had a stretch of enumerating things: my family, hayfields, saddle horses, friends, thirty-aught-six, French and Russian novels. I had a baby girl, colts coming, and a new roof on the barn. . . . I was within eighteen months of my father's death, my sister's death, and the collapse of my marriage. Still, the washouts were repairing; and when a few things had been set aside, not excluding paranoia, some features were left standing, not excluding lovers, children, friends, and saddle horses. In time, it would be clear as a bell. (235–236)

Here, as elsewhere, the balancing point in McGuane's life is his reliance on nature. He invokes the figure of writer and naturalist Aldo Leopold as he reveals what is probably his philosophy of life.

> Aldo Leopold was a hunter who I am sure abjured freeze-dried vegetables and extrusion burgers. His conscience was clean because this hunter was part of a larger husbandry in which the life of the country was enhanced by his own work. He knew that game populations are not bothered by hunting until they are already precarious and that precarious game populations should not be hunted. . . . A world in which a sacramental portion of food can be taken in the old way— hunting, fishing, farming, and gathering—has as much to do with societal sanity as a day's work for a day's pay. (234)

"The Heart of the Game" is a pregnant title for the essay. The word "game" connotes the literal game hunted and the game of life; the two are part of the same game. The description of Aldo Leopold echoes that of Jack Olson: "For Olson, hunting and fishing were forms of husbandry because he guaranteed the life of the country himself." Another resilient echo lies in McGuane's account of why the club's members resented Olsen. "In short, they wanted to kill as he killed without the hard-earned ritual that made it sane" (*The Sporting Club* 62).

McGuane comments on the corruptions in modern life through the metaphor of the hunt. Living a moral life in a degenerate world requires striking a balance. The only power the individual has is control over his own conduct and, for McGuane, developing such personal power lies in negotiating the natural world.

Ayla and the American Girl

While Thomas McGuane uses hunting as a touchstone for judging character, Jean Auel uses hunting to illustrate the possibilities of woman's personal power. Both authors use hunting to define an individual's identity. The character Ayla, created by Auel, represents the experience of American women in the latter part of the twentieth century, especially the 1970s–1990s.

Auel focuses on the concept of "otherness" in her portrayal of Ayla. Ayla is a Cro-Magnon woman, adopted by a tribe of Neanderthal hunter/gatherers. This tribe is unable to appreciate her character and potential. Ayla's many qualities set her apart from the other members of her adoptive tribe.

Auel's premise is that Neanderthals had hereditary memories, hence their ability to inherit knowledge learned over the course of the species' history. The Cro-Magnons' more developed frontal lobes enabled them to reason and innovate. That Neanderthal and Cro-Magnon co-existed and mated drives the plot. Paleoanthropologists believe that about 40,000 years ago the Neanderthal and the Cro-Magnon had coexisted for tens of thousands of years (Fowler 21). Such interaction, especially cross-mating, suggests amalgamating disparate forces in different societies. And this concept echoes the early American colonial ideal of peoples united by intermarriage.

Amalgamation juxtaposes two questions. James Shreeve asks, "What is it exactly that makes us human?" Within the context of our experience on this continent, what is it exactly that makes us American? Fowler cites Shreeve's work and addresses his question by pointing to paleoanthropologists who have found the "origins of our question" by connecting bipedalism, toolmaking, cooperative hunting, and the "very capacity to adapt that allowed us to spread across so much of the planet" (Fowler 21).

Bipedalism, toolmaking, and cooperative hunting are part of the answer, but not entirely. According to Fowler, about 35,000–40,000 years ago, after Neanderthal and Cro-Magnon had coexisted for tens of thousands of years, there was a sudden change. New tools, various forms of symbolic expression—especially Venus figures and cave paintings—appeared. Most paleoanthropologists believe that this is where "we first recognize human beings as they are today." Shreeve has argued that Cro-Magnons were mobile, while Neanderthals were not, and this trait fostered their going farther afield to mate and thus lay "the groundwork for these cultural innovations" (Fowler 21).

Mobility is an enduring characteristic of American culture. Inherent in the freedom of physical movement is a corresponding intellectual freedom. Extending the hunting metaphor, as McGuane does, includes the idea of searching for meaning in life. The physicality of hunting makes the activity particularly apt as a trope. The hunter is one who pursues game for survival and, at the same time, searches for a place in life.

In *The Clan of the Cave Bear*, Ayla begins her adventures as prey rather than hunter. She is searching for a place in life because the earth has literally dropped out from under her: She is a child of five when an earthquake strikes. She is swimming in the nearby river and separated from her family forever when their dwelling is swallowed by the quake. Ayla runs blindly from the rumbling and follows the stream for several days. Weakened by hunger, exposure, and exhaustion, she wanders from the old growth forest into the steppes, where she encounters a herd of aurochs, "the huge reddish brown wild cattle, six feet high at the withers with immense curving horns" (8). She tries to avoid a bull aurochs and faces more peril when the immense cave lions stalking the edges of the herd see her. While the lioness hunts an aurochs, the male lion pursues Ayla. Realizing her plight, the child scrambles along the rock wall and finds a small cave to hide in as the lion attacks.

> In her panic, it was only instinct that led her to the small hole near the ground in the face of the cliff. Her side aching, and gasping for breath, she squeezed through an opening barely big enough for her. It was a tiny, shallow cave, not much more than a crack. She twisted around in the cramped space until she was kneeling with her back to the wall, trying to melt into the solid rock behind her.
>
> The cave lion roared his frustration when he reached the hole and found his chase thwarted. The child trembled at the sound and stared in hypnotized horror as the cat snaked his paw, sharp curved claws outstretched, into the small hole. Unable to get away, she watched the claw come at her and shrieked in pain as it sunk into her left thigh, raking it with four deep parallel gashes. (9)

The portrayal of Ayla as prey, a victim of forces immeasurably more powerful than she, is a central motif throughout the book. That Ayla is clawed by the cave lion becomes important later on. She is marked by the giant cat, and this is a sign of her totem, her symbolic link to the spirit world.

Until she is found by the medicine woman of the Clan, she is nameless, referred to in Auel's narrative simply as "the child" and "she." Her position changes very slowly as the story progresses. Ayla's vulnerability provides tension in the narrative. At first, Ayla is utterly powerless; as she develops skill as a hunter she reverses her position as prey and becomes an almost mythic heroine. She is tall with long, blond hair. These characteristics distinguish her within Clan society, whose members are dark, short, and stocky. Ayla's physical beauty and her epic struggle point to her romantic appeal, accounting—at least to some degree—for the wide popularity the book enjoyed.

The first chapter of *The Clan of the Cave Bear* deals with Ayla alone. After being clawed by the lion, she hovers in the tiny cave for a day and a half with the lion pacing back and forth in front of the only opening.

> The child remained in the small cramped cave through the day, that night, and most of the following day. The leg swelled and the festering wound was a constant pain, and the small space inside the rough-walled cave had little room to turn or stretch out. She was delirious most of the time from hunger and pain and dreamed terrifying nightmares of earthquakes, and sharp claws, and lonely aching fear. But it wasn't her wound or her hunger or even her painful sunburn that finally drove her from her refuge. It was thirst.
>
> She looked fearfully out of the small opening. . . . The lion pride was gone. The lioness, anxious for her young and uneasy about the unfamiliar scent of the strange creature so near their cave, decided to find a new nursery. (9–10)

Ayla crawls across the terrain to the river, manages to drink enough water to stay alive, and collapses. She has reached the limit of her strength. A carrion bird circles above.

At this crucial point the Clan comes upon the almost dead child. The hunters look at her and pass her by; but Iza, the medicine woman of the Clan and sister of the leader, Brun, wants to take her with them. Brun is not anxious to take on anything new and strange, especially since they have just lost their home and six of their members in the earthquake. Now numbering only twenty, the Clan must find a new cave and perform a cave ceremony. The cave ceremony must take place before the Clan can move in, and it is important that the ceremony be performed very carefully to be sure the spirits are satisfied. Should anything go amiss, the process of searching for a new home begins again. Iza is central to this ritual, and if she is upset it might anger the spirits. Brun therefore leaves the decision to Iza, and so begins Ayla's new life.

The society of the Clan is described in detail—to the division of labor and the semi-nomadic wanderings of these hunter/gatherers. Iza is introduced first.

> She was just over four and a half feet tall, large boned, stocky, and bow-legged, but walked upright on strong muscular legs and flat bare feet. Her arms, long in proportion to her body, were bowed like her legs. She had a large beaky nose, a prognathous jaw jutting out like a muzzle, and no chin. Her low forehead sloped

back into a long, large head, resting on a short, thick neck. At the back of her head was a boney knob, an occipital bun, that emphasized its length.

A soft down of short brown hair, tending to curl, covered her legs and shoulders and ran along the upper spine of her back. It thickened into a head of heavy, long, rather bushy hair. She was already losing her winter pallor to a summer tan. Big, round, intelligent, dark brown eyes were deep set below overhanging brow ridges, and they were filled with curiosity as she quickened her pace to see what the men had passed by. (11)

Iza is pregnant, but she carries a load no lighter than she would carry at any other time. All the women are laden with the belongings of the Clan. Iza is distinguished by her medicine bag, which she carries along with her other burdens. "One bag was particularly distinctive. It was made from an otter hide, obviously so because it had been cured with its waterproof fur, feet, tail, and head left intact" (11).

Ayla's physical appearance immediately contrasts with that of the Clan members. She has nearly white hair and a thin body. She is naked when they find her. Brun looks at her, "the thin young girl with the high forehead, small nose, and strangely flat face. 'Not Clan,' the leader gestured abruptly and turned to walk away" (12). Brun is a larger, male version of Iza.

He carried no burdens, only his outer fur wrap, suspended on his back by a wide band of leather wrapped around his sloping forehead, and his weapons. On his right thigh was a scar, blackened like a tattoo, shaped roughly like a **U** with the tops flaring outward, the mark of his totem, the bison. He needed no mark or ornament to identify his leadership. His bearing and the deference of the others made his position clear. (12–13)

Two main schools of thought address the role of Neanderthals in human history. Brenda Fowler notes that, on one side, scientists such as Chris Stringer with the British Natural History Museum maintains that the Neanderthals were "outcompeted" by the Cro-Magnons. According to his 'out of Africa' hypothesis, the Homo sapiens evolved and then moved throughout the rest of the world. This process supposedly began approximately 100,000 years ago, resulting in Homo sapiens replacing all other early humans. However, what is not explained is exactly how this took place (21).

This view has been challenged by a theory of parallel evolution. In opposition to Stringer's theory is Milford Wolpoff from the University of Michigan. Wolpoff is a "multiregionalist" who argues that Homo erectus, the precursor of Homo sapiens and others, evolved down one broad path. Significant differences in human populations are explained by their having "[s]ufficient gene flow among them [that] prevented them from splintering into a new species. In this view, the Neanderthals were the European variety of Homo sapiens, which ultimately evolved into us" (Fowler 21).

Computer "morphs," re-creations/projections of what the Neanderthals looked like, based upon skeletal remains, are a dramatic addition to the information emerging from ongoing study. Great strides have been made since the early 1970s that refute the older view of Neanderthals as "brutes." The "personalities" of the Neanderthals in *The Clan of the Cave Bear* reflect the modern view while reinforcing the element of their foreign appearance. However, in the scientific community, even this foreign appearance is challenged.

Rick Gore describes what he imagines was a typical scene in the lives of the cave-dwelling Neanderthals:

> Staring into the gloom, I imagine the cave's ancient inhabitants, wrapped in bear skins, huddled near a fire. . . . A mother nurses her infant. Children . . . throw . . . bone[s] into the flames. An old woman tends the wounds of a hunter . . . strong smells of smoke, unwashed bodies, and rotting carcasses thicken the air. (6)

Gore refers to "these early humans" when discussing the Neanderthals, rather than "pre-humans" or "sub-humans." Recent excavations have yielded tools that required great skill to make. Indications are that the Neanderthals hunted in highly organized groups for very large animals. They also cared for the sick and the weak, and spoke a primitive language (6). What is striking is not that portrayals coincide in science and fiction, but that desire to establish a link with the Neanderthals as human transcends particular disciples and theories.

In *The Clan of the Cave Bear,* cooperative hunting appears first in Neanderthal society. In Auel's later volumes, cooperative hunting also takes place in the "Other" (Cro-Magnon) populations. Hunting is central to the portrayal of the Clan, to the movement of the plot, and to the power of Ayla's character. Ayla must teach herself to hunt, and then she must hunt alone because women are forbidden to hunt. Later, when her secret is out, she becomes "the woman who hunts" and joins the Clan's men in the cooperative effort.

Ayla's struggle throughout the book is grueling. At the end of this volume, she is banished and forced to make her way in a daunting landscape. The constant danger surrounding Ayla emphasizes her aloneness. Her difference sets her apart, and it sets her up as a model. She contrasts sharply with the rest of the Clan. Not only her looks, but her thinking marks her as foreign. Auel constantly reinforces images of entrapment through descriptions of physical ability and culture. She shows the Clan members in daily life, living in their cave, hunting, gathering, making tools, teaching one another. The way Ayla learns defines her difference.

From the time Ayla is adopted by the Clan, communication is the most dramatic obstacle in her life. Auel creates the internal speech of the various Clan members; they communicate through subtle hand signals and gestures, using only a few guttural sounds. In a sense, she is trapped by her very lack of limitations.

Ayla's tall, blue-eyed blondness is emphasized repeatedly—with resulting negative commentary from the critics. "Auel's Neanderthals grunt. They are a good deal more apelike, physically and mentally . . . and Auel's Cro-Magnon heroine is a typical Aryan—blond, blue-eyed, tall and beautiful" (Mertz 6). When she meets her soulmate, Jondalar, in *The Valley of Horses*, the critics are even more savage. "Of course, this golden couple (their blondness is stressed almost ad nauseam) is no ordinary twosome; they are archetypes" (Isaacs 14).

The Clan of the Cave Bear and *The Valley of Horses,* as well as the rest of the series, have been referred to as "cave operas"—soap operas taking place in the Middle Paleolithic age. But even the severe critics admit the books are fun to read. They combine a wonderful story with scientific information and romantic elements.

For the most part, the reviews praise Auel's research in anthropology, although some find reason to challenge her findings. For example, John Pfeiffer comments that Auel's literary license goes too far when she describes Neanderthals as having practically no frontal lobes in their brains. He also takes issue with her portrayal of the Clan members as bowlegged and thinks it unlikely that their vocal chords were not developed. He does concede that these details do not matter ultimately (7, 20).

Pfeiffer's review indicates that Auel has touched a responsive chord. Even if she employs flawed or debatable evidence, Auel's work remains powerful. She graphically portrays the Neanderthals' speech limitations and weaves them into the fabric of her narrative to underscore Ayla's plight.

Clan society is based on strict adherence to gender roles, which are dictated by the needs of the hunter/gatherers. They must migrate seasonally to pursue the food supply. The women gather plants for food and medicine, and the men hunt according to an inflexible hierarchy of age and status. They must be in tune with nature to survive, and even their spiritual lives are driven by their relationship with nature.

Individual spirits, represented by animals, are believed to guide and protect each Clan member. The influence of these totemic spirits is the Clan's explanation for individual personality traits. Hunters usually have predator totems guiding them in the hunt. That Ayla's spirit is the cave lion or, more accurately, lioness is unprecedented. Mog-ur, the Clan's religious man, assigns each member's totem during the first year of life. Because she is adopted, Ayla's totem is assigned when she is five. The markings on her leg from the encounter with the cave lion secures her claim to the powerful totem. In a society ruled by gender roles, Ayla's departures from tradition lead to her ostracism.

Ultimately, Ayla is banished from the Clan because she is in conflict with the man who rapes her and who becomes the new leader. This banishment curtails Ayla's own motherhood, and her son goes with her former people. He is a mixture of the two peoples, but the Clan is the only way of life he has known. Ayla's hunting deprives her of her son. Unlike the lioness who is her totem, Ayla cannot care for a child by herself and hunt. Clearly, Auel alludes to the choice between motherhood and independence women face in any patriarchal society.

When Ayla moves from Neanderthal to Cro-Magnon society, she finds that their central deity, the Mother, is female. Jondalar, Ayla's lover, introduces her to this belief system in the second volume of the series, *The Valley of Horses*. This belief system centers around hunting as well. A hunter thanks the Mother for her bounty when he or she kills game. In such a society, the women hunt, too. However, Ayla is also special in this culture, but because of her outstanding hunting skills.

Ayla's skills as a hunter are exceptional. She devises a way to use a sling employing two stones instead of one, and her accuracy is deadly. Again, she is portrayed as larger than life and critics deride her character as implausible.

> And no one had ever wielded a sling in rapid-fire fashion, inserting and hurling a second pebble as soon as the first had been released. But Ayla teaches herself that trick, . . . breaking a taboo . . . she uses [her sling] to kill a hyena in the act of dragging off a baby boy. (Pfeiffer 22)

Ayla's talents are even more extensive in *The Valley of Horses,* along with commensurate criticism. Susan Isaacs remarks that Ayla "invents oral sex, horseback riding, a new technique for making fire and a better way of dragging the kill back to the cave." She also refers to Jondalar as a "spear-throwing Cary Grant" (14). But, negative commentary aside, the larger consideration is that Auel has succeeded in connecting us to our most ancient past.

From the point in the first book where Ayla is adopted by the Clan, hunting is used as a touchstone of her difference and independence. Clan society is organized around hunters, and the gender roles reinforce that society's dependence upon maintaining the status quo. With Ayla's introduction into the Clan, the entire society is disturbed and then threatened as a result of her presence. The metaphor of change then becomes primary for Auel, and its expression is couched in terms of hunting. Ayla is the instrument of the shift from strict observance of gender roles, based on hunting, to innovative applications of hunting that delineate the Clan's decline.

Auel emphasizes the Clan's reliance on tradition. Ayla's existence and interaction with the Clan point up its decline. Her ascendance to power points up the limitations and, therefore, the impending doom of the Neanderthals. Auel's message is clear: The Clan is endearing but obsolete. The ideas they embody have been valuable for the time, at least a hundred thousand years of human existence, but that time is passing, The Others, the Cro-Magnons, have emerged.

The Clan finds Ayla because they are displaced by the same earthquake that destroyed her people. They are the Clan of the Cave Bear— Ursus, the gigantic, vegetarian bear. The Clan's legends underscore the integral relationship between the giant cave bear and the tribe's way of life. The Clan's spiritual essence, its totem, is tied to the life of this bear. They revere it beyond all other creatures, but it too will become extinct. Its existence—and the Clan's—will pass as the climate changes because they cannot adapt.

Their holy man (or Mog-ur) is Creb, a misshapen and scarred old man whose personal totem is also the cave bear. He was clawed and almost died as the result of a cave bear's attack when he was a child. He is the only male of the Clan who cannot hunt, but his status is the most sacred and respected. He is the antithesis of Ayla physically, but almost her soulmate spiritually. The opposition of their physical attributes is a constant reminder of Ayla's tenuous position in the Clan. Because Ayla is able to touch Creb emotionally, he protects her and ensures her life with the Clan. She communicates with him on a level more intimate than anyone else in the Clan. She is not awed or repulsed by his appearance.

Creb is the brother of Iza, the medicine woman, and Brun, the leader of the Clan. They each have flashes of insight about Ayla's significance, beginning when they come across the child as they search for a new cave.

They needed a shelter; but almost more important, their protective totem spirits needed a home, if they hadn't already deserted the clan. They were angry, the earthquake proved that, angry enough to cause the death of six of the clan and

> destroy their home. If a permanent place for their totemic spirits was not found, they would leave the clan to the mercy of the evil ones that caused illness and chased game away. No one knew why the spirits were angry, not even Mog-ur, though he conducted nightly rituals to appease their wrath and help relieve the clan's anxiety. They were all worried, but none more than Brun. (17)

The spirits are those of the animals they hunt, the animals that sustain life. Usually, the males are guarded by the more powerful animals and the females by the less aggressive ones. The spirits are also the source of life. According to the Clan's theory of reproduction, a woman's totem struggles with a man's totem. If his totem defeats hers, she conceives. She does this by swallowing the essence of the man's totem. If she has a particularly strong totem, several men's totems may be required to overcome hers. Usually, it is the totem of the man (or men) near her on a regular basis.

In the Clan's scheme of things, there is no connection between sexual intercourse and the birth of babies. It is an entirely spiritual process. A girl is first eligible to conceive when her totem struggles for the first time and bleeds to show it is wounded. If her totem is overcome, she no longer struggles and the child grows within her. The strength of a totem is determined by its association with the strength of the animal it represents. Mog-ur's totem is the cave bear itself, the totem for the entire Clan. Creb's personal totem is the roe deer. Since surviving the attack of a cave bear, he has two totems.

Every night they are without a new home, it is necessary to call upon the spirits to show them the way. An unchanging ceremony is performed night after night and, although the Clan knows the content of the ceremony, they still anticipate it. Their Mog-ur, Creb, calls upon the totem that is his and the Clan's, the totem that makes these people Clan and the most revered of all spirits: Ursus.

> "Great Ursus, Protector of the Clan," the magician said with formal signs, "show this clan to a new home as once the Cave Bear showed the Clan to live in caves and wear fur. Protect your Clan from Ice Mountain, and the Spirit of Granular Snow who begot him, and the Spirit of Blizzards, her mate. This clan would beg the Great Cave Bear to let no evil come while they are homeless. Most honored of all Spirits, your Clan, your people, ask the Spirit of Mighty Ursus to join with them as they make the journey to the beginning." (27–28)

The "journey to the beginning" is a telepathic experience that the hunters of the Clan share, where they visit their origins in a combined racial memory of their own evolution. Mog-ur, who has developed his powers beyond all others, directs the shared memory.

Because they venerated the cave bear, Mog-ur evoked a primordial mammal—the ancestor who spawned both species and a host of others—and merged the unity of their minds with the bear's beginning. Then down through the ages they became in succession each of their progenitors, and sensed those that diverged to other forms. It made them aware of their relationship with all life on the earth, and the reverence it fostered even for the animals they killed and consumed formed the basis of the spiritual kinship with their totems. (29)

The strength and the limitation of the Clan lies in its brain structure. Their brains are "full" and cannot accommodate new knowledge. This limitation makes change very difficult, if not impossible. Their large heads make it hard for the women to give birth, and the Clan is doomed to extinction.

Ayla is special from the beginning. Iza is amazed that Ayla survived the clawing that clearly shows on her left leg. No one can understand how she escaped since the giant beast had to have her in its grasp to do such damage. Iza knows how to treat the infected scratch wounds because she is heir to the healing knowledge of generations of medicine women. She has their memories.

The Clan's hereditary memories are sex differentiated. "Women had no more need of hunting lore than men had need of more than rudimentary knowledge of plants. The difference in the brains of men and women was imposed by nature, and only cemented by culture" (36). The division is nature's attempt to limit the size of the brain to prolong the race, "[b]ut nature's attempt to save the race from extinction carried with it the elements to defeat its own purpose" (37). The sexes are both essential for day-to-day living as well as procreation, but they cannot learn one another's skills; they haven't the brain capacity to store the necessary knowledge.

As the Clan travels, the men hunt and the women gather. They move from the forest to the plains. "Animals were easier to hunt out in the open, easier to see without the cover of forest to hide them, the cover that hid their four-legged hunters as well" (44). Ayla's long, straight legs allow her to move quickly. She explores ahead and discovers the new cave that will become the Clan's home. They explore the cave and find the bones of a cave bear within. It is the best of all possible omens, and they will be able to move in if the first hunt is successful. Brun decides to make the hunt his son Broud's manhood hunt.

The plot of *The Clan of the Cave Bear* consists of one hunt after another. The Clan hunts for a cave. They go on several hunting expeditions. Ayla hunts also. She hunts for her place in Clan society, and she hunts animals. Finally, she must hunt for a new life, alone.

Creb decides upon Ayla's totem and announces it at the cave ceremony. Since Ayla is to be adopted by the tribe, Creb asks to form his own hearth with his sister, Iza; Ayla; and Iza's baby when it comes, if it is female. If the baby is male, there will have to be other arrangements because a boy has to be trained by a hunter. Iza's mate was one of those killed during the earthquake and she must now be provided for. Other babies' totems will be announced at the cave ceremony, and Broud's manhood ceremony will be conducted as well. Creb's psychic connection to Ayla is such that he envisions the appropriate totem for her. However, his reasoning mind initially rejects the message sent by his deepest feelings.

As Creb meditates and waits for a revelation, he visualizes cave lions on the steppes, an entire family of them. He tries to get the vision out of his mind because the cave lion is a male totem, and Ayla is female. Creb tries to get the vision out of his mind, but it remains. He cannot accept that a female could have such a strong totem. Even men did not usually have such a strong spirit. He realizes that she is not Clan, and then he has a flash of insight. She has already been marked by the giant cat. This clear sign links her to the clan members with powerful totems. When young men have their manhood ceremonies after their first hunt, they are marked with the sign of their totemic spirits. The Clan's sign for a cave lion is four parallel lines, cut into the skin of the right leg. Ayla's mark, however, is on her left leg. He also reasons that this is entirely appropriate because she is female. He feels he has been given an undeniable message from the spirit world and, however unlikely, it seems clear.

Creb identifies with Ayla because he has been marked himself. He was born deformed and later mauled by a cave bear. He understands what it is to be born different and removed from society by forces beyond his control. No one comes near him because of his physical deformity except Ayla and Iza. And Ayla is the only one overtly affectionate to him. She reaches up and touches his face without reservation, much as the female cub reaches up to the usually fierce lion.

Creb is a deeply spiritual man who has denied his own emotions all his life. He takes his position of magician in his tribe very seriously. His prayers to the spirits are sincere pleas to understand what he and the Clan are supposed to do.

Creb has a flash of insight that shakes him. He realizes the marks on her leg are the cave lion's message to the Clan to accept her and the announcement that the cave lion himself is her totem. Creb believes Ayla has been chosen by the cave lion just as he was chosen by Ursus and marked by his grasp. Creb also has a feeling of foreboding and hope combined, although he does not articulate this feeling.

Creb's interest in Ayla, and his sense that she is special, is the beginning of her trouble with the Clan, especially with the leader's son, Broud. He becomes the instrument of her totem's test, as she views it. Broud successfully leads the first hunt and his manhood ceremony is a triumph, until it is revealed that Ayla's totem is the cave lion. Then everyone turns their attention to her, attention that Broud needs to feel secure. His jealousy is fostered over several years, and he believes that Ayla is seeking to supplant him. He focuses all his frustrations and blames all his inadequacies on her. He becomes her personal demon. Although she does not intend it, she becomes his.

Ayla embodies female power in a male-dominated society. Auel's work takes the metaphor a step further and shows Ayla as the future, not simply as a remedy for the past. She is not just Cro-Magnon; she is female Cro-Magnon. Her accomplishments are linked to the evolution of mankind. One of the most dramatic incidents is when she shows that abstractions are natural to her. It is Creb who discovers her facility when Ayla asks when she will be a woman. Creb realizes that numbers are difficult for the Clan to grasp, so he makes slash marks on a stick to indicate how old she is, adding more slash marks to indicate how old she might be to give birth. In a flash, Ayla does subtraction, which amazes the magician. It astounds him because he has an inkling of the true significance of her difference.

> "I will be old enough to have a baby in this many years," she gestured with assurance, positive of her deduction. The old magician was rocked to his core. It was unthinkable that a child, a girl child at that, could reason her way to that conclusion so easily. He was almost too overwhelmed to remember to qualify the prediction.
>
> "That is probably the earliest time. It might not be for this many, or possibly this many," he said, striking two more slashes on the stick. "Or, perhaps even more. There is no way of knowing for sure."
>
> Ayla frowned slightly, held up her index finger, then her thumb. "How do I know more years?" she asked.
>
> Creb eyed her suspiciously. They were getting into a realm with which even he had difficulty. (128–129)

Creb explains that after one has used up one's own fingers and put them across slash marks, and then used the fingers of another's hands, one must imagine yet another person's hands. Ayla doesn't miss a beat and extrapolates instantly that one then imagines another person and another and another. Creb is stunned.

> The impact was too much. His mind reeled. With difficulty, Creb could count to twenty. Numbers beyond twenty blurred into some indistinct infinity called *many*.

He had, on a few rare occasions after deep meditation, caught a bare glimpse of
the concept Ayla comprehended with such ease. His nod was almost an after-
thought. He had a sudden understanding of the gulf between the mind of this girl
and his own, and it shook him. He struggled to compose himself. (128)

This exchange is a precursor of many to come where Ayla's superiority is apparent. Her threat to the Clan is doubly felt because she is Cro-
Magnon and female. In the Clan, women are feared if they depart from
their habitual roles. Legends have it that at one time, women controlled
the magic to intercede with the spirit world. They cannot ever be reminded of that time, lest the delicate balance that allows the Clan to
survive be disrupted.

Ayla tries to fit into Clan life, but her mind works so differently that she
cannot remain unobtrusive even though she desperately seeks acceptance.
She loves the legend of Durc, which teaches that one should not deviate
from what is preached by tradition. She focuses on the part of the legend
where Durc takes the initiative and tries to save the Clan. He travels south
despite being told to wait for the return of Mog-ur, who has gone off to
talk to the spirits controlling the encroaching glacier. Durc and his party
are never heard from again. The point of the story is to trust the one in
authority because Mog-ur returns and saves the Clan. Ayla likes to think
that Durc found a new home for himself and his followers.

Her desire to be alone is especially disconcerting to people who are
dependent upon cooperative living. Ayla loves her adoptive mother and
Creb. When Iza gives birth to a daughter, Ayla is delighted with her baby
"sister." But she feels the pressure of constantly suppressing her natural
impulses. She yearns to escape the clan's constant scrutiny. This desire
leads her to become a hunter.

Ayla is out gathering the bark of the wild cherry tree for Iza's medi-
cines and comes across the men practicing with their weapons. This
episode will determine her path for the rest of her life. She wants the bark
that Iza has sent her to collect, but the men are practicing near the grove
where she must collect it. She should turn around and depart. The taboo
against women touching hunting weapons is clear. Women are not even
supposed to touch tools that make weapons, let alone witness the men
when they practice and have private meetings.

But Ayla is determined to collect the wild cherry bark for Iza. She
decides to wait until the men leave the area. She is fascinated by the use of
the weapons and, though intimidated, she is more curious than fearful.
She watches them practice with the sling and sees Broud lose his temper
after he tries to show off. Broud pushes an older man, Zoug, and receives

a severe reprimand from Brun. The men leave the field after the uncomfortable incident. Ayla retrieves the discarded sling. She knows it is wrong, but she is drawn to try the weapon. After several attempts, she manages to hit the practice post. Although her success is attributable mostly to luck, she is encouraged. She also rejoices that she can do something Broud cannot.

Ayla's life now begins to become her own. She practices in secret; she learns to make a new sling by watching the artisans among the men. Ayla decides that if she becomes proficient with the sling she will try to hunt. She is by herself more and more, and discovers a small cave where she caches several articles. She develops competence with the sling but does not realize that her new confidence shows in her demeanor. She has always been indefinably different, but now her composure is apparent to everyone, especially Broud. Ayla's attitude finally sends Broud into a rage. He is driven by his uncontrollable temper to assault Ayla, nearly killing her. Brun considers disowning Broud if he ever shows such lack of control again. Outwardly Broud acquiesces to his father's threat, but he blames Ayla for his state and swears revenge. Once Ayla is aware that Broud will no longer overtly assault her, she engages in a battle of wills to repay him for his tyranny. She oversteps her bounds, however, and once again Broud is in a position to dominate her.

Ayla interprets Broud's treatment as a sign from her totem that she is to be tested. If found worthy, she will be able to hunt, which she has an inexplicable urge to do. Her resolution helps her endure. In the spring, she decides that her totem has given her the sign to begin her secret occupation. Since she cannot bring her kill back to the Clan, she does not kill animals used as food. She kills predators that steal food from the Clan and present a threat to their well-being.

Ayla increasingly takes comfort in ranging far afield, and her skills as a hunter develop rapidly. She teaches herself to use two stones in rapid fire, and becomes self-conscious about her craft.

> She looked at the dead animal at her feet and let the club fall from her hand. Awareness of the implications of her deed came slowly. I killed a hyena, she said to herself as the impact hit her. I killed a hyena with my sling. Not a small animal, a hyena, an animal that could kill me. Does that mean that I'm a hunter now? Really a hunter? It wasn't exultation she felt, not the excitement of a first kill or even the satisfaction of overcoming a powerful beast. It was something deeper, more humbling. It was the knowledge that she had overcome herself. It came as a spiritual revelation, a mystical insight; and with a reverence deeply felt, she spoke to the spirit of her totem in the ancient formal language of the Clan. (208)

When the Clan travels to the nearby inland sea to fish, Ayla saves a baby girl from drowning. She is the only one who swims, a skill she learned before she left her old home—another of her peculiarities. But when she retrieves the child, she distinguishes herself once again. The crucial trial for her comes when she finally reveals her secret: her hunting prowess.

After a successful mammoth hunt, Broud has triumphed and shown his bravery. The women are preparing the meat to transport back to the cave, and scavengers are skirting the camp. Broud's son Brac is playing away from the others, and a hyena grabs him. Again, Ayla springs into action. After the efforts of the others to hurl stones at the beast fail, Ayla flings two stones and has others ready to kill the animal. She kills the hyena immediately and pries the baby's arm from the hyena's jaws.

The Clan is amazed, but they face a dilemma. No woman can touch a weapon, let alone hunt. The penalty is death. Even though she has saved his son, Broud is most vocal against her. The leader considers all the options. He consults with Creb. After much suspense, Ayla is condemned with a death curse, which means no one will see her. Everyone will regard her as dead, and she will disappear. But her curse is only temporary. She is condemned for a month, and winter is coming. No one else could survive alone, but Ayla does. She retreats to the cave where she practiced with the sling in secret. She can hunt and provide for herself. To the Clan's surprise, she returns after her month of loneliness and living death.

Ayla's troubles do not end with her miraculous return. She is repeatedly raped and beaten by Broud and gives birth to his son. Finally, she is banished permanently. In the novel's final scene she must leave her son, but she resolves not to die; she will seek her own people.

Ayla has a moment of solace and vindication when she outfaces Broud at the end. She knows the children see her, and tells her son she loves him. She asks Brun to protect her son, receiving the slightest indication that he understands and agrees. She walks up to Broud.

> "I'm not dead, Broud," she gestured defiantly. "I won't die. You can't make me die. You can make me go away, you can take my son from me, but you can't make me die!"
>
> Two emotions vied within Broud, fury and fear. He raised his fist in an overwhelming urge to strike her, then held it there, afraid to touch her. . . .
>
> ". . . You still don't understand, do you? You acknowledged her, Broud, she has beaten you. You did everything you could to her, you even cursed her. She's dead, and still she won. She was a woman, and she had more courage than you, Broud, more determination, more self-control. She was more man than you are. Ayla should have been the son of my mate." (495)

Ayla is surprised at Brun's eulogy, and it is all the solace she has because she is dead to the Clan. But Ayla must struggle on, which she does in the next volume of Auel's series.

In *The Valley of Horses*, she is still alone. She wanders far from the Clan and finds a valley where she spends lonely years. She raises a colt, which she rides. She also adopts a cave lion cub that mauls two men who wander into her territory. One man is killed. She nurses the other back to health, and he becomes her companion. She will finally be united with her own people, but this leads to other adventures and challenges.

The Valley of Horses begins on the same stark note present in *The Clan of the Cave Bear.* But it shifts once Jondalar enters her world. Ayla has been and will always be defined by what she has suffered and what she has learned. She will also remain between worlds. Ayla has had to be her own world, contain her own universe.

Ayla, like McGuane, has to develop a personal code for conducting her life. When she is unable to meet the expectations of the Clan, she faces both literal and emotional death. Hunting saves her spiritually and physically. She is able to redefine herself precisely because she hunts, and hunting is the way she finds a new life. Like McGuane, she speaks to the power to survive social constriction and offers another illustration of the provocative character of the hunter figure.

Notes

1   See Sara Blackburn, review of *The Sporting Club*, by Thomas McGuane, *Nation* (14 April 1969): 208.

2   See T. O'Hara, review of *The Sporting Club,* by Thomas McGuane, *Best Sellers* (15 April 1969): 28.

Conclusion

At the heart of the American national image is power—no matter what specific form one may argue this image should take. By considering a cluster of images of the hunter rather than seeking an all-encompassing metaphor for the American experience, we gain insight into the process of the creation, emergence, development, challenges, and future of the nation; and the meaning of its nationality. Looking specifically at pairs of American hunter figures, Pocahontas and John Smith represent the power to create a new nation and nationality; Daniel Boone and Natty Bumppo represent the power to develop it; Teddy Roosevelt and "Buffalo Bill" Cody represent the power to expand it both nationally and internationally; William Faulkner's Ike McCaslin in "The Bear" and Ernest Hemingway represent the power to transcend degenerate forces that threaten it; and, finally, Thomas McGuane and the character Ayla from Jean Auel's *Clan of the Cave Bear* represent to power to reinvent it.

From the inception of European attempts at colonization in America, the interactions of European and Indian cultures have shaped the national experience. Looking particularly at the English settlement at Jamestown is instructive since the ideal of amalgamation between these cultures was not realized in practice except in a few notable cases, the most dramatic and enduring of which is the Pocahontas narrative. Her name has been linked with John Smith's in the popular imagination for centuries through the rescue story, even though in reality her marriage to John Rolfe was the union that brought peace for a time to the colony of Virginia. However, the *possibility* of such amalgamation is the idea that underlies our fascination with the Pocahontas figure.

Pocahontas's courage and defiance of authority were and are still appealing qualities to Americans, as well as the romantic implications of a beautiful Indian princess saving a dashing adventurer. However, that the relationship has remained inchoate is also a reason for its appeal, especially to those who might fear miscegenation. The rescue of Smith by Pocahontas also functions as creation myth and founding moment, and it unites the two in the popular imagination. The function of myth is to establish a culture's conception of its own origin and to satisfy the emotional longing for such an original conception and identity.

The basis of the rescue myth's power is that it provides a foundation to create a distinctly American identity, which melds Indian and European into a new and inceptive identity. This American identity begins the process to subvert European notions of aristocracy.

Pocahontas's later marriage to John Rolfe, a gentleman farmer who was responsible for making tobacco a viable and financially lucrative crop for trade, culminated in a union that produced peace for a while and a son whose progeny became the foundation of a Southern "aristocracy."

The heritage of Smith and Pocahontas is a combination of valuable traits from their cultures and individual personalities. They crossed between worlds in their interaction with each other and stand as representatives of the possibility of this kind of mobility.

Pocahontas also exemplifies the duality of the American psyche that on one hand seeks to minimize difference through metaphors like the "melting pot" and on the other celebrates the uniqueness of the individual and his or her ethnic, racial, or historical national ties. The peculiarly American hunter figure that grows from a marriage of European adventurer/settler and Native American warrior is the bicultural hunter/scout/mountain man characterized most notably by Daniel Boone and Davy Crockett, who were later formalized in literary representations.

The most striking figures of Daniel Boone and Natty Bumppo emerged as the historical and literary exemplars of the American hunter of the seventeenth and eighteenth centuries. This is not to suggest that there was one image of this hunter. Again, the flexibility of the hunter's image, his multivalent possibilities, made him at once unique and yet familiar. His melding of Indian and Anglo-American traditions imbued him with admirable qualities and skills, and yet kept him apart with a foot in either world. The hunter shows the way for the farmer to follow. His is the initial foot that traverses the wilderness.

Crevecoeur's question, "What is an American?" is still relevant when posed today. He saw the ideal model in the farmer, with the hunter a necessary evil as the farmer's precursor. This opposition between farmer and hunter has been an operative motif in the American landscape, especially up through the nineteenth century. One immediately thinks of historian Frederick Jackson Turner and "Buffalo Bill" Cody. While Turner represented agrarian expansion across the continent as the benign face of progress through cultivation of the soil, Cody embodied the violence and "glory" of combat with Native Americans as well as the extermination of the buffalo. Cody and Teddy Roosevelt also made the cowboy synonymous with America and Americans.

The one constant in the American hunter's identity is the defining characteristic of individuality. Ultimately, the personal power of the individual comes through self-knowledge gained while immersed in nature. Although the hunter figure can be flawed and may have suffered from the degenerate forces in society like Faulkner, Hemingway, and their fictive characters, it is through hunting that they are able to transcend such forces.

So many images converge in the figure of the American hunter. It was not by design but rather destiny that I began and ended with female figures. Although the hunter is usually a male figure, research indicates women have always hunted in one form or another, and today one of the fastest growing segments of new hunters is women.

The predominant hunter figures of the latter part of the twentieth century once again evidence rebellion against forces in society that subvert the freedom and voice of the individual. Although figures like Thomas McGuane and his characters, as well as Ayla in *Clan of the Cave Bear,* struggle with forms of societal oppression and bouts of self-doubt, they ultimately find themselves in nature through the expression of the hunt. This power over the self represents a power to reinvent oneself in order to face an uncertain future.

Since beginning this project almost a decade ago, I have been amazed by the culture's revisitation of the hunter figures examined in this book. Pocahontas and John Smith have found their way into an animated Disney movie, and a new movie, *Pocahontas II,* has been made and released directly to video. New biographies of Boone, Roosevelt, Faulkner, and Hemingway seemed to be published just as I was about to research each figure. In a rather bizarre twist of popular culture, websites have sprung up for *Clan of the Cave Bear* in response to the 1986 film starring Darryl Hannah. However, Jean Auel has not yet finished her series, Earth's Children, of which *Clan* is the first volume.

The next important question is, How will the American hunter figure evolve in the twenty-first century? The relationship with the landscape must still be at the heart of any discussion of the role of the hunter. The wilderness is not limitless, although it is certainly still vast thanks to conservation efforts started at the dawn of the twentieth century. Perhaps the most valuable perspective for me has been the view of the Native American that we are part of nature, not superior to it—a perspective both humbling and liberating. It is humbling to realize that we are not predominant over the other creatures of the earth even given the weapons technology that is so arguably a factor in discussions about hunting. Most of all, it is liberating to experience the awe that our fellow creatures inspire when we observe them firsthand.

The hunter remains controversial and is still defined by his simultaneous marginal and privileged position in the culture. The term *hunter* is itself emotionally charged especially in today's social climate. Balance is perhaps the operative word to describe what is needed to preserve our wilderness heritage. Hunting is part of maintaining that balance. Through human interference, species have been threatened and have predominated. The American landscape must be managed because the time when man's, particularly the Native American's, presence perfectly harmonized with his fellow creatures is long past. Our lands are not yet as limited as our European cousins; however, many areas of the country are inaccessible unless one belongs to a hunting club, owns land, or can afford to pay for hunting trips and employ guides.

The hunter still travels between worlds of civilization and wilderness. The hunting landscape is perhaps more dramatic when contrasted with the sprawling metropolises of today. I know when I leave my college campus with its computers, briefcases, and books behind in Westchester County in New York State and set out for our hunting cabin in the Berkshires, where there is no electricity, running water, or indoor plumbing, it is like traveling to another world. When I'm sitting in the woods I do not think about what I left behind, only what is happening in the here and now. I notice the birds, ground animals, insects, trees, leaves, sky. It is being perfectly content in the moment. Anticipating the appearance of game keeps my attention focused on each sound and movement. Whether the hunt is successful or not, it is intensity of these experiences that make me feel in tune with nature and with myself as part of the scheme of things.

Works Cited and Consulted

Andrews, Wayne, ed. *The Autobiography of Theodore Roosevelt*. New York: Charles Scribner's Sons, 1958.

Ardrey, Robert. *African Genesis*. New York: Delta, 1961.

——. *The Hunting Hypothesis*. New York: Atheneum, 1975.

——. *The Social Contract*. New York: Delta, 1970.

Auel, Jean M. *The Clan of the Cave Bear*. New York: Bantam Books, 1980.

——. *The Mammoth Hunters*. New York: Crown Publishers, Inc., 1985.

——. *The Plains of Passage*. New York: Crown Publishers, Inc., 1990.

——. *The Valley of Horses*. New York: Bantam Books, 1982.

——. Interview by Oprah Winfrey. *The Oprah Winfrey Show*. Harpo Productions, Inc., 6 March 1991.

——. Letter to author, 23 September 1991.

Bakeless, John. *Daniel Boone*. Harrisburg, PA: Stackpole Co., 1965.

Banks, Charles Eugene, and Leroy Armstrong. *Theodore Roosevelt: A Typical American*. Boston: Home Library Co., 1901.

Barbour, Philip L. *Pocahontas and Her World*. Boston: Houghton Mifflin Co., 1970.

——. *The Three Worlds of Captain John Smith*. Boston: Houghton Mifflin Co., 1964.

Barnett, Louise K. "Speech in the Wilderness: The Ideal Discourse of *The Deerslayer.*" In *Desert, Garden, Margin, Range: Literature on the American Frontier,* edited by Eric Heyne. New York: Maxwell MacMillan International, 1992.

Barrows, Marjorie Wescott, et al., eds. *The American Experience: Non-Fiction.* New York: Macmillan, 1968.

Baym, Nina, ed. *The Norton Anthology of American Literature,* Vol. 1. 1979. 3rd ed. New York: Norton, 1989.

Bellesiles, Michael A. "The Origins of Gun Culture in the United States, 1760–1865." *The Journal of American History* (September 1996): 425–455.

Bercovitch, Sacvan. *The Puritan Origins of the American Self.* New Haven, CT: Yale University Press, 1975.

Blackburn, Sara. Review of *The Sporting Club,* by Thomas McGuane. *Nation* (14 April 1969): 475.

The Booklist and Subscription Books Bulletin. Review of *The Sporting Club,* by Thomas McGuane (15 May 1969): 1060.

Boone, Daniel. In *The Discovery, Settlement and Present State of Kentucke,* by John Filson. New York: Corinth Books, 1962.

Bunyan, John. *The Pilgrim's Progress.* New York: Airmont Publishing Co., 1969.

Byron, Lord George Gordon. *Don Juan.* 1823. New York: Modern Library, 1949.

Campbell, Joseph. *The Hero with a Thousand Faces.* New York: World, Meridian Books, 1949.

———. *The Masks of God.* 4 vols. New York: Viking, 1959–1968.

Campbell, Joseph, and Bill Moyers. *The Power of Myth,* edited by Betty Sue Flowers. New York: Doubleday, 1988.

Cartmill, Matt. *A View to a Death in the Morning: Hunting and Nature Through History.* Cambridge, MA: Harvard University Press, 1993.

Cash, W.J. *The Mind of the South.* New York: Vintage, 1941.

Chase, Richard. *The Quest for Myth.* Baton Rouge, LA: Louisiana State University Press, 1949.

Cody, William F. *The Life of Hon. William F. Cody, Known as Buffalo Bill, the Famous Hunter, Sout, and Guide: An Autobiography.* 1879. Lincoln, NE: University of Nebraska Press, 1978.

Collier, Peter, and David Horowitz. *The Roosevelts: An American Saga.* New York: Simon & Schuster, 1994.

Cooper, James Fenimore. *The Deerslayer: Or the First Warpath.* 1841. New York: The New American Library, 1963.

————. *The Last of the Mohicans: A Narrative of 1757.* 1826. New York: The New American Library, 1962.

————. *The Pathfinder or The Inland Sea.* 1840. New York: Signet, 1980.

————. *The Pioneers: Or the Sources of the Susquehanna: A Descriptive Tale.* 1823. New York: The New American Library, 1964.

————. *The Prairie: A Tale.* 1827. New York: Rinehart, 1960.

Cooper, John Milton. *Pivotal Decades: The United States 1900–1920.* New York: Norton, 1990.

Crevecoeur, J. Hector St. John. *Letters From an American Farmer.* New York: Fox, Duffield & Co., 1904.

Croft-Cooke, Rupert, and W.S. Meadmore. *Buffalo Bill: The Legend, the Man of Action, the Showman.* London: Sidgwick & Jackson, Ltd., 1952.

Cronin, William. *Changes in the Land: Indians, Colonists, and the Ecology of New England.* New York: Hill and Wang, 1983.

Darwin, Charles. *The Origin of the Species and The Descent of Man.* New York: Modern Library, n.d.

Davis, David Brion. "The Deerslayer, A Democratic Knight of the Wilderness." In *Twelve Original Essays,* edited by Charles Shapiro. Detroit: Wayne State University Press, 1958.

Dearborn, Mary V. *Pocahontas's Daughters: Gender and Ethnicity in American Culture.* New York: Oxford University Press, 1986.

Deloria, Vine. "The Indians." In *Buffalo Bill and the Wild West,* edited by Howard R. Lamar. Pittsburgh: University of Pittsburgh Press, 1981; a publication of The Brooklyn Museum; Museum of Art, Carnegie Institute; and Buffalo Bill Historical Center.

Deutsch, Andre. "Foundering Fathers." Review of *The Sporting Club,* by Thomas McGuane. *Times Literary Supplement* (2 August 1969): 927.

Dickstein, Morris. "The Ever-Changing Literary Past." In *Falling Into Theory: Conflicting Views on Reading Literature,* edited by David H. Richter. Boston: Bedford Books of St. Martins Press, 1994.

Diliberto, Gioia. *Hadley.* New York: Ticknor & Fields, 1992.

Dinnerstein, Leonard, and Kenneth T. Jackson, eds. *American Vistas: 1877 to the Present.* 1971. 7th ed. New York: Oxford University Press, 1995.

DiNunzio, Mario R., ed. *Theodore Roosevelt: An American Mind.* New York: St. Martin's Press, 1994.

Donald, David Herbert. "An Easy Man to Crowd." Review of *Daniel Boone: The Life and Legend of an American Pioneer,* by John Mack Faragher. *New York Times Book Review* (17 January 1993): 17–18.

Dyer, Thomas G. *Theodore Roosevelt and the Idea of Race.* Baton Rouge, LA: Louisiana State University Press, 1980.

Elliott, Lawrence. *The Long Hunter: A New Life of Daniel Boone.* New York: Reader's Digest Press, 1976.

Erlich, Gretel. "The Solace of Open Spaces." In *The Winchester Reader,* edited by Donald McQuade and Robert Atwan. Boston: Bedford Books of St. Martins Press, 1991.

Faragher, John Mack. *Daniel Boone: The Life and Legend of an American Pioneer.* New York: Henry Holt & Co., 1992.

Faulkner, William. "The Bear." *Saturday Evening Post* CCXIV (9 May 1942): 30+.

———. *The Faulkner Reader.* New York: Random House, 1953.

Fiedler, Leslie A. "The Legend." In *Buffalo Bill and the Wild West,* edited by Howard R. Lamar. Pittsburgh: University of Pittsburgh Press, 1981; a publication of The Brooklyn Museum; Museum of Art, Carnegie Institute; and Buffalo Bill Historical Center.

——. *Love and Death in the American Novel.* New York: Delta, Dell Publishing Co., 1966.

Filson, John. *The Discovery, Settlement and Present State of Kentucke.* 1784. New York: Corinth Books, 1962.

Fisher, Philip. Introduction to *The New American Studies: Essays from "Representations,"* edited by Philip Fisher. Berkeley, CA: University of California Press, 1991.

Fletcher, John Gould. *John Smith—Also Pocahontas.* New York: Brentano's, 1923.

Fowler, Brenda. "Where Did He Go?" Review of *The Neandertal Engima,* by James Shreeve. *New York Times Book Review* (17 December 1995): 21.

Fox, Stephen. *The American Conservation Movement: John Muir and his Legacy.* Madison, WI: University of Wisconsin Press, 1985.

Frazer, James G. *The New Golden Bough,* edited by Theodor Gaster. Garden City, NY: Doubleday, Anchor Books, 1961.

Freud, Sigmund. *On Creativity and the Unconscious.* New York: Harper, 1958.

Frye, Northrop. *Anatomy of Criticism: Four Essays.* Princeton, NJ: Princeton University Press, 1957.

Gard, Wayne. *The Great Buffalo Hunt.* New York: Alfred A. Knopf, 1959.

Gore, Rick. "Neandertals." *National Geographic* January 1996: 2–35.

Grossman, James. *James Fenimore Cooper.* New York: William Sloane Associates, Inc.; London: Methuen & Co., Ltd., 1949.

Grossman, James R. Introduction to *The Frontier in American Culture,* by Richard White and Patricia Nelson Limerick. Berkeley, CA: University of California Press, 1994.

Hagedorn, Hermann. *The Roosevelt Family of Sagamore Hill.* New York: Macmillan, 1954.

Hallgarth, Susan A. "Across the Great Divide." Review of *West of Everything: The Inner Life of Westerns,* by Jane Tompkins. *Women's Review of Books* (July 1992): 17.

Helmericks, Constance. *Hunting in North America.* Harrisburg, PA: The Stackpole Co., 1959.

Hemingway, Ernest. *Green Hills of Africa.* New York: Macmillan, 1935.

———. *The Old Man and the Sea.* 1952. New York: Twayne, 1992.

———. *The Short Stories of Ernest Hemingway.* New York: Chas. Scribner's Sons, 1927.

Henderson, Joseph L. *Thresholds of Initiation.* Middletown, CT: Wesleyan University Press, 1967.

Heyne, Eric, ed. Introduction to *Desert, Garden, Margin, Range: Literature on the American Frontier.* New York: Maxwell MacMillan International, 1992.

Hicks, Granville. Review of *The Sporting Club,* by Thomas McGuane. *Saturday Review* (15 March 1969): 31.

Higham, John, ed. *The Reconstruction of American History.* New York: Harper Torchbooks, 1962.

Hopkins, Thomas. "Perils of a Prehistoric Pauline." Review of *The Clan of the Cave Bear,* by Jean M. Auel. *Maclean's Magazine* (6 October 1980): 64–65.

Howe, Irving, ed. "William Faulkner." In *Major American Writers,* edited by Perry Miller. New York: Harcourt, Brace & World, Inc., 1961.

Isaacs, Susan. "Ayla Loves Jondalar." Review of *The Valley of Horses,* by Jean M. Auel. *New York Times Book Review* (26 September 1982): 14.

Jameson, J. Franklin, ed. *Narratives of Early Virginia, 1606–1625,* edited by Lyon Gardiner Tyler. New York: Barnes & Noble, 1946.

Johanson, Donald C., and Maitland A. Edey. *Lucy, The Beginning of Humankind.* New York: Warner, 1981.

Jung, Carl Gustav. *Psyche and Symbol: A Selection from the Writings of C.G. Jung,* edited by Violet S. deLaszlo. Garden City, NY: Doubleday, Anchor Books, 1958.

Katzive, David H. Introduction to "The Cowboys." In *Buffalo Bill and the Wild West,* edited by Howard R. Lamar. Pittsburgh: University of Pittsburgh Press, 1981; a publication of The Brooklyn Museum; Museum of Art, Carnegie Institute; and Buffalo Bill Historical Center.

Kelly, William P. *Plotting America's Past: Fenimore Cooper and the Leatherstocking Tales.* Carbondale, IL: Southern Illinois University Press, 1984.

Kerasote, Ted. "The Spirit of Hunting: What Native Americans Knew." *Sports Afield* (June 1994): 52–60.

Kingston, Maxine Hong. *The Woman Warrior. New York:* Vintage, 1989.

Kolodny, Annette. "Dancing Through the Minefield: Some Observations on the Theory, Practice, and Politics of a Feminist Literary Criticism." In *Falling Into Theory: Conflicting Views on Reading Literature,* edited by David H. Richter. Boston: Bedford Books of St. Martins Press, 1994.

———. *The Land Before Her: Fantasy and Experience of the American Frontiers, 1830–1860.* Chapel Hill: University of North Carolina Press, 1984.

———. *The Lay of the Land: Metaphor as Experience and History in American Life.* Chapel Hill, NC: University of North Carolina Press, 1975.

LaBastille, Anne. *Assignment, Wildlife.* New York: Dutton, 1980.

———. *Beyond Black Bear Lake.* New York: Dutton, 1987.

———. *Mama Poc: An Ecologist's Account of the Extinction of a Species.* New York: Norton, 1990.

———. "The Park of Sacred Spaces." *The Conservationist* May/June 1992: 4–7.

———. *White-tailed Deer.* Washington, D.C.: National Wildlife Federation, 1977.

————. *Woodswoman*. New York: Dutton, 1976.

————, ed. *Women and Wilderness*. San Francisco: Sierra Club Books, 1980.

Lamar, Howard R., ed. *Buffalo Bill and the Wild West*. Pittsburgh: University of Pittsburgh Press, 1981; a publication of The Brooklyn Museum; Museum of Art, Carnegie Institute; and Buffalo Bill Historical Center.

Lawlor, Mary. "The Fictions of Daniel Boone." In *Desert, Garden, Margin, Range: Literature on the American Frontier*, edited by Eric Heyne. New York: Maxwell MacMillan International, 1992.

Lawrence, D.H. *Studies in Classic American Literature*. New York: Viking, 1961.

Leakey, Richard E. *The Making of Mankind*. New York: E.P. Putnam, 1981.

Lears, Jackson. *No Place of Grace*. New York: Pantheon, 1981.

Lee, Richard B. *Man the Hunter*, edited by Irven DeVore. Chicago: Aldine, 1973.

Lehmann-Haupt, Christopher. "The Decline of the West." Review of *The Sporting Club*, by Thomas McGuane. *New York Times,* 7 March 1969, 39.

Leonard, Elizabeth Jane, and Julia Cody Goodman. *Buffalo Bill: King of the Old West, Biography of William F. Cody—Pony Express Rider, Buffalo Hunter, Plains Scout & Guide, Master Showman*, edited by James Williams Hoffman. New York: Library Publishers, 1955.

Levi-Strauss, Claude. *The Savage Mind*. Chicago: University of Chicago Press, 1966.

————. *Totemism*. Trans. Rodney Needham. Boston: Beacon Press, 1963.

Levy-Bruhl, Lucien. *How Natives Think*, translated by Lilian A. Clare. New York: Washington Square Press, 1966.

Lewis, Paul. *The Great Rogue: The Life and Adventures of Captain John Smith*. New York: David McKay Co., Inc., 1966.

Lewis, R. W. B. *The American Adam: Innocence, Tragedy, and Tradition in the Nineteenth Century.* Chicago: University of Chicago Press, 1975.

Literary Women. Garden City, NY: Doubleday, 1976.

Loreaux, Nicole. "What Is a Goddess?" In *A History of Women in the West: From Ancient Goddesses to Christian Saints,* edited by Pauline Schmitt Pantel. Vol. 1. Cambridge: Belknap Harvard University Press, 1992.

Madden, D.H. *A Chapter of Mediaeval History.* Port Washington, NY: Kennicut Press, 1968.

Marks, Frederick W. III. *Velvet on Iron: The Diplomacy of Theodore Roosevelt.* Lincoln, NE: University of Nebraska Press, 1981.

Marks, Stuart A. *Southern Hunting in Black and White: Nature, History, and Ritual in a Carolina Community.* Princeton, NJ: Princeton University Press, 1992.

Marx, Leo. *The Machine in the Garden.* London: Oxford University Press, 1964.

McGuane, Thomas. *The Bushwacked Piano.* 1971. New York: Vintage Books, 1984.

———. *Keep the Change.* 1989. New York: Vintage Books, 1990.

———. *The Missouri Breaks.* New York: Ballatine, 1976.

———. *Ninety-two in the Shade.* 1973. New York: Penguin Books, 1979.

———. *Nobody's Angel.* 1981. New York: Vintage Books, 1986.

———. *An Outside Chance: Essays on Sport.* 1980. New York: Penguin Books, 1982.

———. *Panama.* 1978. New York: Penguin Books, 1980.

———. *Something to Be Desired.* 1984. New York: Vintage Books, 1985.

———. *The Sporting Club.* 1968. New York: Penguin Books, 1979.

———. *To Skin a Cat.* 1986. New York: Vintage Books, 1987.

Mellow, James R. *Hemingway: A Life Without Consequences.* New York: Addison-Wesley, 1992.

Mertz, Barbara. "The Novel Neanderthal." Review of *The Clan of the Cave Bear,* by Jean M. Auel. *Book World—The Washington Post,* 28 September 1980, 6, 10.

Miller, Perry, ed. *Major American Writers.* New York: Harcourt, Brace & World, Inc., 1961.

Mitchell, J.G. *The Hunt.* New York: Knopf, 1980.

Moore, Arthur K. *The Frontier Mind.* New York: McGraw-Hill, 1957.

Morgan, Edmund S. *The Puritan Dilemma: The Story of John Winthrop.* Boston: Little, Brown, and Co., 1958.

Morgan, Elaine. *The Descent of Woman.* New York: Stein and Day, 1972.

Mossiker, Frances. *Pocahontas.* New York: Alfred A. Knopf, 1976.

Nash, Roderick. *Wilderness and the American Mind.* 1967. 3rd ed. New Haven, CT: Yale University Press, 1982.

Niethammer, Carolyn. *Daughters of the Earth: The Lives and Legends of American Indian Women.* New York: Collier Books, 1977.

Oates, Joyce Carol. Review of *The Sporting Club,* by Thomas McGuane. *New York Times Book Review* (23 March 1969): 4–5.

Oates, Stephen B. *William Faulkner: The Man and the Artist.* New York: Harper & Row, 1987.

Oelschlaeger, Max. *The Idea of Wilderness: From Prehistory to the Age of Ecology.* New Haven, CT: Yale University Press, 1991.

O'Hara, T. Review of *The Sporting Club,* by Thomas McGuane. *Best Sellers* (15 April 1969): 28.

Olsen, Larry Dean. *Outdoor Survival Skills.* New York: Pocket-Simon & Schuster, 1976.

Ortega, Jose y Gasset. *Meditations on Hunting,* translated by Howard B. Wescott. New York: Charles Scribner's Sons, 1985.

Pascoe, Peggy. "America Slaps Leather." Review of *Gunfighter Nation*, by Richard Slotkin. *New York Times Book Review* (21 March 1993): 21.

Paugh, Tom. "Predator or Prey?" *Sports Afield* (January 1993): 10–11.

Pfeiffer, John. "Prehistoric Characters." Review of *The Clan of the Cave Bear*, by Jean M. Auel. *New York Times Book Review* (31 August 1980): 7, 20.

Phillips, Leon. *First Lady of America: A Romanticized Biography of Pocahontas*. Richmond: Westover, 1973.

———. *Pioneers and Caretakers: A Study of Nine American Woman Novelists*. Minneapolis: University of Minnesota Press, 1965.

Pringle, Henry F. *Theodore Roosevelt*. New York: Harvest Books, 1956.

Proulx, Annie E. *Heart Songs*. New York: Harper & Row, 1990.

Publishers Weekly. Review of *The Sporting Club*, by Thomas McGuane (20 January 1969): 267.

Quammen, David. "The Disappeared." *Outside* (April 1991): 31+.

Reynolds, David S. *Beneath the American Renaissance: The Subversive Imagination in the Age of Emerson and Melville*. New York: Knopf, 1988.

Richter, David H., ed. *Falling Into Theory: Conflicting Views on Reading Literature*. Boston: Bedford Books of St. Martins Press, 1994.

Riggs, Rev. Thomas L. "The Last Buffalo Hunt." *Sports Afield* (April 1993): 110–118.

Roosevelt, Theodore. *African Game Trails*. New York: Chas. Scribner's Sons, 1910.

———. *Autobiography*. New York: Chas. Scribner's Sons, 1920.

———. *Cowboys and Kings: Three Great Letters by Theodore Roosevelt*. Cambridge, MA: Harvard University Press, 1954.

———. *Ranch Life and the Hunting Trail*. 1888. New York: Winchester Press, 1969.

————. *Theodore Roosevelt: An American Mind, A Selection From His Writings,* edited by Mario R. DiNunzio. New York: St. Martin's Press, 1994.

————. *Theodore Roosevelt's Letters To His Children,* edited by Joseph Bucklin Bishop. New York: Chas. Scribner's Sons, 1919.

————. *The Winning of the West.* Six volumes in three. New York: G.P. Putnam's Sons, 1889.

Rosa, Joseph G. *They Called Him Wild Bill: The Life and Adventures of James Butler Hickok.* Norman, OK: University of Oklahoma Press, 1964.

Rowlandson, Mary. "A Narrative of the Captivity and Restoration of Mrs. Mary Rowlandson." In *The Norton Anthology of American Literature,* edited by Nina Baym.Vol. 1. 3rd ed. New York: Norton, 1979.

Rubin, Louis D. *William Elliot Shoots a Bear: Essays on the Southern Literary Imagination.* Baton Rouge, LA: Louisana State University Press, 1975.

Ruitenbeek, Hendrick M., ed. *Psychoanalysis and Literature.* New York: Dutton, 1964.

Russell, Don. Foreword to *The Life of Hon. William F. Cody, Known as Buffalo Bill, the Famous Hunter, Scout, and Guide: An Autobiography,* by William F. Cody. Lincoln, NE: University of Nebraska Press, 1978.

————. *The Lives and Legends of Buffalo Bill.* Norman, OK: University of Oklahoma Press, 1982.

Sales, Grover. "Primordial Passion of Pleistocene Times: The Flesh is Willing, But the Diction is Weak." Review of *The Valley of Horses,* by Jean M. Auel. *Los Angeles Times Book Review* (12 September 1982): 2.

Saveth, Edward N. "Theodore Roosevelt: Image and Ideology." In *American Vistas: 1877 to the Present,* edited by Leonard Dinnerstein and Kenneth Jackson. New York: Oxford University Press, 1995.

Scheckel, Susan. "Mary Jemison and the Domestication of the American Frontier." In *Desert, Garden, Margin, Range: Literature on the*

American Frontier, edited by Eric Heyne. New York: Maxwell MacMillan International, 1992.

Schlissel, Lillian. *Women's Diaries of the Westward Journey.* New York: Schoken Books, 1982.

Schorer, Mark, ed. "Ernest Hemingway." In *Major American Writers,* edited by Perry Miller. New York: Harcourt, Brace & World, 1961.

Schullery, Paul. *The Bear Hunter's Century.* New York: Dodd, Mead, & Co., 1989.

Seboek, Thomas, ed. *Myth: A Symposium.* Bloomington: University of Indiana Press, 1965.

Seduction and Betrayal: Women and Literature. New York: Random House, 1974.

Shi, David E. *The Simple Life: Plain Livng and High Thinking in American Culture.* New York: Oxford University Press, 1985.

Shreeve, James. *The Neandertal Enigma: Solving the Mystery of Modern Human Origins.* New York: William Morrow, 1995.

Silverberg, Robert. *The Morning of Mankind.* New York: New York Graphic Society Publishers, Ltd., 1967.

Skinner, Constance Lindsay. *Pioneers of the Old West: A Chronicle of the Dark and Bloody Ground.* New Haven, CT: Yale University Press, 1921.

Slotkin, Richard. *The Fatal Environment: The Myth of the Frontier in the Age of Industrialization, 1800–1890.* New York: Atheneum, 1985.

———. *Gunfighter Nation: The Myth of the Frontier in Twentieth Century America.* New York: Atheneum, 1992.

———. *Regeneration Through Violence: The Mythology of the American Frontier, 1600–1860.* Middletown, CT: Wesleyan University Press, 1975.

———. "The 'Wild West.'" In *Buffalo Bill and the Wild West,* edited by Howard R. Lamar. Pittsburgh: University of Pittsburgh Press, 1981; a publication of The Brooklyn Museum; Museum of Art, Carnegie Institute; and Buffalo Bill Historical Center.

Smith, Bradford. *Captain John Smith: His Life and Legend.* New York: J.B. Lippincott Co., 1953.

Smith, Captain John. *The Generall Historie of Virginia, New England & The Summer Isles.* 1624. 2 vols. Glasgow: James MacLehose and Sons, 1907.

Smith, John. *The Complete Works of Captain John Smith,* edited by Philip L. Barbour. Three volumes. Chapel Hill, NC: University of North Carolina Press, 1986.

Smith, Henry Nash. *Virgin Land: The American West as Symbol and Myth.* New York: Vintage, 1950.

————. Introduction to *The Prairie: A Tale,* by James Fenimore Cooper (New York: Rinehart, 1960)

Spiller, Robert E. *The Cycle of America Literature.* New York: The New American Library, 1956.

————. Afterword to *The Pioneers: Or the Sources of the Susquehanna: A Descriptive Tale,* by James Fenimore Cooper. New York: The New American Library, 1962.

————, ed. *A Time of Harvest: American Literature 1910–1960.* American Century Series. New York: Hill and Wang, 1962.

Stratton, Joanna L. *Pioneer Women: Voices from the Kansas Frontier.* New York: Simon and Schuster, 1981.

Striker, Laura Polyani. "Captain John Smith in Seventeenth-Century Literature." In *The Life of John Smith, English Settler,* by Henry Wharton. Chapel Hill, NC: University of North Carolina, 1957.

Tilton, Robert Steven. "American Lavinia: The Pocahontas Narrative in Ante-Bellum America." Ph.D. diss., Stanford, 1992.

————. *Pocahontas: The Evolution of an American Narrative.* New York: Cambridge University Press, 1994.

Tompkins, Jane. *West of Everything: The Inner Life of Westerns.* New York: Oxford University Press, 1992.

Trefethen, James B. *An American Crusade for Wildlife.* Alexandria, VA: Boone and Crockett, 1975.

Turner, Frederick Jackson. *The Frontier in American History*. New York: Holt, Rinehart and Winston, 1962.

Twain, Mark. *Mark Twain: Collected Tales, Sketches, Speeches, & Essays, 1891–1910*, edited by Louis J. Budd. New York: Library of America, 1992.

Utley, Frances Lee, Lynn Z. Bloom, and Arthur F. Kinney, eds. *Bear, Man, and God: Seven Approaches to William Faulkner's "The Bear."* New York: Random House, 1964.

VanDerBeets, Richard, ed. *Held Captive by Indians: Selected Narratives, 1642–1836*. Knoxville, TN: University of Tennessee Press, 1973.

————. *The Indian Captivity Narrative: An American Genre*. New York: University Press of America, 1984.

Van Noppen, John James, and Ina Woestemeyer Van Noppen. *Daniel Boone, Backwoodsman: The Green Woods Were His Portion*. Boone, NC: The Applachian Press, 1966.

Vidal-Naquet, Pierre. "The Black Hunter and the Origin of the Athenian Ephebia." In *The Black Hunter*, translated by Andrew Szegedy-Maszak. Baltimore: The Johns Hopkins University Press, 1986.

Wagenknecht, Edward. *The Seven Worlds of Theodore Roosevelt*. New York: Longmans, Green & Co., 1958.

Wallis, Velma. *Two Old Women*. Seattle: Epicenter Press, 1993.

Ward, John William. *Andrew Jackson—Symbol for an Age*. New York: Oxford University Press, 1962.

Watts, Alan. *Myth and Ritual in Chrisitianity*. London: Thames and Hudson, 1953.

Wecter, Dixon. *The Hero in America*. Ann Arbor, MI: University of Michigan Press, 1963.

Westrum, Dexter. *Thomas McGuane*, edited by Frank Day. Twayne's United States Authors Series. Boston: Twayne, 1991.

Wharton, Henry. *The Life of John Smith, English Soldier*, translated by Laura Polanyi Striker. Chapel Hill, NC: University of North Carolina Press, 1957.

Whisker, James B. *The Right To Hunt*. Croton-on-Hudson, NY: North River Press, 1981.

White, Richard, and Patricia Nelson Limerick. *The Frontier in American Culture*. Berkeley, CA: University of California Press, 1994.

White, T.H. *The Once and Future King*. New York: Putnam, 1958.

Wilkinson, Rupert. *American Tough*. New York: Harper & Row, 1986.

Williamson, Joel. *William Faulkner and Southern History*. New York: Oxford University Press, 1993.

Wilson, James Q., and Richard J. Herrnstein. *Crime and Human Nature*. New York: Simon and Schuster, 1985.

Winter, Yvor. "Fenimore Cooper or the Ruins of Time." In *In Defense of Reason*. Denver: Alan Swallow, 1947.

Wolff, Dick. "Parting Shot." *Guns & Ammo* (January 1991): 98.

Woodward, Grace Steele. *Pocahontas*. Norman, OK: University of Oklahoma Press, 1969.

Yost, Nellie Snyder. *Buffalo Bill: His Family, Friends, Fame, Failures, and Fortunes*. Chicago: Swallow Press, 1979.

Young, Philip. "The Mother of Us All: Pocahontas Reconsidered." *Kenyon Review*, XXIV (1962).

Index

Studies on Themes and Motifs in Literature

The series is designed to advance the publication of research pertaining to themes and motifs in literature. The studies cover cross-cultural patterns as well as the entire range of national literatures. They trace the development and use of themes and motifs over extended periods, elucidate the significance of specific themes or motifs for the formation of period styles, and analyze the unique structural function of themes and motifs. By examining themes or motifs in the work of an author or period, the studies point to the impulses authors received from literary tradition, the choices made, and the creative transformation of the cultural heritage. The series will include publications of colloquia and theoretical studies that contribute to a greater understanding of literature.

For additional information about this series or for the submission of manuscripts, please contact:

Peter Lang Publishing
Acquisitions Dept.
516 N. Charles St., 2nd Floor
Baltimore, MD 21201

To order other books in this series, please contact our Customer Service Department:

800-770-LANG (within the U.S.)
212-647-7706 (outside the U.S.)
212-647-7707 FAX

Or browse online by series at:

www.peterlang.com